For Heaven's
Sake

FOR HEAVEN'S SAKE

CYRIL HARRIS

Chief Rabbi of the Union of Orthodox
Synagogues of South Africa

VALLENTINE MITCHELL

LONDON • PORTLAND, OR

First published 2000
Copyright © 2000
Chief Rabbi Cyril Harris

First published in 2001 in Great Britain by
VALLENTINE MITCHELL
Crown House, 47 Chase Side, Southgate
London N14 5BP

and in the United States of America by
VALLENTINE MITCHELL
c/o ISBS, 5824 N.E. Hassalo Street
Portland, Oregon 97213-3644

Website: http://www.vmbooks.com

Copyright © 2001 Cyril Harris

ISBN 0-85303-418-4

Printed and bound by NBD
Drukkery Street, Goodwood, Western Cape

Cover design by Boss Repro Centre
Homemaker Village
69 Turf Club Road, Turffontein

NEW INTRODUCTION

This book is a journey. The Chief Rabbi takes the reader along with him through the highways and byways of his well-stocked memory. No feature of the rabbinic task is left unadorned by recollection and comment. No necessary rabbinic relationship remains unexplored. It was Simeon Singer of prayer-book fame who immortally declared: 'divines are so human'. In all the better senses, Rabbi Harris is no exception.

His moments of nostalgic sentiment are sometimes poignant, never obtrusive, always natural. The pages are far more than a personal record. They are a mine of experience, rich in guidance to all men and women in communal or public service, whether professional or lay, or aspirants thereto. He allows his impatience to be markedly discerned in the face of small-mindedness, more so when confronted by the occasional swollen pretences of holders of office. Injustice or unfairness he cannot abide. His sense of humour is happily as unflagging as his Scottish accent.

Underlying his notable incumbency of three significant successive synagogues in London, as well as his work as national director of the British Hillel Foundation, and if I may say so, his Chief Rabbinate of the Union of Orthodox Synagogues of South Africa, there has been an unalterable sense of personal duty. This was, and is, connected with his passionate belief in the credo of his fathers, and his conviction that the rabbi's responsibility for the continuity of that faith is bound up under divine providence both with the future of his own people and the betterment of the human family. For him, unless Judaism speaks out, it is less than true to itself. His life-long religious Zionism belongs to the same style of thought.

From the time of his sitting on the Hillel Education Committee – even much earlier, to judge by what he writes of his days in Jewish youth movements – his unaffected talent for friendship and jollity was prominent. It blossomed into his later characteristic flair for enlightened informality, a form of familiarity without patronage or any injury to inherent dignity or moral example.

His wife, Ann, shares his instinct for friendship. They are a team. Certainly they have their own lines of reasoning and their own platforms. But a team they are, in their active concern for human rights and social welfare, in their courage and compassion, and in their mutual devotion.

They left Britain in mid-careers to meet the challenges of South Africa. We soon heard their voices from afar and rejoiced with a family-like pride at their standing and influence.

Cyril Harris now tells his own story. It is about an epoch which is not yet over in a land ever in the spotlight. Among those rabbis who over the generations left these shores for that magnificent and divided land – a noble gallery – he stands high. May his hopes for its future be realised.

People of all ages and walks of life will be drawn to read his tale and, if wise, may ponder wherein lies his appeal. Perhaps part of the answer is found in his laudatory reference to his well-remembered rabbinics tutor at Jews' College in London, Rabbi Koppel Kahana Kagan. That sage would 'continually' remind his students that 'anyone could say no' but that 'it took a *talmid chacham* [a truly learned and wise scholar] to find a way to say yes within the parameters of the law'. If out of the many spheres of Anglo-Jewish life where he made his mark, one was to make the difficult choice of selecting the most crucial, the answer would probably be in the development of the Anglo-Jewish rabbinate. There were long negotiations between representatives of the rabbinate of the United Synagogue and its lay leadership. Rabbi Harris was a leading figure on the rabbinic side. The extended discussions were directed to considering how to enhance the rabbinic status, expand rabbinic responsibility, engineer effective regular consultative machinery, and significantly enlarge the salary structure towards recognised professional levels.

He was not the sole spokesman of the comparatively younger rabbinate but his influence on the proceedings, to which he makes brief reference in the book, was rightly deemed substantive and substantial. In this smiling, tough, outspoken, sport-loving Scot, hard-headed lay negotiators were meeting their match and welcomed it. Long gone was the old deference. With it had gone any notion that the rabbi's role was confined to the synagogue. Not for nothing was the published report of the proceedings entitled 'Beginning Anew'.

He had long preached the policy of broadening the practical role. His successful pursuit of higher university qualifications was characteristic of the new age, as was the intensification of rabbinic attention to the increasingly important fields of inter-faith and inter-group relations.

His acceptance of his strenuous post at Hillel was, as he observes, a new kind of departure from earlier phases of United Synagogue thought and practice. He did not enjoy student politics – only students do. If they sharpened their communal teeth during his four years with them, he did not regret it. By the time he and Ann had come to the United Synagogue's flagship in St John's Wood, they had long become a rabbi and a rabbi's wife for the times.

His Hon. Israel Finestein, QC

London, September 2000

CONTENTS

FOREWORD

South Africa, and especially its Jewish community, was blessed in 1988 when Cyril Harris accepted the call to become the orthodox community's Chief Rabbi.

Little did that community's leaders anticipate the changes that were soon to overtake this country and the need for unusual moral and religious leadership for which they would call.

I know from the Chief Rabbi that the decision he and his wife, Ann, took to move from England to South Africa was an excruciatingly difficult one which was opposed by members of their immediate family.

South Africa was then the pariah of the international community and in the midst of emergency rule which denied elementary justice and all fair process to its citizens, many thousands of whom were being held without trial in prisons and police cells. The apartheid leaders led the majority of white South Africans to believe that this method was a justifiable defence to the "total onslaught" designed to instal an anti-white, communist government.

From his first days in South Africa, Chief Rabbi Harris, to the dismay of many of his congregants, spoke out against the iniquities of racial discrimination and preached the inconsistency between Jewish ethics and the policy of apartheid.

His empathy for the oppressed black majority enabled him to build bridges with many of the liberation movement's leaders and an especially warm relationship with Nelson Mandela after his release from prison in 1990.

In this book the personality and character of Cyril Harris emerge. Those of us who have been privileged to have experienced his company and friendship will enjoy having this record of his humour, wisdom and, above all, his humanity.

Here is a rabbi who understands the frailty of the human spirit yet who has absolute faith in the triumph of good over evil. He has abiding optimism even in the face of adversity. His confidence in the future success and prosperity of South Africa is founded on pragmatism and realism and without ignoring the serious problems facing it and the time and effort needed to solve them.

The care and thought characteristic of all the Chief Rabbi's teachings in South Africa were obvious from the start. In his address delivered during his induction into office at the Wolmarans Street Synagogue he focused on three issues which have become emblematic of his tenure of office:

"... the continuity of traditional Judaism as a living force; the preservation of the bonds of the Jewish people with the State of Israel; and the practical application of Jewish ethical teachings to the South African scene."

These themes are like fixed stars. They do not wax and wane according to ephemeral moods brought about by this or that event in Israel, South Africa or elsewhere.

The frustration and disappointment which many of us feel when the peace process in the Middle East breaks down or is impeded by right-wing intransigence is no reason to weaken our bonds with the centre of Jewish life. Fanaticism, evidenced by one party or another and rooted in religious belief, is no reason for the faith of those who adhere to traditional Jewish ethics and observance to be tempered. So, too, it should not diminish the respect and tolerance which all decent people should exhibit towards their own or other religions.

It is in respect of the third theme, the application of Jewish ethical teachings to the wider community, that Chief Rabbi Harris has made an essential contribution. In that endeavour he has had the full and active support of his wife, Ann. For many years she gave of her time and professional ability to the work of the Law Clinic run by the Law School of the University of the Witwatersrand. As a team they have lost no opportunity in making an important Jewish contribution to the wider South African society and especially in the upliftment of its many victims of apartheid.

The Chief Rabbi frankly explains his views on many subjects, both religious and secular. I feel compelled to comment on some of his remarks on our new Constitution.

He adds his own acclaim to the general praise "rightly given to the South African constitution for being an excellent guiding document for a truly democratic society." Nevertheless, he identifies a tension which inevitably exists between some provisions of the Bill of Rights and the principles of many religious citizens. The tension is not surprising, and presents a challenge to our courts to minimize that discord to the extent possible.

I would question, however, Chief Rabbi Harris's cautious appraisal that the constitution "tends to give preference to the rights of the individual over those of society as a whole". I would suggest that the history of the second half of the twentieth century demonstrated that societies which have prospered and advanced the interests of the majority of their citizens are those in which individual rights have been respected. States which have placed the interests of society above those of individuals, failed at the cost of the misery and worse of the individuals who lived in them.

Nevertheless my position is that the abolition of the death sentence should not properly be seen as preferring the rights of the individual over those of society. In 1995 our Constitutional Court unanimously held the death sentence to be a violation of our Bill of Rights. Principally the judges found that it was inconsistent with the core values of human dignity and the right to life. These are values essential for any truly democratic society. When they are violated, it is not only at the expense of the criminal but at the expense of the whole society.

I do not believe that the answer lies in the interpretation of the Talmud "to keep the death penalty on the statute book but to carry it out rarely". If it remains law the death penalty will be carried out, and having regard to high crime rates in most countries, it will be carried out only too frequently. In my opinion it is a great relief that we are no longer counted with Russia and the United States as countries which judicially allow the killing of substantial numbers of their citizens each year.

Finally, on this score, one has to accept and respect the tension with religion when the constitution and the courts recognise and give effect to the human dignity of those who are homosexual.

I can put it no better than my colleague, Justice Albie Sachs, in his judgment in the case in which the Constitutional Court held the sodomy laws to be unconstitutional:

"The fact that the State may not impose orthodoxies of belief systems on the whole of society has two consequences. The first is that gays and lesbians cannot be forced to conform to heterosexual norms; they can now break out of their invisibility and live as full and free citizens of South Africa. The second is that those persons who for reasons of religious or other belief disagree with or condemn homosexual conduct are free to hold and articulate such beliefs. Yet, while the Constitution protects the right of people to continue with such beliefs, it does not allow the State to turn those beliefs — even in moderate or gentle versions — into dogma imposed on the whole of society."

Of course, the value of this outstanding book is that it enables issues such as these to be discussed openly between rational and intelligent people. And, how refreshing it is when one of the protagonists is one of this country's most eminent religious leaders.

What emerges from this book are the difficult and complex obligations which are thrust upon our religious leaders. Their relationship with their congregations, their synagogue committees, their colleagues and their flock is frequently a difficult one. One is left in no doubt that Chief Rabbi Harris enjoys his calling despite the difficulties he may encounter. And so he should.

In one chapter he discusses "the ideal rabbi". I would suggest that unintentionally he has accurately described himself. At the ceremony for Joe Slovo which he recounts in perhaps the most memorable chapter of the book, he said:

"There is an old Rabbinic teaching, a beautiful one, that just before a person dies, an angel comes to him from heaven and asks the vital question: 'Tell me, is the world a better place because of your life which is about to end? Is the world a better place because of the efforts you exerted? Is the world a better place because you were around?'"

In the case of Chief Rabbi Harris we do not need to wait for the angel to come from heaven to ask the question. We can with an assurance answer that question immediately. There can be no doubt at all that the South African Jewish community is a better one for his outstanding leadership, both spiritual and secular. We should be grateful that he decided to write this book.

Justice Richard Goldstone
Judge of the Constitutional Court of South Africa

April 2000

PREFACE

Memoirs are usually written after one has retired. Breaking with that tradition, I have preferred to write them while I am still active and while my recollections are fresh and unclouded by forgetfulness.

By no means a comprehensive treatment, the items here are a selection of cameos from communal life in Anglo-Jewry and South African Jewry. Much of this book deals with my pastoral work in the London of yesteryear; however, I trust I have also communicated the sheer exhilaration of living in the new South Africa as it goes through its birth pangs. Sharing one's experiences and the insights gleaned from them may have some bearing on the current challenges facing South African Jewry.

That the veil of charity is drawn over the many flaws of one's own character and over events one would rather not mention are just two of the advantages of a subjective treatment of one's own career.

There are numerous people who helped shape my career - members of the family, beloved teachers, close colleagues, helpful lay leaders, and considerate Jewish staff - and to whom I am personally or professionally grateful. Unfortunately, it has been impossible to include all of them in this book, but they have my most grateful thanks.

Over the years I have written for numerous journals and broadcast on many radio and TV religious programmes. Some of the themes dealt with here derive from those contributions, and although the pieces have been considerably reworked, I would like to acknowledge my thanks to *Jewish Tradition*, *Jewish Affairs*, the former *SA Jewish Times*, *Business Day* and the *Sunday Times* (South African publications) and the *Jewish Chronicle* (London), SABC Religious Programmes and BBC's "Thought for the Day".

Throughout the Diary, I have quoted freely from diverse sources and in case I have omitted any attribution, I would like to express my omnibus thanks.

I appreciate the help and encouragement of my publisher, Benjamin Trisk, and editor Jeremy Gordin, and wish to express my gratitude to my secretary, Debby Rabinowitz, for her indispensable assistance.

CKH

GLOSSARY

The following translations and explanations are given in the order in which the Hebrew, Yiddish or Aramaic terms, phrases or names first appear.

H: Hebrew

Y: Yiddish

A: Aramaic.

Throughout the colloquial usage is preferred, not always the grammatically correct form.

The acronym z'l, "May his (or her) memory be for a blessing," appears throughout the text.

PERSONAL
1 A Holy Start

Fast of Gedaliah:
Commemorates the assassination of Gedaliah, the governor of Judah appointed by the Babylonians after the fall of Jerusalem in 586 BCE. His death led to the final elimination of Jewish autonomy in Judah.

Bris:
The act and ceremony of circumcision. Ashkenazi pronunciation. H: *brit*: covenant.

Rabbi:
"My master" or "my teacher" (H). Jew qualified to expound and apply Jewish law; official leader of a Jewish congregation.

Shul:
Yiddish word for synagogue, from German for "school", used by diaspora Jews. H: *bet ha-knesset*, house of gathering.

Beth Din:
"House of law" (H); religious court made up of rabbis who oversee and control all aspects of Jewish law and life, from dietary laws to divorce, in specific communities. Must comprise a minimum of three ordained rabbis.

Gaon:
Title used for the heads of Babylonian academies in the post-Talmudic period and for outstanding sages;

Eliyahu, the Vilna Gaon (1720-1797), was the most famous gaon of modern times. H.

Litvak: Yiddish term for Jew from Lithuania. Originally used by Polish and central European Jews as a term of opprobrium for someone unsophisticated. Some 90 percent of Jews who immigrated to South Africa from the end of the 19th until the middle of the 20th century were Litvaks.

Barmitzvah: Ceremony at which the Jewish male child of 13 attains religious maturity; he becomes responsible for keeping the *mitzvot* (commandments). H.

Shabbat: The Sabbath, the most important Jewish holiday, on which no profane work is allowed. H.

2 The Oldest Chaver

Chaver: Friend, comrade, associate. H.
Madrich: Leader. H.
Mazkirut: Secretariat or administrative body. H.
Ve'idot: National Conferences. H.
Bachad: Acronym for *Brit Chalutzim Dati'im*, Organisation of Religious Pioneers. H.
Aliyah: "Elevation" (H); used both as a term for (1) immigrating to Israel and (2) for being called up to the reading of the weekly portion in the synagogue.
Torah: The teachings; the Law; the entire body of Jewish wisdom including the Talmud, the compendium of oral law. But may also be used to refer specifically to the Pentateuch. H.
Mizrachi: The Zionist movement of the mainstream orthodox. H.
Shiur: Lesson; in religious context, a lesson on a sacred text. H.
Zemirot: Table hymns sung at a Sabbath or Festive meal. H.
Benshing: Saying grace after a meal. Y, lit. "blessing".

3 Influences

Gabbai:	Elected synagogue trustee or warden. H, lit. "collector" of charity.
Shivah:	The seven days of intense mourning after the death of a close relative. H.
Menschlech-keit:	Decency. Y.
Halachah:	Jewish law. H, lit. "the way to go".
Talmid Chacham:	A person renowned for his Jewish learning. H.
Mapam:	Formerly the left wing of the Israeli labour bloc. H.
Knesset:	Israel's parliament. H.
Bagrut:	Israeli matriculation. H.
"Shavua Tov":	"(May you have) a good week" — generally said just after the end of the Sabbath about the forthcoming week. H.
Tsaddik:	A saintly person. H.
Mitzvot:	Commandments. H.
"Hob nit kein fardruss":	"Don't have any regrets." Y.
Sephardi:	Strictly-speaking a Jew whose family originally came from the Iberian peninsula, but now used for Oriental and North African, as well as Spanish and Portuguese, Jews. H, lit. "Spanish."
Mezuzzah:	The small parchment scroll affixed to the "doorpost" of a Jewish home. H.

4 "Rabbi of the Match"

Derashah:	Sermon; address; speech; a scholarly interpretation. H.
Rabbonim:	Plural of rabbi. H.
Chazonim:	Plural of *chazan*: cantor. H.
Tsoros:	Trouble. Y.

Chupah:	Wedding canopy; used as a synonym for wedding. H.
Yarmulke:	Skull cap. Y.
Derech Eretz:	Respect, good manners. H, lit. "the way of the land".
Rabbonon	Prayer said after communal study, asking for a
Kaddish:	blessing upon rabbis and scholars. A.
Chutzpah:	Effrontery; cheek. H. & Y.
Nachas:	Pleasure, gratification. H. & Y.

5 Three London Synagogues & A Myriad of Students

Shammas:	Synagogue beadle. H: *shamash*: servant.
Cheder:	Elementary religious school. H, lit. "room".
Simchat	Last day of the festive season, following Tabernacles
Torah:	and Shemini Atzeret, on which the annual cycle of the reading of the Law ends and begins once more. H, lit. "the rejoicing of the Law".
Kol hanearim	The calling of all the children to the *bimah* to
aliyah:	celebrate the Law. H.
Bimah:	"Elevated platform" in the centre of the synagogue where the Torah is read. H.
Talleisim:	Colloquial plural of *tallis*, fringed shawl worn by male Jews during prayers. H.
Siddurim:	Plural of *siddur*, the week-day and Sabbath prayer book. H.
Chumashim:	Plural of *chumash*, the five books of Moses (Pentateuch). H.
Noch:	"In addition to!" Y.
Berachot:	Blessings. H.
Kashrut:	Jewish dietary laws. H.
Bat chayil:	H, lit. "A worthy daughter," from *Eshet Chayil*, "a woman of worth".
Batmitzvah:	Ceremony at which the Jewish female child of 12 attains religious maturity; she becomes responsible for keeping the *mitzvot* (commandments). H.

Pesach:	Passover. H.
Chol Hamoed:	The intermediate days of Tabernacles and Passover when ordinary work must be limited. H.
Yom Tov:	A festival on which most work is prohibited. H, lit. "a good day".
Seder:	The special home ceremony on the first two evenings of Passover. H, lit. "(the correct) order".
Shomrei Shabbat:	Those who abide by the Sabbath laws; religiously observant people. H. Singular: *shomer Shabbat*.
Gemara:	The part of the Talmud that consists of interpretation and discussion of the oral law presented in the *Mishnah*. A.
Rosh Hashanah:	The Jewish New Year. H.
Selichot:	Penitential prayers said prior to, and during, the Ten Days of Penitence. H.
Nusach:	The traditional melody for given prayers. H.
Mishnah:	The oral law, as compiled by Rabbi Judah the Patriarch, circa 200 CE. H.
Sefer:	Book. H.
Motzei Shabbat:	Saturday night after Shabbat has ended. H.
Ketubah:	The Jewish marriage document. H.
Unterfihrers:	Those who lead the bride and groom under the Chupah in instances when the parents are not present. Y.
Layening/Lein:	Reading the Torah aloud in shul, from the German word "to read". Y.
Kol Nidrei:	The solemn annulment of vows between a person and G-d at the commencement of the Fast of Atonement. H.
Yizkor:	The special section of the synagogue service for remembering the dead. H.

6 Induction Into Office

Aron Kodesh: The holy ark in which the Torah scrolls are kept. H.
Berich Shemai:A prayer in praise of G-d and of petition to Him. A.
Shalom Bayit: Domestic bliss. H, lit. "peace in the home".
Yiddishkeit: Jewish religious values. Y, lit. "Jewishness".

7 The African Chief

Tehillim: Psalms. H.
Meshuggah: Crazy. H. & Y.
Sholem: Peace. Yiddish pronunciation of Shalom.
Shabbat   The reception in the synagogue hall immediately
Brochoh: following the Sabbath morning service. H.
Haftara: The section from the Prophets directly after the
                Sabbath Torah reading. H.
Kiddush: Sanctification over wine at the beginning, and on mid-
                day, of the Sabbath and Festivals. H.
Minchah: Afternoon prayers. H.
Shalosh   The third meal prior to the end of Sabbath. H, lit.
Seudos: "three meals".
Divrei Torah: Verbal explication of a section of the Torah. H.
Parashah: The weekly reading from the Torah, or a specific
                portion of it. H.
Av Beth Din: Head of the Beth Din. H.
Gittin: Plural of *Get*, the Jewish bill of divorce, delivered by
                the husband or his representative to the wife. H.
Chavrusa: Collegiality. H. & Y. & A.
Mitzvah: In this case, a religiously prescribed act or good deed. H.
Minyan: Quorum of ten adult male Jews necessary for the
                whole prayer service to be recited. H.
Shnorrer: A beggar. Y.
Yeshivah: Rabbinical academy. H.

8 Likes and Dislikes

Challah: Special bread baked for the Sabbath and Festivals. H.
Faribbel: Grievance. Y.
"A nechtiker   "It's simply not going to happen"; lit. "the day
tog":   that has gone". Y.
Rachmones: Mercy, pity. Y.
Treif: Unfit to eat; contrary to the dietary laws. H, lit. "torn".
Kosher   May be eaten during Pesach. The phrase is
l' Pesach: written on the labels of those comestibles ratified by
the Beth Din. *Chametz*, i.e. leavened bread or anything
else containing flour and water that has been allowed
to rise. H.
Adon Olam: "Lord of the universe," the closing hymn of the Shabbat
morning service. H.

PASTORAL
2 The Long Day

Punkt: "Precisely at the point at which ... ." Y.

3 Happy Ever After?

Talmud: The basic body of Jewish oral law consisting of the
interpretation of laws contained in the Torah.
Midrash: Homiletical commentary on the Bible.

5 Together With the Community

Machzor: Festival prayer book. H.
A gut yohr: "A good year". Y.
Al chait: The long confessional prayer on the Fast of
Atonement. H, lit. "For the sin ...".
Vidui: Confession. H.

Avinu
Malkeinu: "Our Father, Our King", Fast Day prayer. H.
Anim Zmirot: Hymn praising the beauty of G-d. H.
Yigdal: Final hymn of the Friday night service. H.
Gemar Tov: "A good completion". H.

7 The Permanent Shadow

Bnai Brith: Worldwide Jewish philanthropic organisation. H, lit.
                "Sons of the Covenant".
Goyim: Term for Gentile; has become pejorative. Plural of goy.
                H, lit. "nation".

9 Old Bones

Chanukkah: Eight-day festival of light. H.
Mi sheberach: The first two words of a blessing. Used here
                euphemistically for "a telling off".
Oi vei iz mir: "O, woe is me". Y.
Nu: So ...? Y.
Refuah
Shelemah: A complete recovery. H.

10 Defeating El Nino

Hoshana   The seventh day of *Succot*, Tabernacles, on which
Rabbah: the special seven Hoshanos circuits are made. H.
Sifrei Torah: Plural of *Sefer Torah*, scrolls of the Law. H.
Hoshanos: The prayers, calling for G-d's salvation, recited on
                Hoshana Rabbah. H.
Lulav: Palm branch. H.
Etrog: Citron. H.
Musaf: Additional service for New Moon, Sabbaths and
                Festivals. H.

Shemini Atzeret:	Festival following Succot on which special prayers are offered for rain. H, lit. "Eighth Day of Solemn Assembly".
Succah:	The "booth" in which Jews live for the duration of Succot. H.
Piyyut:	Poem. H. & A.
Tashlich:	Ceremony of casting away one's sins. H.

11 The Thread of Life — Thin and Thick

Nach:	Acronym for The Prophets and The Writings/ Hagiographa (i.e. everything except the five books of Moses). H.
Berachah:	Blessing. H.
Hashem:	The Almighty. H, lit. "the Name".
Modeh Ani:	The first two words of the prayer recited on rising in the morning. The first two words of the last prayer recited before death. H, lit. "I give thanks / acknowledge ...".

COMMUNAL
1 The Ideal Rabbi

Shlemiel:	Fool, person always out of place. Y.
Machers:	Active people in the community; lit. "those who do". Y.
Mikveh:	Ritual bath. H.

2 The Ideal Gabbai

Ba'al Teshuvah:	Someone who has turned to a religious life from an irreligious one. H.

3 Good Jewish Schools

Simchah:	Happy occasion. H.

Shabbatonim: Special weekend retreats for educational purposes. H.

4 The Power of Community

Kehilla: Community, pl. Kehillot. H.
Klal Yisrael: The people of Israel; the general Jewish community. H.
Bachurim: Young men. H.
Shtetl: One of the small Jewish villages of eastern Europe. Y.
Chesed: Kindness. H.

5 Proper Prayer

Tefillah: Prayer. H.
Amidah: The 19 benedictions, recited while standing and facing the Ark. H.
Shtender: Lectern. Y.

6 Seven Up!

Aufruf: The ceremony of the bridegroom reading the section from the Prophets in the synagogue, on the Saturday prior to his wedding. Y.
Keriat haTorah: Reading of the Law. H.
Sidra: Prescribed portion of the Torah read out in synagogue. H.
Yahrzeit: Yiddish term for the anniversary of someone's death.
Segan: Lay synagogue official. H, lit. "deputy".
Chiyyuv: "A must". H.
Gantse Mishpochoh: "The entire family". Y.
Tsutshep-penish: A distant cousin. Y, lit. "stitched on".
Ashkenazim: Jews of central or east European origin. H.
Chassidim: Most commonly, members of the sect initiated by

Israel Baal Shem Tov in the 18th century. H, lit. "the pious ones".

Cohen: Direct descendant of Aaron and the Temple priests. H.

Levi: Direct descendant of Levi, third son of Jacob. H.

Shelishi: The third portion of the Shabbat morning reading of the Torah. H.

Maftir: The person who reads the Haftara. H.

Cholent: Since Jews are not allowed to cook on the Sabbath, this stew — of, say, meat, beans and potatoes — is pre-cooked before Shabbat and then left to simmer. Y.

8 Unions of Synagogues

Lehavdil: "On the contrary". H.

9 Of Commas and Baritones

Kedushah: "Holiness". The goal of ethical behaviour and self-discipline; also used to refer to sections of the liturgy that emphasize the holiness of G-d. H.

Kichel: Thin, dry but tasty biscuit. Y.

Tochachah: The two sections of the Torah which list the dire punishments which will befall the Children of Israel should the Torah not be kept. H, lit. "rebuke".

Mechitsah: Partition between the sexes in an Orthodox synagogue. H.

Magen David: Star of David. H.

Shtiebl: Yiddish term for an "informal" synagogue. "Little room".

Ne'ilah: The "closing" service of Yom Kippur. H.

10 What Makes Synagogue Services Effective?

Ba'al Tefillah: Person conducting the prayer service. H.
Kavanah: Intention; purpose. H.

NATIONAL
1 The First Elections

She'heche-   Blessing of thanks extolling achievement or
yanu: completion. H.

2 Communist Friends

Kneidlach: Dumplings. Y.
Kippah: Skull cap. H.
Mensh: A decent person. Y.

5 Getting the Get Bill

Get: The Jewish bill of divorce, delivered by the husband or his representative to the wife. H.
Agunot: Plural of *agunah*: primarily a wife whose husband has disappeared, and she is unable to remarry; here refers to women whose husbands refuse to give them the Get. H, lit. "chained".
Kiddush
Hashem: "Sanctification of the Name". H.

6 Madiba

Lubavitch: A sub-group of Chassidim who follow a path of intellectualized mysticism. Y.
Luach: Calendar; diary. H.

10 "Egbok!"

Keinenhora: "May there be no evil eye!" Y.

FESTIVE
1 New Year Wishes

Bobba: Grandmother. Y.

2 The New Me

Galut: Exile. H.

3 Following-Through

Nasherei: Snacks. Y.
Havdalah: The ceremony at the conclusion of Shabbat, separating the holy (Shabbat) from the profane (the rest of the week). H.

5 The Dance of Pesach

Haggadah: The text recited before, during and after the festive home meal on Pesach, telling the story of the Exodus from Egypt.
Chametz: Leavened bread and anything else containing flour and water that has been allowed to rise. May not be eaten during Pesach. H.

8 The Touch of Beauty

Rishonim: The early Rabbinic authorities. H., lit. "the first ones".
Shofar: Ram's horn blown on various occasions, especially at the New Year. H.

Tefillin: Phylacteries; two black boxes containing parchment with Torah passages, worn during weekday morning services. H.

HUMANITARIAN
2 The Moral Repudiation of Apartheid

Tosefot: Franco-German commentators on the Talmud. H, lit. "additions".

3 Giving and Taking

Shulchan Aruch: The main code of Jewish law compiled by Joseph Caro. H, lit. "the prepared table".

5 The Incomplete Family

Shalom aleichem: In this case, a Shabbat song. H, lit. "peace unto you all".

Eshet Chayil: "A woman of worth" — in this case, the chapter of praise to the Jewish wife from the Book of Proverbs. H.

SPIRITUAL
1 The Efficacy of Prayer

Shechinah: The Divine Presence. H.

Sheva Berachot: The seven marriage benedictions. H.

3 The Essential Jewish Identikit

Pirogen: Oval-shaped pastry filled with meat or chicken. Y.

Zeide: Grandfather. Y.

Zecher Tsaddik Livrochoh: "May the memory of this righteous person be for a blessing". H.

Der heim:	The home, referring to Jewish habitation in Eastern Europe. Y.
Tisha B'Av:	The fast of the 9th of Av, remembering the destruction of both Temples. H.
Mizrach plate:	Plate hung on the wall to denote the direction of East for prayer purposes.
Besamim (box):	Spices used for *Havdalah*.
Kaddish:	Prayer in praise of G-d, marking the break between the sections of the synagogue service, and also, in a slightly different version, recited by mourners. Needs presence of a *minyan* to be recited. A.

4 "Even Stevens"

Kohelet:	The Book of Ecclesiastes. H.

5 Approaching the Kotel

Kotel:	The Western Wall of the Temple. H.
Am Yisrael:	The Jewish People. H.
Shabbat Shacharit Kedushah:	The section ascribing holiness to the Almighty in the Amidah of the Sabbath morning service. H.

6 Holiness Sublime

Megillah:	The Book of Esther. H, lit. "scroll".
Kittel:	White garment usually worn on Rosh Hashanah and Yom Kippur. H.

I

PERSONAL

1.   A Holy Start

I have three birthdays.

Born on Shabbat Shuvah, the special sabbath between New Year and the Fast of Atonement, I usually celebrate that day as my main birthday. But the Hebrew date in the year in which I was born was the third day of the month of Tishrei, 5697, and that day is generally the Fast of Gedaliah.

This fast cannot be commemorated on the sabbath — unlike Yom Kippur, the Fast of Atonement, the only one which can — so if it falls on the sabbath, it is moved to Sunday, the day afterwards. Hence I also keep the third of Tishrei as a birthday, on whichever week day it falls!

The English date when I first appeared was September 19, 1936 which I also keep as my birthday. I can therefore look forward every year to three separate lots of birthday presents, a neat arrangement that is pleasing to a good Scotsman like myself, except that every twenty years or so, two of the three dates coincide, leaving me without my triple bonus.

On the day of my birth The Times of London carried news of the end of the 63-day siege of Toledo in the Spanish Civil War ("Red Flag Flying Over Ruins") and mentioned that Anthony Eden had begun negotiations for a new Western European security pact to replace the Locarno Treaty. It also mentioned the "impressive ceremonies" marking the 300th anniversary of Harvard University and ran a short item from its Jerusalem correspondent noting that "the Jewish New Year holiday, added to the Arab strike, has made the towns of Palestine exceptionally quiet".

It was reported that the trial had opened at London's central criminal court of the proprietor and the printer of the newspaper Fascist on charges of libelling the Jews by publishing "divers scandalous statements regarding his Majesty's Jewish subjects with intent to create ill-will between his Majesty's subjects of the Jewish faith and those not of the Jewish faith, so as to create a public mischief". The Attorney-General led the prosecution.

King Edward VIII, later to abdicate, "left Euston Station last night for Balmoral to pay his first visit since his accession", DJ Rees won the final of the professional golf tournament at Oxhey, TS Eliot's *Murder in the Cathedral* was showing at the Mercury Theatre, and a gift box of choice Devon anemones could be purchased for two shillings and sixpence. The weather forecast was "mainly fair".

My bris was in shul on Yom Kippur. I was born in Camphill Avenue in the district of Langside in Glasgow — the business magnate Sir Isaac Wolfson, at the half-way stage of his illustrious career, lived next door at the time — and as I was to be named after my grandfather z'l, who had died the year before and who had been the spiritual leader of the Langside Hebrew Congregation, the Beth Din allowed my non-Jewish nurse to carry me to the synagogue for the ceremony.

As Yom Kippur is a fast day and as the benedictions at a circumcision are always recited over a cup of wine, there is, of course, a problem: who is supposed to drink the wine? Answer: the baby! I have it on the good authority of several persons who were present that when I was given the wine to drink, I took my week-old arm and pushed the cup aside, as if to remonstrate at the very idea of expecting me to drink on a fast day.

"One day this boy will be a rabbi," one of the onlookers joked.

Our family are direct descendants of the famous Vilna Gaon. Of course every Litvak claims this honour, but unlike most of them we can prove it. My mother's maiden name was Bloch and our family is descended from the Gaon's youngest daughter, Tova. Incidentally, we, the Scottish branch of the family, are known to our cousins in other climes as "the Blochs from the lochs".

Evacuated to Annan in Dumfriesshire for a short while, we lived in Ayr throughout the Second World War. I started primary school at the age of four in 1940. I have never, by the way, been able to understand the South African educational system in which proper schooling does not start until the age of seven, so that a Barmitzvah boy is still at primary school whereas in England he will have been at high school for two years already.

I recall that there were 54 of us in a class-room designed for 25.

But the war was on, so we crushed together in the desks and made the best of it. The war did not affect us much at all. Ayr is next to Prestwick, and when the Americans came it was their main air force headquarters in Europe. The Jewish personnel used to visit us regularly; my mother, despite war-time rationing, showed them hospitality, and as my father was a chess champion they loved to challenge him to a game. They all seemed incredibly friendly, and kept bringing us presents from the PX, the store for servicemen, at Prestwick Aerodrome. My elder sister and brother and I were among the very few children to enjoy a constant supply of sweets throughout the war.

Every morning when school began we were obliged to practise putting on our gas-masks, which we kept in a cardboard box beneath our desk; we merely had to put them on, and then after a minute or two take them off. They were heavy in those days and smelled of rubber, and I used to loathe the morning drill.

Years later, visiting Israel during the "Scud War" of 1991, we were obliged to be fitted with gas-masks on arrival at Ben Gurion airport. As soon as I put the gas-mask on, I felt the same feeling of nausea I had experienced fifty years before. The officer at the airport could not understand my adverse reaction and insisted I had to persevere.

In Primary 3, every Friday afternoon before school finished for the week, our teacher would tell us a long and exciting story. He was a marvellous raconteur and made the content, whether cops and robbers or cowboys and Indians, come to life. In the Scottish winter, Shabbat begins before school finishes, and I still remember having to put up my hand in the middle of the story to ask permission to go home.

I used to wonder how those stories ended. My little mind thought how wonderful it would be if only there could be Jewish schools one day — at my school there were only three Jewish pupils out of 170 — so that we did not have to interrupt the routine and would not have to miss the end of a good story.

Our father z'l, used to work all day on Sundays in a basement room full of maps in the county buildings about five minutes walk from our house. So, one after the other, my elder sister, Leila, and my elder brother, Victor — both of whom have always been most supportive of me — and I, used to carry a hot lunch from home to him. He would open a basement window adjacent to the street and we would hand in the dishes to him. I still remember his smile as he took each course of the meal through the window without ever spilling any of the contents.

The Ayr Hebrew Congregation, of which my father was the proud chairman — I was introduced to shul politics as an infant — was very close-knit and intimate, and the hundred or so Jewish souls of the seaside town really seemed to care about each other. Perhaps it was the war which brought everyone closer together but I believed every community was as warm as that, and it was one of the reasons I decided early on to become a congregational rabbi.

When I was nine, our school was visited by the inspector of education for the county. He marched into our class, looked at us imperiously, and in a loud voice said: "Tell me, boys and girls, if there are twelve pennies in a dozen, how many half-pennies are there?"

Everyone's hand shot up and he was repeatedly given the answer, "twenty four". I waited for everyone else to finish and raised my hand. He looked at me. "Twelve," I said.

"Come here," he ordered and, with my face the colour of beetroot, I rose from my seat and went to the front of the class.

"Pupils," he said, "look at this young man. He knows there is always twelve in a dozen."

He patted me on the shoulder, shook my hand, and then released me from my embarrassment.

When pupils reached the age of eleven, the Scottish education department sorted out grammar school pupils from secondary school pupils by means of a qualifying examination. Whether this was too early an age to categorise pupils occasioned much heated debate but in any event for me the "Qualy" fell on a Shabbat.

So I had early experience of sitting an "alternative examination". A dozen of us Jewish children wrote a specially set paper on the Monday morning. Fifty years later, dealing with exams set on holy days is still a contentious issue.

In my last year at primary school, I sat at the back of the tiered classroom, not that I was so well-behaved but teacher wanted to keep an eye on the more mischievous pupils who were deliberately placed at the front.

On the wall behind me there was a large relief map of the then Union of South Africa. I used to look at it every morning before I took my seat, at the magnificent Drakensberg range of mountains, the diamond mine at Kimberley, the gold on the Witwatersrand, the Limpopo River separating South Africa from the then Rhodesia, and the Atlantic and Indian Oceans merging on the south coast.

"Now, that looks a nice place," I used to think to myself.

2.   The Oldest Chaver

I have been a member of Bnei Akiva, the orthodox Zionist youth movement for more than fifty years. Indeed I believe I am the oldest chaver in South Africa.

Fully committed to the ideology and rejoicing in the company, I attended thousands of Shabbat and Sunday afternoon meetings as a youngster in Glasgow and as a teenage madrich in London. I have been drenched to the skin at summer and winter camps from East Lothian in Scotland to Devon in south west England. I have participated in innumerable Days of Study, mazkirut meetings, regional conferences and ve'idot. And I have loved every moment of it.

From the age of sixteen I used to spend as much of the summer holidays as possible at the farm at Thaxted in Essex. Run by Bachad as a training centre for those wishing to go on aliyah to kibbutz, usually to Lavi in the Galilee, the farm had a serious vocational purpose and was replete with agricultural experts and complicated machinery. We were kindly allowed "to help a little" in the summer months.

The simplest jobs were allocated to us. As I was tall, I was usually instructed to pull dock, a coarse weed which grew very high, from the potato fields.

One morning, by way of change, I was asked to hoe the kale field. Kale is a variety of cabbage with wrinkled leaves and the problem for the inexperienced farm hand is that kale is virtually indistinguishable from weeds of the same size.

I began work at about nine o'clock, conscientiously loosening the top soil with a hoe, and scraping up what I thought were weeds. At about midday the manager, Benno Landau, came along and after one glance took the hoe away from me.

"Chaver," he said pointedly, "you've taken out the vegetables and left the weeds." He looked around him. "You've done about 500 pounds' worth of damage." He paused for a moment.

"Tell me," he said," wouldn't you rather be a rabbi?"

Notwithstanding my lack of agricultural skill, there is something to be said for working in the open air. Largely lost in our world, which has nearly everyone marketing or servicing rather than directly engaged with their own hands in production, is the deep sense of satisfaction which comes from association with the soil.

One can identify with the Psalmist's truism: "When thou eatest of the labour of thine hands, happy art thou and it is well with thee." Going down to the village pub by the cricket green for a pint of beer in the evening, with two of the farm dogs at my feet, having spent a hard day in the fields, I have rarely felt so genuinely contented.

The concepts of Bnei Akiva have always appealed to me. The motto of the movement, "Eretz Yisrael l'am Yisrael al pi Torat Yisrael" ("the land of Israel for the people of Israel according to the Law of Israel"), constitutes a philosophy that in my view renders all others significantly deficient.

All three components, "the full house," are essential: not the love of the land without the love of Torah; not the love of Torah without loving all Jewish people; and not loving the people and Torah without our ancestral homeland. The greatest mischief, especially in our days, is done by fracturing the tripartite structure by rejecting one or even two of the basics: Torah-true Jews who despise those who are not; secular Israeli Jews who cannot abide the Torah; and diaspora Jews who feel no need for Israel.

I have always disapproved of the description "centrist" — the term is borrowed from modern orthodoxy — being applied to Bnei Akiva and Mizrachi philosophy. I prefer "maximal," which is a more accurate way of depicting our beliefs.

On one notable occasion I was privileged to see all three together, as they should be. Visiting a new kibbutz, Bet Rimon, with a group of British rabbis in 1980, we were thrilled when everyone suddenly downed tools and crowded into one of the huts in order to hear a shiur by the district rabbi who had come to visit them.

A sister kibbutz to Lavi, and only a few hills away from it, Bet Rimon has unfortunately not proved all that successful. But that afternoon, seeing the men, women and children who lived on the kibbutz concentrating intently on the Torah lesson was for me the fulfilment of the orthodox Zionist dream. All three components were at long last together.

Most of us cheat on our Zionism. We are "Israel-without-tears" Zionists, visiting the country for a cosy holiday and, in the comfort of a plush hotel, blissfully ignoring the real Israel and its problems. We are "emotional Zionists," knowing in our hearts that the destiny of our people is irrevocably linked to our homeland, yet our level of concern fluctuates according to Israel's latest crisis.

Or we are "nervous Zionists," anxiously observing the actions of the Israeli government and the reactions of our host country and constantly assessing the consequences for the Jewish community. We are "hesitant Zionists," our commitment wavering uneasily between our reluctance to see the diaspora disappear and the required degree of support to ensure Israel makes even more progress.

Viewed in this light, Bnei Akiva and all that it stands for has much to commend it and I can confirm that dozens of my contemporaries have (unlike me) gone to live in Israel and that, despite its problems, they feel happy and fulfilled, all recognising that there, more than anywhere else in the world, they are part of Jewish destiny.

In later years I assisted Bnei Akiva as an adviser and supporter. For I have taken much from it during half a century of belonging. The Hebrew word chaver can mean a friend, a fellow student, a spiritual associate or a comrade supporting the same cause. All these roles and more I have enjoyed and it has resulted in my firm conviction that Judaism and Zionism are indissolubly intertwined, two sides of the same ideological coin.

But the greatest boon is to be part of its ruach, or spirit, which in South Africa is at its best at the annual summer camp near Mossel Bay. The traditional zemirot at Shabbat lunch time, with five hundred youngsters participating, usually last for at least a couple of hours and it is the thrill of a lifetime to be caught up in their joyous singing.

"Baruch ha-gever...," the campers chant enthusiastically at the end of benshing, and then they stand on the tables and sway to the music. "Lala-la-lala-la, pumpum-pumpum-pumpum..."

The whole building rocks and one is caught up in the ecstasy. Ah, what it is to be young.

3. Influences

When I was sixteen I played board number two in the chess team for my school, Queen's Park, in Glasgow. Board number one was my friend, Danny Aharoni. But at the beginning of 1952 he contracted leukaemia and he died in May, the week before the final of the Inter-Schools Chess Competition, in which we were scheduled to play.

We all moved up one board but were so upset at not having him with us that we all lost. Our opponents found out the reason why we were off form and very sportingly, when they accepted the trophy, indicated that the second-best team had won.

Then in November of the same year, Uncle Aby z'l, died. He was only in his early forties and, because he was quite remarkable, his loss was really acute.

A brilliant mathematician, during the Second World War he was a boffin stationed at Malvern where he helped to perfect radar and ground control approach systems which proved of inestimable value to the Royal Air Force. Coincidentally, his sister, my Auntie Minnie z'l and her husband, my Uncle Wolf z'l, lived in Worcester nearby. Uncle Wolf was a hard-working general practitioner and Aunt Minnie the most hospitable person in the world, so Uncle Aby was able to spend every Shabbat with them, a luxury in war time.

Uncle Aby was fair, tolerant and widely read and taught his nephews and nieces a great deal. I recall as a youngster that he spoke up on behalf of the Palestinian Arabs after Israel's War of Independence; he was always prepared to see the other person's point of view. A heavy pipe smoker, he contracted lung cancer.

Then in January 1953 my father suffered a heart attack on the way home from shul and died ten days later in the Victoria Infirmary across the road from my school. He was only 47 and had always been absorbed in shul life. In Ayr where we grew up he was the chairman of the shul and in Glasgow the gabbai of Queen's Park Shul and he certainly passed on to me his passion for Jewish communal life. My father's death was a devastating blow for the family. Indeed it got to the stage that, when I reached home after school, I was reluctant to walk up the path to our front door lest there was further bad news.

An extraordinary coincidence occurred when my father died. The same afternoon I was sitting a preliminary examination in French for the Scottish Highers and, as my watch wasn't working, my mother had given me my father's. It stopped at one minute past four and I had to keep turning round to see the clock at the end of the hall to know how much time I had left to finish the paper.

When my brother Victor and I went to the hospital to fetch our father's belongings, the staff nurse in his ward was most comforting. I don't know what made me ask but as we were leaving I wanted to know what time he had died.

"I had just given him his 4 o'clock cup of tea," she replied, "when he had his last attack. I put the time of death in his file at 4:01."

So in the space of under a year I had lost three people very close to me. It was my Bnei Akiva madrich, Arnold Rosin, who restored my faith. He was studying medicine — later on he had a distinguished career as head of geriatrics at Shaarei Zedek Hospital in Jerusalem — and while we were sitting shivah for my father z'l, he wrote me a long letter which was so full of religious common sense and honest sympathy that I kept referring to it during the following months and it certainly helped pull me through my difficult time.

My mother z'l, who possessed a fundamental faith in heaven accompanied by a deeply emotional exposition of it — any spiritual sensitivities I may have stem from her — was never quite the same person after my father's death.

Many teachers have influenced me in important and diverse ways. Because I held a United Synagogue studentship I was seconded while at college to various London shuls. The rabbi who was most encouraging to me was Louis Jacobs, and in 1957, seven years before the famous "Jacobs Affair", which split London Jewry over the issue of the Divine authority of the Torah, I was attached to the New West End Synagogue. Dr Jacobs went out of his way to help me, and whatever difference there may be regarding his approach towards Judaism, when it comes to menschlechkeit he can teach his colleagues a thing or two.

When I came to the Rabbinical Diploma class, Rabbi Koppel Kahana Kagan z'l, made an immediate impression. A Lithuanian gaon, he was also a master of modern legal studies and he taught all his students the crucial relevance of comparative assessment. As an expert in Talmudic, Roman and English jurisprudence, he was able to pinpoint the superiority of Torah over other systems.

The same legal problems face all societies, whether in procedural or substantive law, public or private, civil or criminal, and unless one is able to compare the manner in which each legal system attempts to solve them, one is relying on blind faith. How does one know that the answers of Torah are better unless one also has an acquaintance with the answers offered by other systems?

His endorsement of secular studies profoundly affected all his disciples. Additionally, he was wonderfully lenient in his approach to halachah, continually reminding us that anyone could say "no", but it took a talmid chacham to find a way to say "yes" within the parameters of the law. How he would have objected to the current trend of extreme orthodoxy and its tendency to heap prohibition upon prohibition on an over-burdened religious public.

The Israeli ambassadors to South Africa have had an influence, not always benign, on me. When Nelson Mandela embraced Yasser Arafat at the Namibian Independence celebrations in 1990, the then Israeli ambassador, a retired brigadier-general who had little grasp of politics, lambasted Mandela a week later at the opening of the South African Zionist Federation conference. As we were leaving the platform, I remonstrated with him and we had words with each other. Unbeknown to me, a freelance Israeli journalist was listening in and the argument between us appeared in the following day's Israeli newspapers.

The pick of the bunch was Ambassador Alon Liel, who prior to the first elections deliberately befriended the African National Congress and built up a multitude of useful contacts with them. His efforts undoubtedly helped to ensure a more even-handed stance by the ANC than might have been in its policy towards the Middle East.

In September 1993 Dr Liel phoned me, his excitement unconcealed. "Rabin and Arafat are definitely going to sign a peace agreement on the White House lawn in Washington. Come and join us at the embassy in Pretoria [technically Israeli territory] and we can watch the ceremony on TV together."

With a welter of mixed emotions — hope and trepidation, joy and anxiety — we witnessed the historic handshake. As both of us are firmly in the peace camp, we felt deeply moved at the possibility that decades of hostility might at last be over. Peace as a goal is surely worth striving for and a window of opportunity was opening up.

We were not to know at the time that Yitzhak Rabin z'l, would be assassinated, that Benjamin Netanyahu, the next prime minister, would back track, and that the negotiations would have to go through endless, volatile convolutions. At that precious moment, peace really seemed at last within reach.

Ambassador Elazar Granot, who had formerly been the leader of Mapam in the Knesset proved to be an engaging personality. Surprisingly, he is a poet — one of his books is set for the bagrut in Israel — and he was fond of telling me his maternal grandfather was a Rabbi and that he himself "took inspiration, though not direction" from Jewish sacred sources. The first time he and his wife came to dinner at our home I asked him for an example of his poetry. In response he gave me a rough translation of his poem, Grandma's Birds.

"Grandma loves to feed the birds with stale bread and cake crumbs every morning on the verandah outside her apartment. On Yom Kippur morning she comes out to feed them as usual and a neighbour complains to her that as it is Yom Kippur she should not be handling food. Grandma replies to the effect that she personally has sinned and has to fast but the birds have not sinned so she doesn't think they should suffer. She dies at a ripe old age and her friends, the birds, come to the funeral and they fly a circle of tribute over her grave. But her grandchildren do not observe Yom Kippur at all — and the birds go hungry."

The Saturday night Rabin was assassinated he phoned to tell me what had happened. "Shavua tov," I said to him, recognising his voice. "Not such a good week at all," he replied and told me that Rabin had been shot and was on the operating table. Twenty minutes later he phoned to tell me the worst.

Of all the Jewish personalities in South Africa, the one who benefited me the most was Rabbi Yirmiya Aloy z'l. He epitomised all the qualities which one associates with a tsaddik: genuine warmth and kindness, a pleasant and peaceful approach and an exemplary love of Torah, which was always sweetly expressed and gently inspiring. He got on so well with everyone that when he passed away in 1998, there was a real void in our community. His quiet advice was always a great source of strength.

During the first of — alas! — too many controversies I have been involved in during my time in office, he kept me going. It was over beauty queen Anneline Kriel, who underwent a "quickie" conversion to Judaism in Zurich, one which was unacceptable to the Beth Din in South Africa. We discovered that she had only spent a short time in Switzerland and that Rabbi Mordechai Piron, who was authenticated by the Tel Aviv Beth Din, had converted her. Not only was this unfair to all the converts who spend years in the process of understanding Judaism and becoming acquainted with the mitzvot, but we had considerable doubts as to the standard of observance of Anneline and her then husband.

So we refused to accept it, and a furore, covered by the world press, ensued. In the middle of it all, Rabbi Aloy came and told me not to worry — "Hob nit kein fardruss," he said — and assured me it would all work out.

Subsequently Rabbi Piron, due to his involvement, lost the nomination to become chairman of World Mizrachi because my Mizrachi associates in Israel, Britain and Canada had been shocked at the whole affair. Anneline eventually revealed the truth during a television interview when she was asked what religion she was.

"Jewish," she answered hesitatingly, and then added, "Well, really Jews for Jesus."

Since my arrival, I have had the honour of meeting all the country's state presidents. PW Botha entertained me to tea at Tuinhuys, his official residence, and I found him affable. The first time I officially met FW De Klerk was on February 1, 1990, the day before his famous Parliamentary speech unbanning the ANC and the South African Communist Party and announcing the release of Nelson Mandela.

Together with Joe Fintz, my favourite Sephardi, and Mickey Glass, the director of the Union of Orthodox Synagogues in Cape Town, we met De Klerk in the Cabinet Room at 8 am. He came in smoking a cigarette and said that he had fifteen minutes only for us because of the pressures of the opening of parliament next day. Three-quarters of an hour later we were still chatting and in answer to a question on behalf of the Jewish Board of Deputies as to any possible threat from the Afrikaanse Weerstandsbeweeging (AWB), the ultra right-wing Afrikaner paramilitary organisation, he smiled and suggested that we had nothing to worry about and told us he himself was probably their number one target.

I asked him about his speech the following day.

"I will not disappoint you," he said with a smile.

I met him on numerous occasions during the hectic period of negotiations leading to the new dispensation and always found him kind and courteous. There has been much speculation as to the possible reasons for his change of heart, his decision to turn the country from a white minority ruled one into a democracy. My sense is that while he was acting president, when PW Botha was ill, and he visited Europe in the latter part of 1989, he came face to face with reality.

Helmut Kohl's insistence when they met in Bonn that the European community was going to put up the shutters against South Africa, Margaret Thatcher's informing him in Downing Street that she could no longer hold out against the rest of the Commonwealth, and Mario Suares of Portugal's reminder to him of what had happened in Angola and Mozambique must have turned the tide. True, there were many pressing internal reasons besides, but the realisation that South Africa could no longer hold out against the rest of the world must have dawned on De Klerk during that trip.

Whatever the reasons, when he had made up his mind to concede, in my opinion and that of many others he did it with considerable grace. Mandela has often stated that the peaceful revolution came about in no small measure due to the steady and dignified manner in which De Klerk conducted himself and at a banquet which the Jewish community made for me and my wife in Johannesburg, I praised De Klerk's historic role.

I am full of confidence in Thabo Mbeki and believe the future of our country is in very good hands. Somewhat shy and reserved, Mbeki is a great thinker and an excellent strategist. His speeches are always deep and worthwhile, and Africa in general — South Africa in particular — can be filled with hope now that he is at the helm.

At his inauguration, I was again privileged to represent the Jewish community and deliver a prayer. As five religious leaders were participating, my colleague, the Reverend Cedric Mayson of the ANC Commission for Religious Affairs, came to me a month before and handed me the text of what I was supposed to say. Each of us were given a theme — mine was confession — but I thought that what I had been given was far too depressing. So with permission, I changed it and wrote my own text.

"Our country at this time has too much violence and crime, too little love and laughter. Pardon us, Lord, for so often despairing instead of always hoping, for looking down at our feet instead of beholding the horizon," was a key part of my prayer.

The past twelve years in South Africa have been enriched by a range of personalities whose acquaintance and friendship my wife and I have been privileged to enjoy. In the first place, we would not have come here had it not been for the persuasive powers of the normally genial Anthony Spitz.

Then, among those no longer in the land of the living are Clive Menell, a gentleman par excellence, and Jackie McGlew, a devotee of religion in his later years when we met quite often, he to discuss theology and me to talk about cricket.

I have also been privileged to admire at close quarters the qualities of a number of well-known South Africans: the super efficiency of

Reserve Bank deputy governor, Gill Marcus, the intellectual prowess of education minister Kadar Asmal, entrepreneur Mendel Kaplan's infectious love of history, the sensitivity of Gauteng agriculture chief, Mary Metcalfe, the incisive thought of Nobel literary laureate Nadine Gordimer, the indomitable courage of Helen Suzman, the deep faith in G-d and man of the world-renowned anthropologist Phillip Tobias, the genial philanthrophy of businessmen Eric Samson and Jonathan Beare, Desmond Tutu's jovial piety, and the sheer integrity of president of the constitutional court, Arthur Chaskalson.

The two people who have influenced me more than any others are my wife Ann and our son Michael. Ann has a searing honesty which does not allow any pretence or duplicity and a regard and respect for fellow human beings which made it natural for her to visit Russian Jews several times when it was dangerous — she took mezuzzah parchments with her, hidden in her toothbrush kit — and which has moved her to take the lead in upliftment programmes in South Africa. She is a lawyer and I have been happy to be "in the arms of the law" for the last forty years and, please G-d, many more.

Michael is painstaking in his studies; he is a philosopher as well as a rabbinic expert on Jewish sacred texts and often helps his father, who tends not to be quite so painstaking. Michael is also a thoughtful and articulate proponent of modern Jewish orthodoxy and his parents are very proud of him and of his energetic and talented wife, our daughter-in-law Sara.

Whom have I influenced? The answer to that question lies in the realm of biography not autobiography. But, as far as some of the many thousands of fellow Jews I have been privileged to serve are concerned, I trust that I have managed to instil a lively definition of being Jewish, promoted solid bonds with Israel, and urged a positive, not reluctant, involvement with the new South Africa.

4. "Rabbi of the Match!"

Of all the many and varied ways of raising funds for worthy Jewish causes, London's Annual Charity Cricket Match is pretty unique.

There is something very special about cricket as a game. Spiritual leaders of all denominations are somehow attracted to cricket more than any other sport. Perhaps, despite the popularity of the limited over game, this has something to do with the length of regular cricket matches; it is not a hectic and rushed game, but steady and persistent. Maybe it is because of the pleasant sound of bat on ball and the invariably picturesque background against which cricket is played.

It could also be because the game has an undoubted contemplative quality, appealing to the spiritual as much as the physical. "It's not cricket" is the heartfelt protest the game has given to any deviation from principle. And in the age before metal visors for close-in fielders and extensive protective padding for batsmen, cricket was indeed a game for gentlemen. Certainly it gives such true and long-lasting pleasure that a major championship match, knockout competition or test match is rarely played without the attendance of some members of the cloth.

In my first derashah at the prestigious St John's Wood Synagogue, which is situated around the corner from the headquarters of cricket, I informed my new congregants: "I come here to bring you closer to the Lord — and me closer to Lord's!"

My wife knows little about cricket but loves to accompany me — not to watch, but because she likes the setting and the background noise, while reading the book she invariably brings with her.

On one occasion, while on holiday in the south-west of England, we went with the boys to see the semi-final of the Nat-West Trophy at Taunton. There was a huge crowed overfilling the small ground and Ann could only find a seat next to an ice-cream van behind the spectators. Halfway through his innings, Ian Botham opened his shoulders and hit an immense six. As it went over my head I suddenly realised it was going to land too close to my wife for comfort.

As the crowd yelled "Six!", I yelled "Ann", but the ball bounced on top of the ice-cream van and landed on the ground three inches away from her.

But even she has caught the addiction. Once at a limited overs match in Weston-super-Mare, Allan Lamb scored a century and it was quite obvious that his team was going to win. I wanted to go, but she insisted we see the match out to the very end.

Shortly after South Africa returned to test cricket, I was very kindly invited to the Long Room at the Wanderers to see the first day's play against Australia. When I arrived late at 12.30 pm, the score for our team was unfortunately 124 for 5.

My friends Ali Bacher, Joe Pamensky and Jackie McGlew turned to me as soon as I sat down and said "Rabbi, start praying". So I did — and Jonty Rhodes and Dave Richardson built up a splendid century partnership and we won the match.

To get back to the Annual Charity Cricket Match. This was held five years running on August Bank Holiday in Edgware, a district of London with many Jewish residents.

I was given the honour of being appointed captain of the MCC — not the famous Marylebone Cricket Club, but the Ministers' Cricket Club — a scratch team of rabbonim and chazonim who happened to be available for the occasion.

Now I must tell you that no captain in cricket history ever had such tsoros, or trouble, as I had. My star batsman, a young chazan of considerable talent, 'phoned me on the morning of the first match to tell me he had to officiate at a chupah at 2.30 pm. My wicket-keeper, a rabbi who was young many decades ago, had to officiate at a tombstone unveiling at the nearby cemetery on the same day at 4 pm. It was, well, a miracle that I managed to field a team at all.

The first time we played, against a young, strong team called Catch 22, their captain won the toss and they went in to bat. My Gateshead-trained fast bowling rabbi kept losing his yarmulke on the run-up to the wicket, much to the hilarious delight of the good-humoured crowd. It was not until we borrowed a couple of hair clips from a

woman sitting on the boundary that play could continue uninter-
rupted.

Our opponents' main batsman raced to 50 in twenty minutes and
my team looked to me in desperation to do something about the dire
situation. I went up to the batsman and said, "Jeremy, listen to me. I
have eleven different shuls represented in my team. If you don't get
yourself out soon, you will never get an aliyah in any of those shuls
ever again!"

Apparently derech eretz still exists, because he got the message
and the very next ball he received, he hit a "dolly catch" to mid-off. He
gave me a big wink on his way back to the pavilion.

My team — its average age forty (and that's being charitable) were
exhausted after fielding for a couple of hours — but we tried to make
a few runs. When I went in to bat I was partnered by a rabbi who had
a very long beard and ear locks.

When we had been in for about ten minutes, I called for a run
which wasn't really there. I got safely home, but I left him stranded.
The sports reporter of the local newspaper, which was always kind
enough to report our match, wrote the following day: "Rabbi Harris
did a most un-Christian thing and ran out his colleague!"

We lost that match by one run, simply because the other team,
sporting to the end, remembered the Talmudic rule not to shame others in public. But we had lost, so I took my team to the middle of the
pitch and together we recited Rabbonon Kaddish!

These matches were always special occasions, both for the teams
and the spectators, and witnessed not only a worthy total of runs but
of funds raised for key Jewish charities. If the standard of play of the
rabbis and cantors left much to be desired, the invariably good weather must have resulted from their prayers, and in any event, walking off
as happy losers, they knew better than anyone that it is the spirit that
counts.

I never imagined that the Anglo-Jewish experience would be
matched by our South African Jewish community.

But lo and behold, a few seasons ago the Mother Synagogue, the beautiful Gardens Shul in Cape Town, had the chutzpah to challenge the Chief Rabbi's XI to a match on the Herzlia School's playing field.

Under Action Cricket rules, this proved unbelievably entertaining. When the shul's team was in, one of their batsmen called for a run, and when it was completed, there was a shout of "Quick, let's go for another".

But it wasn't his partner speaking, it was one of our close fielders giving the instruction, so when the second batsman was duly run out and turned to walk back, we owned up to the mischief.

They asked me to bowl — a rash thing to do! The wicket-keeper muttered that as befits a preacher I was "giving it a lot of air". Nevertheless Providence was with me. By the sheerest fluke I took four wickets in the last over, one bowled and three caught, the "Angel of Safe Catches" being on our side.

So we managed to win and they made me Rabbi of the Match, a piece of undeserved nachas, or Jewish pride. Of all the honours I have been given throughout the years, this one is quite special.

5. Three London Synagogues and A Myriad of Students

We spent thirty happy years in London. The three congregations at which I worked were different in almost every way, especially in terms of the dominant age group and stage of communal development and thus presented a stimulating variety of challenges.

Kenton was a fledgling community when we arrived in 1958 but its members had the good sense to build solid, multi-purpose premises in a central location. Situated between Wembley and Stanmore in the outer north-west London suburbs, the district was modern and pleasant, while property was not too expensive and very suitable for young married couples. It was ideal for growth.

Taken for granted at the time, the sheer enthusiasm of everyone involved in building up the community was the most vital factor in making progress at a quite phenomenal rate. The board of management met fortnightly, often till well past midnight. Everyone worked overtime, from the part-time secretary — Saul Goldstein, a genuinely helpful administrator with a heart of gold, who did a full-time job — to the honorary officers and board members who ungrudgingly took synagogue chores to their own offices, the ladies guild who worked their fingers to the bone, and even the caretaker for whom nothing was too much trouble.

The honorary Shammas, Eli Kanerick z'l — a successful dress manufacturer, known to all the cheder children as "Uncle Mick" — used to sweep the hall after classes on Sunday when there was a chupah in the afternoon to ensure that everything was just right for the wedding.

Incidentally, the United Synagogue did not in those days pay princely salaries. My wife Ann took one look at my first monthly pay cheque which, after deductions, came to forty-two pounds, seven shillings and fourpence and promptly went out to work. She eventually ended up a partner in the prestigious law firm of which Martin Mendelsohn, a dear friend of ours and a world expert on franchising, was senior partner.

Fighting the establishment, an energy-sapping activity if ever there was one, was likewise undertaken with lively vigour by all of us in the congregation.

"*Three* more teachers for next term?" queried the London Board of Jewish Religious Education. "Impossible."

"*Another* overflow service?" exclaimed the United Synagogue incredulously. "But you've only recently built a new shul!"

A community, we were told in no uncertain terms, was not supposed to grow so large so soon. It was somehow against the constitution.

But grow we did, and I vividly remember the astonishing problem we had in 1962 when we literally ran out of room. Simchat Torah fell on Sunday and when we called up all the children for the traditional kol hanearim aliyah, not only was there insufficient room for them on the bimah, we only just managed to squeeze them all into the shul itself.

Like the fulfilment of the Divine promise that the Children of Israel would become as numerous "as the stars of heaven and as the sand on the sea-shore", the talleisim, a billowing wave of white, spread from the centre of the bimah to the walls on all sides, which resounded to the joyous blessings of the hundreds of excited children.

In the late 1960s we had so many services for the Days of Awe that I spent more time walking and preaching than praying. I used to buy a new pair of slippers before Yom Kippur, and having walked from the synagogue to the youth service at the Grange, then to the Parallel Service at the Methodist Church Hall, and from there to the Parallel Service at the Churchill Hall, I used to throw the worn-out slippers away the next day. Kenton was admirably egalitarian in that "overflow" was considered pejorative and changed to "parallel," and it was one of the few synagogues in the world where everyone paid the same membership subscription whether they sat in the front or back row.

Throughout its development the synagogue depended on a veritable army of voluntary helpers. The Parents' Association used to turn up in force very early every Sunday morning to take siddurim, chumashim and exercise books for the cheder classes from the shul over to Uxendon Manor School and to St Gregory's, a Catholic school which was happy to provide facilities for Jewish religious education, on Sundays noch. At one new members' evening we counted no less than 200 committee members from over twenty assorted synagogal and local Jewish organisations.

A warm and welcoming atmosphere surrounded all the congregations' endeavours. The unspoken philosophy was that no fellow-Jew, however unknowledgeable about Judaism or irreligious in observance, was turned away. Genuine attempts were made to educate and to inspire. Those who could not read a word of Hebrew were called up to the Torah after crash courses of ten weekly lessons. On one memorable occasion a proud father of the Barmitzvah boy faultlessly recited the berachot much to the delight of his teacher, my wife, and all the members of the mostly female class.

The chazan, Michael Rothstein, not only sang to the congregation but taught the congregation how to sing. Instead of the "big service" with chazan and choir so predominating that the congregants are reduced to virtual spectators, everyone joined in as one massive choir, and the joyous voices collectively expressing their devotion produced a thrilling and infectious atmosphere of prayer.

Thus the unity and friendliness of the community brought about admirable spiritual dividends.

Kenton had the distinction in the early 1960s of reviving the Batmitzvah ceremony for girls. A feature of the pre-war years, it had unfortunately fallen away with the result that most girls left cheder by the age of eleven, unlike their brothers who had Barmitzvah to look forward to.

Encouraged by my dear friend Bent Melchior, later to become Chief Rabbi of Denmark, I introduced a special syllabus for girls in our Hebrew classes. It concentrated on the traditional basics of the Jewish home, the laws of kashrut and the preparation of Shabbat and holy days being given prominence. A working knowledge of the siddur, especially becoming acquainted with the Shabbat morning service, was included, and the history section concentrated on the women of the Bible.

Our philosophy was quite simple. Judaism is a domestic religion, the home being even more important than the synagogue, and thus the education of Jewish girls in running it properly is vital to Jewish continuity. We went so far as to say that Batmitzvah was as imperative as Barmitzvah. The course proved very popular and seventeen girls passed the first examination and participated in a Sunday afternoon ceremony at which the synagogue was packed to capacity.

For this innovation, we were attacked by almost every rabbi in London, the bat chayil (as it was then known) course and ceremony being denounced as "not in accordance with Jewish tradition". We hit back by pointing to our success at retaining the girls in cheder and at how genuinely enthusiastic they were in becoming familiar with the domestic aspects of Judaism.

Within five years all the mainstream synagogues in London — and many beyond — were offering special classes for girls and conducting a variety of graduation ceremonies.

I did not require validation for what we had done, but it came my way the Pesach after the second group of girls had completed the course. During Chol Hamoed, an elderly grandmother telephoned me.

"I want to tell you how wonderful your classes for girls are," she began. "Unfortunately my daughter took ill last week two days before Pesach began. My grand-daughter Gillian, bless her — you know, she did your course last year — finished all the Yom Tov preparations."

"The seder was so good," she went on, pride in her voice, "better than I used to do, better than her mother's." She paused.

"Rabbi, whatever else you do, don't ever give up these classes for the girls."

When we came to Kenton in 1958 there were under 100 families and a few dozen pupils in the Hebrew classes. When we left early in 1972 there were more than 1 200 members of the shul and 674 children in the cheder. This growth was the direct result of the spirited and compelling way the congregation was run. After thirteen hectic and fulfilling years it was time to move on.

As I had always been closely involved with student affairs in my college days, I accepted the offer of the Bnai Brith Hillel Foundation to become National Director. Hillel provided a variety of services — accommodation, a Jewish library, kosher meals and, vitally, a focal point for Jewish students — on many university campuses throughout the country. Because most students chose to study away from their home town, the Hillel Houses were popular and well-used by the students — by no means the majority — who wished to maintain contact with Jewish life.

My appointment was greeted with something approaching incredulity by the leadership of London Jewry, who were of the narrow opinion that rabbis belonged in the pulpit and occasionally in educational positions but not anywhere else. In vain did I point to the dozens of rabbis in the United States and Israel who filled communal positions, but the establishment could not wait for me to return to what they perceived as normality.

Indeed, after I had been with Hillel for two years, the United Synagogue honorary officers offered me the prestigious post of dayan, or judge, of the London Beth Din. Three close friends said to me "it isn't you," so I politely declined. Then the chairman of the London Board of Jewish Religious Education offered me the director's post. I was tempted but declined.

Hillel proved a fascinating but exhausting job. There was a huge organisational, educational, counselling and fund-raising load to carry, and on top of it all the student leaders tended to be highly politicised and were often more interested in controversy than getting things done.

"Why are our students revolting?" was the apt ambiguity coined at the time by Lionel Simmonds, the campus correspondent of the *London Jewish Chronicle*. There was constant friction and futile power struggles and often the only way to achieve results was to make out that the idea being implemented originated with the students themselves.

The immaturity of some of the student representatives was not always harmless. On one occasion when we were demonstrating outside the Russian Embassy in Kensington on behalf of Soviet Jewry, one of the executive members of the Union of Jewish Students left his briefcase containing confidential letters from the Israeli ambassador in the embassy garden. The Russians found the case, opened it, and an international furore, reported by all the daily newspapers, ensued.

But there were ample rewards in the work. The serious students insisted on high-level programmes, the favourite themes being mysticism, anti-semitism, and the origins of Zionism. The Hebrew classes, at all levels, were invariably packed. Photocopying had just become fashionable and I helped pioneer a system of having the diverse source material copied, cut out and pasted on one sheet so that it was easy to follow the discourse. My "bingo sheets," as I called them, have been instrumental to this day in introducing newcomers to the primary texts of Jewish sacred literature.

I recall encouraging whichever students were around to join me on Shabbat morning on occasional visits to Bevis Marks, the beautiful old Spanish and Portuguese synagogue in the city. It was an hour's walk from Euston but even the non-orthodox students enjoyed the experience. To sit in the old wooden pews — the synagogue was built in 1701 — gave one a keen sense of history, and the contrast between bustling London outside and the dignified interior of the majestic Sephardi synagogue was compelling.

Pioneered by the affable Henry Shaw z'l, Friday night dinners were utterly memorable. Often there were Jewish students from all over the world, not just from all over Britain, and the zemirot were truly international. Because London University comprised dozens of scattered colleges, London Hillel was indeed a convenient regular central meeting-place and fulfilled an essential social function.

It did this so well that a large number of life-long liaisons came about due to meetings at Hillel. My wife Ann, a former law student at

University College, and I first met there, and there are hundreds of similar happy examples.

During my four years at Hillel I succeeded in establishing Jewish facilities in "Hillettes" at universities where the number of Jewish students was modest, such as Cardiff, Hull and Southampton, and I can honestly claim to have driven, at some time or another, usually in the early hours of the morning, on all the motorways of England and Wales.

The University Jewish Chaplaincy Board eventually superceded much of the educational and welfare work of Hillel. But it has always been cash-strapped. Why the students' own parents have not contributed towards it but have left the burden to communal organisations like the United Synagogue is beyond me.

The late Professor Sir Ernst Chain, who discovered penicillin with Sir Alexander Fleming, once described Hillel Houses as "rallying-points for Jewish students and a firm anchor in a world of drifting values." In my time they were.

We moved to Edgware, a huge synagogue — it is listed in the Guinness Book of Records — in the outer London suburb at the end of the Northern Line of the tube system. There are many advantages of a large congregation. The Shabbat morning services were attended by never less than 500 congregants and the atmosphere was lively and enthusiastic. Somewhat unusual for London in those days, several hundred members were Shomrei Shabbat. They lent an aura of devout respectability to congregational proceedings and it was a real advantage to be able to deliver a Gemara shiur every Shabbat afternoon to such a large and appreciative group.

But there are drawbacks to being so big. The routine work was enormously demanding so that by the time one had dealt with life-cycle events from circumcisions to tombstones and attended the meetings and events of the dozens of local Jewish organisations — the evenings were usually treble-booked — there was precious little time for anything else. My wife has the fixed view that there is an invisible wire connecting the soup-ladle to the telephone: no sooner had we sat down to eat the evening meal when the 'phone would ring.

For the Days of Awe we had the largest services in the Orthodox world. This was due to a bizarre arrangement whereby the adjacent and very large shul hall, instead of being utilised for a separate over-flow service, was incorporated into the synagogue itself by disman-tling the huge connecting wooden partition.

It is not easy to speak to 2 000 people without a microphone. I have been blessed with a loud speaking voice — those who try to sleep during my sermons can attest to that — and I managed the first Rosh Hashanah to project it from the pulpit to the very back row, which seemed miles away. But I became hoarse half-way through Yom Kippur and lost it completely on the first day of Succot.

A notable occasion in the Edgware shul calendar was the first Selichot service. As it was held after Shabbat, transport could be used and there was always a full congregation of locals and visitors. Commencing at midnight and lasting till 3 am, it never failed to be spiritually uplifting. The choir was augmented for the special service and the superlative rendition of Chazan Asher Hainovitz — a melodi-ous tenor voice with meticulous nusach and fluent Hebrew — inspired those privileged to attend and set the right tone for the forth-coming holy days.

In all my congregations I have produced a shul journal. In Edgware I was spoiled because we enjoyed a veritable embarrassment of riches when it came to journalistic talent. On the editorial board of Muse, Magazine of the United Synagogue Edgware, we had four luminaries of the London Jewish Chronicle, a newspaper as necessary for Anglo-Jews at the end of the week as chicken soup. They were the late John Shaftesley, then the editor, the genial Joe Finkelstone, a prize-winning foreign affairs writer, my friend Hyam Corney, the paper's current deputy editor, and Geoffrey Gilbert who was an expert in advertising. The team was completed by Gita Zarum, a highly gifted journalist.

Our editorial board meetings were relaxed and enjoyable and I learned a great deal. Needless to say, the results were faultless.

A genuine difficulty in ministering to the congregation was that my predecessor, the genial Reverend Saul Amias, who served Edgware for forty years, lived in the district. He was given the title "emeritus minister" (having a good sense of humour he used to say that "emeritus" must be some kind of skin disease) and because he knew all the families of the community so well, many of them could not accept that he had in fact retired. He was so used to the pastoral work that he himself sometimes gave the impression that he had not retired.

Among its many failures, the United Synagogue has never tackled the problem of retired rabbis who continue to live locally and to frequent *their* synagogue. There have been serious consequences. One of my colleagues used to have to suffer the "emeritus" pushing his hat forward over his face and going to sleep the moment he went into the pulpit. It was a factor in my colleague leaving that congregation. Another retired minister used to ostentatiously open a sefer when the sermon began. My colleague left for overseas. I personally found the relationship tiresome.

In the end I left Edgware over a point of principle. The local Jewish school, Rosh Pinah, where I taught Mishnah twice a week, was much in demand and there was an annual clamour for places. The management admitted the child of a Reform convert (halachically non-Jewish) to the detriment of a bona fide Jewish child whose parents were justifiably upset and complained to me about it. I protested. I was told to "mind my own business."

As there were strong links between shul and school, I felt it was my business, particularly as the cheder did not permit non-Jewish children — to prevent subsequent problems with regard to Barmitzvah and marriage — and the school's admission policy was causing confusion.

A special board of management meeting was convened to discuss the issue. After many hours of debate late into the evening my point of principle was rejected.

"In which case," I said quietly as I rose to leave (I am at my most resolute when I speak softly), "you can find yourselves another rabbi."

The 'phone rang at midnight. It was Jeffrey Milston, the synagogue's financial representative and a good friend. "You meant it, didn't you?" he asked.

"Yes," I said.

That was on a Monday night, and that very week on Motzei Shabbat Levi Stern z'l, a prominent member of St John's Wood Synagogue, telephoned to tell me that its rabbi had announced that morning that he was leaving. Stern wanted to know whether I might be interested in the job.

SJW was a lovely community. Founded in 1876, it was still going remarkably well a century later (like my favourite whisky) and in contrast to most of the founding and early synagogues of the United Synagogue, which had either closed or seen better days, it retained its strength and its prestige. Other districts fluctuated regarding Jewish popularity, but St John's Wood, an elegant and highly agreeable part of London, kept its reputation as a highly desirable place of residence.

Most of the members were successful in life and, although they were well-off, they were pleasant — an unusual combination. Disparagement of the rich — that you can tell what G-d thinks of money when you look at some of the people He gives it to — did not apply to the congregants of St John's Wood. They were largely unspoilt, exceptionally generous and even somewhat shy. It is the only congregation I have ever known in which millionaires did not mind sitting inconspicuously towards the back.

A fashionable venue for weddings, I spent most Sundays under the chupah. The setting was ideal and the flower-bedecked synagogue quite splendid. They were invariably warm and happy occasions, despite the photographers who delighted in turning my synagogue into a film studio, the videotape of the wedding apparently being more important than the wedding itself.

Once the proceedings were nearly ruined before they had even begun. The parents of the bride and groom were divorced and it so happened that all four had remarried. As this presented a choice of eight possible parents and step-parents to stand under the bridal canopy, I gave the bride, who wanted her step-father and not her natural father to give her away, the option to choose whom she preferred in the entourage.

I recall it was a very sunny afternoon in June, a large number of family and friends were assembled, and the ceremony was due to begin at 3 pm. I had signed the ketubah with the groom, and we were waiting to begin. At ten minutes past three, the Shammas signalled to me desperately from the entrance to the shul that something was amiss.

I went out as surreptitiously as possible and discovered an appalling row taking place in the Bride's Room. Arguing furiously as to who should accompany the bride, the assorted parents were shouting at each other at the top of their voices. Pale, upset and on the verge of tears, the bride appealed to me to do something.

"Right," I remonstrated with them, "that's enough. We made the exact arrangements for the procession weeks ago. Either we stick to them — that's what the bride wants and it's her day — or I'm going to pick unterfihrers from the congregation and you can just all stay here."

They all calmed down, and we went ahead according to plan but it was a close call.

I had three "slips" for the layening. The public reading of the Torah is a matter of precision, and the text being sacred, no mistakes whatsoever are allowed. The preparation is thorough and painstaking, quite a few years of experience being needed before one reads well. Encouraged by my father z'l, right after I became Barmitzvah, I have been reading the weekly portion regularly for well over forty years — the first thirty years are the most difficult and then one gets used to it — and I am now quite proficient at it.

My rendering is somewhat dramatic on purpose, following the meaning of the text, especially in the narrative parts of Chumash, and despite the necessity of constant revision to avoid making mistakes I enjoy the exercise, and close acquaintance with the text has enabled me the easier to be able to pinpoint a scriptural verse when required.

By the time I began officiating at St John's Wood, I was fairly fluent. This is not to say I did not succumb to the occasional mistake. Now whenever the reading is incorrect and changes the proper meaning of the text, it must immediately be put right — not only is the reader obliged to be accurate, the congregation is obliged to hear a correct rendition. However, how mistakes are corrected in practice is a matter of some contention.

As the reading of the Law is public, it can of course be highly embarrassing if corrections are brusquely shouted out. Fortunate indeed is the officiant who has a knowledgeable gabbai standing by him on the bimah who can gently indicate the error sotto voce.

So I had three slips, friends of mine — Norman, Bill and Louis, all of whom were capable of reading the Torah — who delighted in catching me out at least once every Shabbat morning. Imagine me bent over the open scroll and a few yards behind me to the right, exactly where the slips field for the person batting, they would wait patiently for a chance.

When it came one of them, often all three of them, would rise up in their seats and triumphantly, but always good-naturedly, voice the correction. Nowadays I usually only lein a particular portion when I am called to the Torah (many worshippers are surprised the Chief Rabbi can do it) and when I make a mistake — a rare occurrence, of course! — and am pulled up and corrected, I automatically turn my head to the right and nod at the invisible slips.

The presiding warden was a benign and altogether helpful lay leader named Zeno Filipsohn z'l. To any difficulty which arose from whatever source, regarding any request which was made, whether by me or by close friend and colleague, Chazan Chaim Abramovitz, by the Synagogue secretary, by the well-meaning Shammas, Hymie Hinden z'l, or by the non-Jewish caretaker, he had one reply: "No problem."

Seldom could a shul have been run so agreeably and graciously with such genuine good will and with such commendable results and, although some of the board members considered him far too indulgent, the air of tranquillity which hovered over all the affairs of the community was largely due to his temperate character.

Across the road was the Hospital of St John and St.Elizabeth, staffed by the appropriately-named Sisters of Mercy. Of all the hospitals I have visited over the years none has made more impact on me in terms of natural friendliness and sheer kindness to all the patients — who were of all religions and none — than these nursing sisters. Their sense of responsibility was unconditional, their devotion to duty inspirational and it was a privilege to be the Jewish chaplain of such a hospital.

One of the many items my wife introduced was the periodic communal Friday night dinner. A large number within the community were widows or widowers and many of the elderly, for one reason or another, had no close family in London. The first time we organised this function there were about 70 people. Instead of spending Shabbat on their own, forgotten and miserable, they were hosted by their own synagogue in a congenial atmosphere.

An 85-year old man told me that the magic of Friday night, which had faded from his memory years ago, had been revived. One 80-year old lady with tears in her eyes said that she had not heard zemirot for over twenty years. All of them were deeply touched. Their own congregation had remembered them.

The most efficacious sermon I delivered from that pulpit was at the Kol Nidrei service several days after the Sabra and Chatilla massacre. Israel had taken a heavy pounding in the media; morale in the Jewish community was very low. It was the custom in Anglo-Jewry to devote the Kol Nidrei Appeal to the JIA — I introduced the same concept to South Africa when funds were desperately needed to aid the rescue of eastern European and Ethiopian Jewry — but opinion against Israel was so relentless that it was feared the appeal would meet with a pitiful response.

I spoke about the power of Yom Kippur to bring us close to everything that mattered. Close to the congregation in prayer and fasting, close to our personal roots with Yizkor, and close to the Almighty whose presence we often ignored during the year but who was recognised by us on this holy day. And close to our people with whom we were inextricably bound, and close to Israel, our home from home.

"Israel does not need our criticism, too, that we should join all those pushing her down," I implored the congregation. "Israel at this time needs our understanding, our help, our love."

Dozens of congregants came up to me after the service to tell me that they had come to shul intending to give nothing to the appeal but I had succeeded in convincing them otherwise.

The years at St John's Wood were active and satisfying and we could quite easily have remained there till the time came to retire. But a more strenuous challenge beckoned. South Africa.

6. Induction Into Office

The amazing thing was the number of people.

On March 20, 1988, the huge Wolmarans Street Synagogue — alas now desolate, but shortly to be resurrected in a slightly different form in Oaklands — was teeming and there was the electric atmosphere of a state occasion. Those who could not get a seat, and there were hundreds who came along for the rare spectacle, irrespective of whether or not they had been invited, sat in the aisles with dozens standing squashed at the back.

So my entry to office was characterised by all the traits which make South African Jewry so special — warmth, informality and noisy liveliness.

Television and radio had likewise commandeered the large area in front of the Aron Kodesh, so there was precious little room for the three Chief Rabbis present, who spent most of the duration of the service trying to avoid knocking into cameras and tripping over wires.

I recall the warm endorsement given to me by the late Chief Rabbi Bernard Casper z'l, a man of towering dignity, and the splendid advice given to me by my late mentor, Chief Rabbi Lord Jakobovits z'l, a leading spiritual personality of the 20th century.

For me the most moving moment was the recitation of the pledge from Berich Shemai. I looked up at my wife and late mother-in-law z'l, smiling down from the packed ladies' gallery, turned my back on the mammoth congregation, and facing the Ark began to say the prayer:"I am the servant of the Holy One, Blessed be He, and I prostrate myself before Him and before the glory of His Torah at all times...".

The Talmud tells us that whenever the Ark is open here below, the Gates of Prayer are open above. I remember praying with humility that I should be blessed from on high to fulfil the responsibilities of office and be worthy of the challenges that would face me.

Because it was a once in a lifetime occasion, I had spent an inordinate amount of time in preparing my induction sermon. Normally preferring to speak from a few notes, which allow me the freedom to elaborate within the framework of the theme and to give the address, although fully prepared, an air of spontaneity, no such luxury was permitted on this special occasion. Every single word was chosen in advance, the text was already with the press and the full manuscript had to be delivered as prepared.

Beginning with a plea for togetherness with the entire community — "its leaders spiritual and lay, its organisations ancient and modern, its members young and old, its adherents and its backsliders" — I called for partnership with everyone and especially with my rabbinic colleagues to be the hallmark of my tenure of office.

"The touchstone of any chief rabbinate lies in its ability to promote co-operation and concord, the extent to which it is effective as a positive integrating force."

I then deliberately focussed on three issues, which I considered to be by far the most crucial: the continuity of traditional Judaism as a living force; the preservation of the bonds of the Jewish people with the State of Israel; and the practical application of Jewish ethical teachings to the South African scene.

Contrary to the view of assimilationists that Judaism had run its course and had no viable role at the end of the twentieth century, I wished to stress that the tenets of Judaism were more relevant than ever before.

"In the domestic chaos of one-in-three divorces, Judaism teaches the supreme importance of family life and the bliss of shalom bayit; amidst the seething scramble of the acquisitive society — man possessed by his possessions — Judaism provides the oasis of Shabbat, the holy Sabbath day; in a world which has lost control over its appetites, Jewish tradition offers the discipline of Kashruth; at a time when HIV-AIDS threatens the very future of a permissive society, Judaism holds out the dignity of an unchanging code of morality; when a pluralism of conflicting ideologies, most of which breed anarchic life-styles, menace the fabric of civilisation, the Torah retains a clear distinction between right and wrong behaviour. Judaism, the only intellectual heritage and guide on how to live, still extant after 3 500 years ... Judaism has more to say now, to the Jew and to the world, than ever before."

The second area I wanted to address was the need to recapture the Zionist dynamic. As the leading Zionist community of the diaspora, South African Jewry should work with more enthusiasm for the recognition of the centrality of Israel and its pivotal significance for the destiny of the Jewish people.

The paradoxical situation in which Zionism *before* the establishment of the state fired the imagination with visions of a noble Jewish future, but which *after* the founding of the state searches around for high purpose, was a pivotal challenge.

"We have become used to the idea of a Jewish State; it no longer grips us with the same emotional appeal or level of commitment." We had to fight the apathy which was resulting in Zionism losing its impetus. "We must never give up the sense of wonder and elation at Israel reborn in our lifetime, we who have been privileged to witness the miraculous rebirth of the Jewish homeland...".

I then moved to the disturbing general situation in South Africa and the Jewish community's responsibility regarding it.

Contrasting the option of non-involvement — "the efforts may be misconstrued as political interference; the comfort and security of the Jewish community may be jeopardised; the help may be resented rather than welcomed..." — with that of involvement, I came down heavily in favour of the latter, supplying what I considered compelling reasons.

"The self-respect of every member of the Jewish community is at stake in this issue more than any other, for it has always been an established principle that the distinctive honour of being Jewish carries with it corresponding responsibility ... the doctrine of the Chosen People does not imply the conferment of special privilege ... rather the imposition of extra obligation ... we are 'chosen' for duty, however uncomfortable ... 'chosen' to be an example of good, whatever the circumstances."

I asked for a real identification with suffering and degradation, for a sharing with the underprivileged of the blessings we enjoyed — "if anyone cries in the beloved country, let it never be our fault, let it not be due to us".

"Of all the responses to the current dilemma, confusion, resignation, indifference, despair or escape," I concluded, "the only genuine one is a mighty effort by all people of good will to build bridges across the divide, to believe in, and work for, the evolutionary process, and to harness all positive energies to allow South Africa to hope for the future."

My address, delivered probably too loudly into the battery of microphones, received a somewhat mixed reaction. Whereas the exhortations concerning Yiddishkeit and Zionism met with approval, those regarding Jewish involvement in black upliftment were considered unnecessarily controversial.

This response was to recur with monotonous regularity throughout the first six years of my chief rabbinate. At meetings and organisational gatherings, from the pulpit and at seminars and conferences, whenever I urged higher standards of Torah observance it was fine — "That's his job, to tell us to be better Jews". Whenever I spoke about Israel, it was well received: "Our chief is a Zionist."

But when I spoke about the urgent need to help the majority black population, there was an eerie silence and a coolness in the atmosphere. "Oh dear," the audience was thinking, "what on earth is he going to say next?"

This reaction happened so often, the change of mood was so marked it was as if a switch had been thrown, that I became inured to it. It is still around, but thankfully has faded to a large extent, among the older generation into a kind of reluctant acceptance, and with the younger generation usually into eager approval.

So on my great day I went for it by abjuring the role of a "nominal, decorative, restrictive Chief Rabbinate," and by stating categorically that "rather do I come to serve the needs of our time".

One sentence sticks in my mind, and it sums it all up: "The members of the Jewish community are urged to exemplify Jewish values in their relationships with the underprivileged sections of the society in which we live."

More than a decade later, the words still apply.

7. The African Chief

Purely by chance, before I was appointed Chief Rabbi of South Africa, I had the opportunity of gaining experience in almost every branch of rabbinic endeavour, educational, welfare, managerial, communal and (even on occasion) spiritual.

Since the age of sixteen, I had been teaching Torah and giving shiurim. Always close to the youth movements I was given the youth portfolio in Chief Rabbi Jakobovits's first "cabinet". A student leader in my college days, I was in 1956 elected vice chairman of the Inter-University Jewish Federation, predecessor to the Union of Jewish Students, and I served as national director of the Hillel Foundation in the early 1970s.

Acquaintance with the military was gained as senior Jewish chaplain to Her Majesty's forces. For several years I was joint chairman of Mizrachi in Britain, my colleague Menny Klausner and our president, Arieh Handler, doing most of the work. I was active on the rabbinical council of the United Synagogue for two decades, on the committee and as secretary and as chairman. Quite often appearing on radio, I was taught a great deal by Michael Freedland who successfully ran BBC Radio London's "You Don't Have To Be Jewish" programme for many years.

I think I have visited every hospital in London, those hospitals where I was Jewish Chaplain many hundreds of times. I have been at the Middlesex Hospital in Mortimer Street in London's West End at all hours of the day and night; when a Jewish patient was dying it was correctly expected that the chaplain would be at the bedside helping the patient, saying tehillim and consoling the family.

Teenage, marital and bereavement counselling was a regular occurrence. For a decade in the 1960s, I was chaplain at a maximum security prison.

Real depth of experience I cannot claim, but for one reason or another I am able to claim range of experience. Also the way things worked out, without knowing that I would ever become a chief rabbi,

I had the good fortune in St John's Wood of being near to Chief Rabbi Lord Jakobovits z'l. A mentor of rare quality, his staunch adherence to principle on all issues of moral well-being, his capacity, ably assisted by his energetic wife Amelie, to develop cordial and notable relationships with the highest in the land, and the finely-honed balance he always brought to bear in solving controversial issues, were lessons of immense value that I picked up subconsciously and which were to stand me in good stead.

The work of the chief rabbinate is pressurised. All week could easily be spent dealing with incoming telephone calls. The post is voluminous. Meetings of all shapes and sizes are so frequent and conferences and seminars at all levels so regular — like a shul committee, South Africans in authority actually believe in talking one's way out of problems — that all the time available for work could be spent, several times over, simply attending them.

Even in these days of communication by fax and e-mail as well as letter, the well-ordered office divides the treatment of mail into In, Out and Pending compartments. Due to the regrettable tendency of most Jewish people to insist on "going to the top" (as they see it) — blissfully ignoring the possibility that the matter in question may have nothing whatsoever to do with the chief rabbi — my mail is divided into six categories: In, Out, Pending, Tsoros, Meshuggah, and Impossible.

Managing the office smoothly is never easy and while it is flattering that so many people wish to make demands on one's time, and while one wishes one had the time to deal with all of them, the real problem with the hordes of telephone callers and appointment seekers is that the valid often gets lost among the unnecessary, the trivial, the extraneous and the absurd. Short of being rude, I do not know of an effective and fail-safe way of screening requests, and the problem is aggravated by most callers imagining their problem to be the most urgent in the world and, furthermore, that I have the ideal solution at hand.

The scope of the demands is unbelievable. Here are some examples. Someone's son and daughter-in-law have just moved house but the nearest synagogue is three kilometres away, so could I arrange forthwith for a new shul to be built close to their new home? There is a family row that has been going on for many years: a large sum of inherited money has led to two brothers, who had a severe personality clash apart from the money, not speaking to each other for twenty years. Could I please sort out matters? The family is absolutely convinced that if I were to intervene I could make sholem in no time. "You're a Zionist, aren't you, Chief Rabbi? Please contact the United Nations and tell them the Palestinians don't need a state of their own."

The positive aspects of the work may be loosely categorised into the pastoral, the rabbinic, the communal and the general.

My wife and I have visited every place in southern Africa where a Jewish community exists. In fact, I believe I have sung the haftara in nearly every shul in southern Africa. The welcome is always effusive and heart-warming; the smaller the community the more the visit is appreciated. In addition to participating in religious services and communal gatherings, we have consumed delicious braais in Oudtshoorn and Paarl, been entertained royally from Pietersburg to Plettenberg Bay, enjoyed the sumptuous Shabbat berochoh in Bloemfontein and Muizenberg, and eaten countless delectable Friday evening congregational dinners from Klerksdorp to East London. Our spiritual mission is everywhere accompanied by gastronomic delight, but we have been likewise thrilled to sense the genuine desire across the country to keep Judaism alive.

Of course the pastoral visits necessitate a great deal of speaking on my part. In Johannesburg itself, in order to maintain contact with the congregations as frequently as possible, I quite often "appear" at three different shuls on the same Shabbat by giving the derashah at one on Friday night, speaking at the kiddush of a second in the morning, and delivering the shiur at a third after Minchah. One year during Pesach I officiated at twelve different synagogues in the main Jewish areas of Johannesburg and once on Yom Kippur in Cape Town managed to fit in five separate venues.

If there were an entry in the Guinness Book of Records for the greatest number of rabbinic speeches on one Shabbat, I think I could claim it.

About ten years ago my wife and I were spending Shabbat with the Sandton community — they now boast a large and beautiful new shul which is a remarkable affirmation of a future for South African Jewry — and the programme went as follows. At the invitation of my colleague Rabbi Ziggy Suchard (whose personality is as sweet as his name suggests), I gave the Friday evening derashah. Half-way through the service, more than a hundred black school pupils turned up and I spoke to them in the crowded youth service.

After shul, the congregation had arranged a dinner in our honour in the old Jewish Guild across the road. Five hundred congregants attended a traditional Friday night dinner at which I gave the after-dinner speech.

On the Shabbat morning I was invited to pop in to the youth service and to the children's service to "say a few words." I spoke at the berochoh. The shul had organised a special lunch for all the members of the management committee, adjacent committees and their wives, and I spoke before benshing.

In the course of the afternoon, I addressed the local Bnei Akiva group for half-an-hour. I gave a shiur before Minchah. I spoke at Shalosh Seudos.

That's ten times on the one Shabbat. Just in case you imagine my colleague, who loves nothing better than to expound Torah, had an easy time of it, I would mention that he gave a couple of divrei Torah during the meals, introduced the parashah in detail before the reading of the Law, addressed the Barmitzvah boy on Shabbat morning and slipped in two shiurim during the course of the day.

If our colleagues of the Rabbinical Union ever found out we had spoken no fewer than 16 times between us, they would call an emergency meeting, at which I trust we would not be allowed to speak!

The specifically rabbinic side of my responsibilities is very much worthwhile. I have always believed the Chief Rabbi's prime duty is to encourage and support his fellow rabbis in every way possible. This entails helping them to find and obtain a suitable congregational or educational position. Often it means being involved in local synagogal controversies, some of them serious, others unbelievably petty. I do not invariably side with the rabbi, but I help sort the problem out if I can. I hope I am a fair "third umpire".

It also means trying to obtain the best possible financial deal for rabbis. I am frequently called upon to intervene in unpleasant disputes over remuneration, bearing in mind that congregations vary considerably in size and substance.

Wishing to find out precise information concerning income and emoluments, I asked all my colleagues at our Annual Rabbinical Conference in 1992 to fill out a questionnaire on salary, housing, medical aid, pension, and so on. To avoid any embarrassment, I requested them not to put their name on the form, only the financial details.

The results caused considerable consternation: there was an alarming difference of R60 000 a year between the lowest and highest paid part-time rabbis and an outrageous discrepancy of no less than R130 000 between the lowest and highest paid full-time rabbis. Some rabbis lived in their own house, others in a house belonging to the shul. Some had proper expense arrangements for car and telephone expenses; others had to fight to recover what they spent. Some had adequate pension arrangements, others none.

I resolved there and then to try to gain the agreement of the Union of Orthodox Synagogues to a minimum salary structure and to basic conditions of service. This would serve to protect the rabbi, especially when negotiating his package with a new congregation, and would at least offer guidelines and a basic framework in an uncertain and often haphazard situation.

We set up a special committee of leading and experienced lay and spiritual leaders and met regularly over many months to try and come up with an acceptable formula. Regrettably we were unable to reach agreement as it was strongly felt that each shul was independent and had to retain its prerogative to come to terms on its own without recourse to overall regulations.

This remains an unacceptable state of affairs but in many instances I am called upon by rabbis moving to another position "to have a word" with their new shul chairman to try to obtain a better deal. These interventions quite often meet with some measure of success but it would be infinitely preferable if there were fixed scales so that where necessary the incoming rabbi could at least point out that what he was being offered did not match the minimum recommended rate.

Of course there is always a price to pay. I recall the protracted negotiations in the early 1980s in London when a high-powered committee composed of the top honorary officers of the United Synagogue and senior rabbis tackled the issue of salaries. At the time there was a shortage of rabbis, some six large congregations were searching for incumbents, and the Rabbinical Council politely pointed out that if the financial provisions were made more attractive, candidates were more likely to be forthcoming.

The imperatives of supply and demand apply as much to synagogues as elsewhere, and to their credit the lay leaders instituted vastly improved salary scales over a period of three years. But there was a catch.

"There is a quid pro quo arrangement here," Victor Lucas z'l, the then President of the United Synagogue, who admirably endeavoured to bridge the gap between lay and rabbinic leadership, announced to the rabbis on the committee.

"You will get the quid. But we want the quo!"

It transpired that a major segment of the salary increases for rabbanim and chazanim would be subject to an annual vote of the local synagogue's board of management. If the incumbent's performance was deemed satisfactory the entire amount would be awarded. If the board was not fully satisfied, a partial increase would be given. If the board was dissatisfied and wished to send a signal to the poor rabbi or cantor, the entire amount would be withheld. So we got our quid and they kept us on our toes.

Fortunately for me, the halachic aspect of my work is made all the easier by the excellence of the Batei Din in both Johannesburg and Cape Town. Under the expert guidance of the Av Bet Din, Rabbi

Moshe Kurtstag, and ably assisted by his colleagues, the supervision of kashrut, arrangements for gittin and conversions, and all matters appertaining to the proper religious functioning of our community are smoothly carried out. We meet weekly to discuss a wide range of policy matters and consult with each other regarding all decisions of communal importance.

All the rabbis of South Africa come together before Rosh Hashanah for the Annual Rabbinical Conference, an event organised by my office in conjunction with the Southern African Rabbinical Association and the Union of Orthodox Synagogues. This annual get-together always proves of value, in that we are able to debate current problems of Jewish and general concern, listen to experts in the educational and welfare field, tackle fascinating ethical dilemmas caused by technological progress, and generally recharge our batteries in the company of our colleagues.

The conference is particularly appreciated by the rabbis of the smaller and country communities who are often quite isolated most of the year and who deserve the boost to morale that the chavrusa invariably engenders. Organised in recent years by my capable and level-headed assistant, Rabbi Ron Hendler, the conference provides a serious forum for the consideration of enhancing professional standards and an ideal opportunity of sharing views on key issues, among them priorities in communal funding, rationalisation of facilities, and the tension and interaction between the Jewish community and the majority population of the country.

Over the years a number of successful mitzvah campaigns have been held throughout the country, the Taste of Shabbat being conducted twice and proving influential with the younger married couples. One rabbi told me with pride that due to the widespread publicity and collective impact of the campaign, "the number of sabbath observant Jews in my small community has doubled from five to ten. We now have a minyan of shomrei Shabbat."

The Taste of Kashrut campaign was also remarkably beneficial, as was the Jewish Family Values week in which the strong attempt was made to counteract the pernicious forces causing so much damage to traditional norms.

Encouragement to ameliorate areas of concern is also provided. My Durban colleague, Rabbi Dr Pinhas Zekry, has pioneered a support system for converts so that there is proper follow-up once the candidate has been passed by the Beth Din. This help can make all the difference to the effectiveness of the conversion in terms of maintaining standards of observance and helping converts feel they belong to the community. Such attempts deserve the widest application.

The advent of the Jewish Studies matriculation exam has created an ideal opportunity of strengthening the Jewish educational content of our mainstream Jewish schools. I am involved with the Independent Examination Board as a moderator. Although the innovation got off to a slow start, the momentum has rapidly increased and nearly all of our Jewish schools throughout South Africa enter a larger number of pupils every year.

To be sensitive to the needs of our numerous Jewish organisations, I retain close contact with the majority of them. To the best of my knowledge no other Chief Rabbi in any other country is regularly co-opted onto the national management committee of the Board of Deputies and the Zionist Federation, but I have been happy to serve, and despite the innumerable meetings and mountains of paper work, have been able occasionally to make some input on policy decisions affecting the well-being of the community.

Delicate and critical issues arise from time to time, especially concerning the standing of the Jewish community vis-a-vis the government and it is good that Jewish leadership is usually united in dealing with them.

All the organisations in the Jewish community, educational, welfare, charitable, student, youth and sporting, keep in regular touch with my office, and whenever my presence or advice is requested I try to oblige.

Needless to say I am heavily involved in fund-raising for multifarious causes. I am not sure whether I am a good shnorrer or not, although by and large the results have been positive thanks to some wonderfully generous people. But I have never been able to summon up huge reserves of enthusiasm for the task of relieving people of their own money, however worthy the cause.

Fund raisers everywhere should be familiar with the anonymous poem, first shown to me by Ronnie Kaplan, chairman of the Rabbi Aloy Foundation Trust, about one of their kind who passes away and applies for entry to heaven. "Come straight in and choose your harp," the fund raiser is bidden, "you've had your share of Hell."

At the farewell reception the Hillel Foundation gave me, I recall thanking "several Anglo-Jewish millionaires for teaching me humility".

One of the exceptions to my distaste for raising funds is the Yeshivah of Cape Town. The brainchild of Rabbi Jonathan Glass, the yeshivah has had a major impact on Cape Town Jewry, bringing higher Torah learning and genuine appreciation of Jewish religious observance to the community.

Clearly leadership involves the duty, sometimes painful, of pointing out where one believes others are wrong. Among the many rows I have been involved in, one of the most hurtful to the collective South African Jewish identity was the furore over the 1989 Maccabiah. Our teams were adamant they wanted to participate as South African Maccabi but the World Maccabi Union was frightened that South Africa's participation as South Africa might severely prejudice the international sporting status of Maccabi as a whole.

I recall a furious Zionist Federation meeting — uniquely in the Jewish world Maccabi is part of the South African Zionist Federation — during which almost everyone, except one Poale Zion delegate and me, was insistent that the local teams participate as South Africans.

Explaining that we had no right to prejudice Maccabi's standing in the world of sport, and quoting my good Maccabi friends from London, Ken Gradon and Fred Worms, concerning the damage we might cause, it was eventually but reluctantly accepted that we would participate under the banner She'ar Ha-olam, the Rest of the World.

It is rarely necessary to berate one's colleagues but when Rabbi Dr

Jack Steinhorn of the Sea Point synagogue went too far in insulting the Beth Din in a case in which he was wrong in fact and in Jewish law, action to defend the authority of the Beth Din became imperative.

Together with all the other rabbis of Cape Town, the Beth Din and I declared Rabbi Steinhorn persona non grata. His congregants, the majority of whom did not understand the first thing about the matter, rallied to his support and only after Judge Dennis Davis arbitrated the matter was Rabbi Steinhorn reinstated. But he agreed to abide fully by the authority of the Beth Din and his shul committee also guaranteed his future behaviour.

All chief rabbis agonize, I believe, over the dilemma of whether they should publicly represent the consensus of rabbinic opinion or whether they should "do their own thing". I plead guilty to advancing my own views on two issues — support for the "peace process" between Israel and its neighbours and the level of involvement required by the Jewish community in the new South Africa. But I have propounded these views in my own name and been at pains to point out that my views are not necessarily shared by my colleagues.

Acute communal problems that warrant active and serious consideration surface from time to time. A case in point was the setting up of the Jewish Divorce Commission.

Much concern about the continuing high rate of divorce was evident in the Jewish community and at my initiative a commission consisting of Jewish social workers, psychologists, psychiatrists, divorce mediation lawyers, specialist rabbis and family doctors and representatives of the women's organisations was instituted. They were mandated to identify the issues, both general and specific to the Jewish community, that contributed to marriage breakdown, and to make recommendations as to how to solve or ameliorate them.

Under the expert guidance of Brenda Solarsh and Etta Goldman of Jewish Community Services, the commission, on which I sat, met regularly over a period of two years and consulted widely with local and international authorities.

In its incisive report, the commission specified an alarming list of external factors. Among these were the changing roles of women, affluence and overindulgence, the stressful nature of South Africa's transition, the destabilising effect of emigration on family life, enmeshed family relationships that blur the boundaries between a couple and their parents, and the lack of suitable role models.

Included among the internal factors were unrealistic expectations of marriage, an unhealthy emphasis on so-called self-realisation, the belief that most things including relationships are disposable, a lack of relationship skills, and "unfinished business" from previous marriages.

Prevention, the commission determined, was the way towards stemming the high divorce rate. It strongly recommended that marriage preparation programmes be expanded and that relationship awareness programmes be conducted for standard eight pupils in all Jewish day schools. An innovative idea was a pilot project testing the feasibility of a Relationship Marketing Model, tracking couples from the time of engagement to their first anniversary and so on, the stages being computer-linked to sponsors and relevant workshops.

More research needed to be undertaken, the commission insisted, into all aspects of Jewish marriage and divorce, but it certainly accomplished the initial task of rousing awareness of a key problem, and in many valuable ways it pioneered a collective process as to how vexed communal issues should be tackled in future.

Much of my time and energy is devoted to representing the Jewish community to the wider public and engaging in inter-community activities. A wide range and fascinating variety of responsibilities is involved here, from advancing Tikkun's outreach programmes at national, provincial and metropolitan level to motivating the ongoing attack against crime, from consulting with colleagues of the National Religious Leaders' Forum on how best to promote basic moral values, to sitting as a trustee on the Job Creation Trust, from attending the state opening of parliament to lecturing about Judaism to church groups.

This is not only enthralling, but in the course of making contacts and building bridges with a host of welcoming and well-meaning organisations, I have met so many kind, genuine and reliable people — from government personalities to the person in the street — that this aspect of my duties has become a source of deep and increasing satisfaction.

I am the first to admit that my personality and approach are riddled with contradictions somewhat unusual in a Chief Rabbi. I am utterly traditional and at the same time like to think of myself as thoroughly modern.

I am strictly Orthodox yet liberal enough to work with Reform associates for the common good. I am intensely passionate — oy, am I passionate! — on all matters of principle but I loathe fundamentalism and much prefer moderation. I deal in the main with absolutes, yet politically espouse the centre — well, just left of centre. I live in an inner world of concepts and ideals and constant spiritual reflection yet I am equally at home watching my favourite soccer or cricket team.

Whether such hybrid qualities are an advantage is debatable.

All those who think of themselves as "prime movers" and "major players" would do well to keep in mind the astute observation of marketing man Phillip Kotler. He tells us there are five kinds of people. Those who make things happen, those who think they make things happen, those who watch things happen, those who have to ask what has happened, and those who do not even realise anything has happened.

In fulfilling my role in our frenetic, excitable and volatile South Africa, I can honestly claim a personal acquaintance at some time or another with all five categories.

8. Likes and Dislikes

Let's start with South African English. Quaint and animated, reflecting a multi-cultural hotch-potch and competing with no fewer than ten other "official" languages, the South African brand of English can make you smile or drive you mad.

That the same word can have a different nuance depending in which English-speaking country it is used — "presently" in Britain means "soon" but in the United States means "at present" — is to be expected. That the same word means the opposite is disconcerting, to say the least. My introduction to this phenomenon came on my first weekend in the country.

I had delivered my first sermon at the Friday evening service in the Great Synagogue at Wolmarans Street in central Johannesburg. Coming out of shul afterwards, I happened to be behind two old men who were discussing my "performance".

"What did you think of the derashah?" the one asked the other.

"Ach, shame" was the reply.

Now my address that night was not all that bad and I was a bit shaken at such a negative reaction. So I tentatively inquired an hour later at the Friday night table whether the word shame had a different connotation in South African English than elsewhere. My fellow guests were highly amused at the query and put me out of my misery by explaining that locally the expression does not signify reproach but is used to denote warm approval or sympathy.

My wife Ann had a similar experience when we moved into our first South African home. On asking the workmen to attend to several urgent practical jobs, the foreman nodded and replied that the work would be done "just now". Weeks later the jobs had still not been done, "just now" apparently meaning some time before the end of the next millennium. Thus we learned that if you want anything done immediately, you have to use the magic South Africanism, "now-now".

There are myriad quirks of language. The cinema is still referred to by some as the "bioscope" while the radio is the "wireless". A decimal point is not a dot but for some peculiar reason a comma. When problems arise, those in authority tell us they will "address" them. Everywhere else problems require to be solved not addressed.

That Afrikaans has influenced South African English is obvious but the result has lead to hilarious linguistic combinations and much illogicality. Instead of "how are you?", we have "how's it?". My wife likes to reply "how's what?". In place of "is that so?" or "did you really?" we have "is it?".

The one that really drives me up the wall is the use of the negative when the affirmative is meant.

"Is everything okay?"

"No, everything's fine."

"Are you feeling alright today? "

"No, I've never felt better. "

Afrikaans has this infuriating ja-nee, an emphatic affirmative, which comes into English as "yes-no," the trouble being that the "no" on its own is also often used as an affirmative. Hence whenever arrangements are made for me, I double-check.

"Are all the arrangements for this trip made?"

"No, all the arrangements are in order."

"Do you mean no or yes?" I ask, raising my voice.

The question is considered unfair, anyone with brains surely being able to understand in context whether "no" means "yes" or whether "no" means "no." I get a little of my own back when people ask me, as they often do, if I enjoy being Chief Rabbi.

"No," I say, which brings a puzzled look to their face, and then "I love it!"

Key Yiddish expressions in South Africa also differ from other countries and are a source of surprise to the uninitiated. The special Shabbat loaf of plaited bread is called a kitke, everywhere else a challah. An argument between two people or, more precisely, a grievance — both favourite Jewish pastimes — is called a faribbel. The kiddush on Shabbat mornings after the service is uniquely called the berochoh. Whereas kugel and bagel to Yiddish speakers around the world are

FOR HEAVEN'S SAKE

delicious edibles, to South African Jewry they also denote a spoilt young Jewish woman and man, respectively.

Yiddish is unfortunately a dying language but its South African form is full of colour and charm, and to hear the older generation speak it is a delight.

One of the most beautiful shrubs in the country, Brunfelsia, blossoms in three different colours, purple, light lavender and white, at the same time. It is known colloquially as "yesterday, today and tomorrow". On being told its name, I immediately suggested that in Yiddish it should be called a "nechtiker tog"!

Among my many likes are animals. I never used to care for them. They are smelly, get in the way and have peculiar diets. But my wife loves animals, insisting that they are more trustworthy than human beings, and gradually I've grown used to them and have even come to like them.

When the boys were young we had a guinea pig called Snoopy. She nibbled at anything and everything from the sides of her wooden box to the insulation around the wire of the electric clock in the kitchen. But her special treat was grass. Whenever I started mowing the lawn she would squeak in joyous expectation and not stop until I had given her a huge handful of freshly-mown grass. She lasted nearly nine years, something of a record for guinea-pigs.

Incidentally I love mowing the lawn. In addition to the exercise, there is something deeply satisfying about trying to keep the lines straight, the noise of the mower is therapeutic, and besides it is a good time to think about sermon themes. Our former house in Johannesburg had a front lawn large enough for our cricket knock-up for an hour every Sunday in between commitments, but the first time I tried to mow it — and I was really looking forward to the job — I was stopped before I started. I had just taken out the electric lawn-mower and the extension lead from the garden shed when four black hands descended gently on my shoulder. It was two of our domestic staff and they were shaking their heads in disbelief.

"Not for you, Rabbi," they told me respectfully but firmly.

55

"But I enjoy mowing the lawn," I insisted.

It was to no avail. Most white men simply do not mow their own lawn in South Africa, and in any event the look in their eyes implied I was taking the work away from them. As I went back indoors I wondered briefly whether Snoopy would have liked the Johannesburg grass.

We have had numerous cats. Some we have acquired, some we have saved from being put down, and some were strays who wandered into our kitchen, seemed to like it, and stayed for several years.

Before I was appointed Chief Rabbi, I was summoned to South Africa House in Trafalgar Square to meet the then ambassador, Ray Killen, either out of courtesy or perhaps so that he could ascertain whether I was any kind of threat politically. I ran the gauntlet of the anti-apartheid demonstrators at the entrance and we had a long chat that seemed to satisfy him.

"Anything I can do for you, Rabbi?" he asked when I was about to leave. I cleared my throat.

"Well, we have three cats and we'd like to bring them with us."

"Say no more," he smiled, and the cats got diplomatic clearance and VIP treatment before we did.

Josh, the oldest of our cats, whose style had been somewhat cramped by our small garden in St John's Wood, found the huge garden in Johannesburg very much to his liking. A British Blue — which, of course, means he was jet-black in colour — he struck up an immediate affinity with the African National Congress and took an intense dislike to the ginger cat in the house next door who in his opinion must have been a member of the AWB. So they fought, over the future political landscape of the country as a whole and over territorial rights in our road in particular.

My neighbour at the time, a lovely old man called Harry Judes, used to walk with me occasionally to Berea shul, only a few streets away.

"Funny thing, Rabbi," he said to me as we strolled along, "my cat is limping very badly on his hind legs."

"Yes, Harry," I chipped in, "and you should see my cat's right ear!"

We thought we had lost Josh for good when he suddenly disappeared without trace. After four days awol, when we were quite frantic about his whereabouts, we heard a scraping noise on the outside steps while we were watching the 8 o'clock news. It was Josh. He was covered in mud, limping very badly and ravenous.

The vet diagnosed a fractured pelvis; we think he was knocked down by a car during one of his marauding escapades in the vicinity, had managed to crawl into bushes at the side of the road and, when he had summoned up enough energy, courageously made it back home. The vet operated on him and he was banished for six weeks' convalescence to the spare bedroom where he noisily recuperated.

Possessing more than the proverbial nine lives — the only cat who had more was the famous Mikolo who crossed almost every night from the Russian sector over the Berlin Wall and kept going backwards and forwards despite all attempts to shoot him — Josh resumed active duty for a few more months. Then his kidneys failed and he reluctantly passed on to the cat heaven.

The best name for a cat I ever heard was Rachmones. She belonged to Grandma Tilly z'l, in Waterloo Road in Manchester and because Grandma, who was a wonderful cook, was so pedantic and had the cleanest and neatest kitchen in the world, every time the cat entered the kitchen she promptly threw her out.

"It's a rachmones for the cat," Grandpa was heard to mutter behind the pages of the Guardian. And the name stuck.

My favourite cat is called Pik. She is black with a white collar and rubs against my legs with approval every time she sees me. I give her treats and she purrs with pleasure. She is fifteen years old and still going strong and there is only one thing wrong with life. She hates dogs.

We used to have a Labrador called Blackberry. Since the cats were in residence first, he showed them great respect and they, including Pik, more or less tolerated him. Surprisingly, cats and dogs need not spell endless strife and friction and they certainly manage to live together in the same house.

Blackberry was thoroughly loyal and, being a retriever, the best finder in the world of a lost cricket ball. The only thing was he would not give it back to you except in exchange for a dog biscuit. He was also something of a celebrity. His favourite trick went like this. My wife would put a biscuit on the floor in front of him.

"It's treif, Blackberry," she would say, "you can't have it."

And Blackberry would sniff the biscuit, walk round it, push his snout in the air, but not eat it. Ann would then put another biscuit in front of him.

"Blackberry, it's kosher," she would say, and the dog would gobble it up with great relish.

This provided me with splendid illustrative material for sermons on the dietary laws.

"My wife's dog knows the difference between kosher and treif. Why are there Jewish families who do not know the difference?"

Blackberry's feat became so well-known throughout the Jewish world that on delivering a paper at an international conference in Jerusalem, I was introduced not by own qualifications but "as the owner of the dog who knows the difference between kosher and non-kosher".

He gave much joy to everybody and was full of fun. But he contracted a disease of the pancreas, and despite the valiant efforts of our vet, succumbed after a few weeks. There was such a vacuum in the house after he went that my wife replaced him with two dogs: Jackie, a handsome collie who is unfortunately frightened of thunder and Toffee, who looks like a lioness and loves to eat the daily newspaper and the books on the bottom shelf of the bookcase in my study. Pik loathes both of them.

One of my pet dislikes — it must be shared by thousands — is the habit of most politicians to indulge in false promises. I suppose sensible people simply ignore what is being proffered or divide by ten, but the lack of morality irks me. Do we have to live in the unprincipled world of Lewis Carroll's Humpty Dumpty who says to Alice in *Through the Looking-Glass*: "When I use a word, it means just what I choose it to mean."

It is related of Earl Lang, governor of Louisiana in the early 1950s, that he decided he wanted to serve another term and so offered himself for re-election. On being asked by the populace what he would do if returned as governor, he promised he would substantially reduce state taxation.

He was duly re-elected by a large majority and the first thing he did was to increase taxes substantially. The citizens came to demand an explanation.

"Mr Governor, you promised us faithfully that if we re-elected you to office, you would decrease our taxes. But instead you have increased them. Do you have an explanation?"

"Yes," the governor replied, "it's quite simple. I lied to you."

"Oh," the people said, "what an honest politician."

Dissembling of any sort never really succeeds. A quite unprecedented mistake occurred a number of years ago in Windhoek when a Jewish man passed away and his non-Jewish wife wished to honour her dead husband by having some Hebrew inscribed on his tombstone.

Unfortunately the only item she could find in the house was an old Pesach food wrapper. She recognised that it was Hebrew wording and the stonemason duly carved Kosher l'Pesach, upside down, on the stone over his grave. Of course she meant well, but the Jewish Board of Deputies, to avoid further embarrassment, eventually arranged to have the phrase erased.

In Jewish terms South Africa is extraordinary. One of the loveliest customs is that on Shabbat morning congregants leave their seats when the Torah is being ceremoniously returned to the Ark, to crowd around the scroll and kiss it. By contrast, Anglo-Jews bow solemnly from their pews.

And when Yom Tov is approaching, the national newspapers carry on the front page good wishes to all their Jewish readers for a "A Happy New Year" or "A Happy Passover". I have not seen that in any country other than Israel.

Real dislikes? On the list are chazanim and choirs who insist on singing synagogue prayers to totally inappropriate tunes, like Adon Olam to O Sole Mio; Jews who make derogatory remarks about blacks but are the first to complain of anti-semitism when they hear derogatory remarks about Jews; cricketers at one-day games who wear coloured pyjamas instead of whites; having to speak at a funeral when I never knew the deceased; someone who misses a meeting and then has the chutzpah at the next one to insist that we consider the previous meeting's agenda all over again; children who misbehave in shul; Parktown prawns.

Likes? Very many, but especially Bruch's violin concerto in G; Friday night zemirot; the superb concerts given by the Johannesburg Jewish Male Choir; the par-3 golf course at Hengistbury Head on the Solent when the wind is not blowing; my Wednesday evening shiur; imbibing my favourite Scottish tipple against the glorious background of an African sunset; the joy on a Zulu's face when I greet him hesitantly in his own language; Jonty Rhodes's fielding; ceremonial properly done; George airport; the interior of the Gardens Shul in Cape Town.

And my gorgeous grandchildren.

II

PASTORAL

1.   The Reviving Touch

Maternity is at one end of the corridor; at the other is a ward for the chronically sick, mostly elderly and often terminal patients. This unfortunate proximity, probably devised by some neat civil servant, is noticed by visitors to the hospital, to say nothing of the patients.

The problem for the hospital chaplain is whom to visit first? Do you visit the gravely ill and then go into the maternity ward looking morose and melancholic, or do you visit them first and carry their cheerful glow along the corridor to the dying?

Recalling Stanley Holloway's old monologue — "O my, you do look queer!" — and its dampening effect on someone who until then was feeling perfectly well, I opt instead for the advice by the medieval sage Eliezer ben Isaac, applicable to every situation: "Enter cheerfully for the patient's heart and eyes are on those who come in".

Ample instruction is offered by the sacred codes on the theme of sick visiting. Do not visit too early in the morning or too late in the evening. Never outstay your welcome. If the illness is embarrassing, do not go at all, but rather enquire if you can be of any help.

On the fascinating question as to whether a person is obliged to visit someone with whom he has had a bitter quarrel, the authorities are divided. One opinion says no. Imagine the patient coming round after an operation and, on opening his eyes, sees his adversary standing over him. It might finish him off altogether! Certainly, the motive may be misconstrued, the sick person thinking it was occasioned not by goodwill but by a wish to gloat over his condition.

Another opinion pronounces favourably. The patient may appreciate the visit so much that the opportunity will be seized to make up the dispute between them. Despite the abundance of wise counsel regarding visitation, an extraordinary degree of care must be exercised, even casual conversation being full of booby traps. The simple greeting, "How are you?", a well-meant and apparently innocuous question should be avoided whenever possible with Jewish patients. The reason is that they may tell you.

A half-an-hour and dozens of gory details later, the patient is just warming to his or her answer, but you may have five more wards to visit. Of course when time allows one should indulge such patients because sharing their medical condition really seems to make them feel much better.

Another reason for not asking is the unforgettable telling-off I received many years ago when I greeted a patient I had not met before with a gentle "Hello, how are you?"

"How am I?" he thundered at me.

"How do you think I am? If I were all right, do you think I'd be lying here in bed? In hospital, noch? How am I? What kind of question is that?"

His voice rose to a crescendo, disturbing the whole ward. His health may have been delicate but his lungs were in good order. "I'm ILL, that's how I am!"

Since that time I have begun such conversations with: "Tell me, are you feeling a little better today?"

To incorporate a valid religious dimension — surely the primary task of a chaplain, the lay visitor being able to help the patient at least as well, if not better, in every other direction — is easier said than done. With present-day sanitised hospitals and antiseptic clinics, designed not so much to keep body and soul together as to keep the body itself in working order, it presents a daunting challenge.

Amid blood transfusions and anaesthetics, saline drips and catheters, X-rays and scanners — sophisticated technical equipment so abounds in coronary care units one is surprised there is room for the beds — the spiritual seems absurdly out of place.

Yet the rabbi can be supportive in so many ways. Lifting flagging spirits, countering feelings of helplessness, offering encouragement to get well soon, or simply by being there. The rabbi's visit to a hospitalised congregant is usually more appreciated than a hundred sermons. In times of stress he can also alleviate worry by being a valuable link between the patient and his or her family.

For every patient who is embarrassed by the rabbi's visit, or startled by it — "What have you come to see me for? I'm not dying am I?" — there are dozens who are genuinely grateful for the reassuring presence and bedside chatter of the rabbi.

In moments when the patient is feeling really down, the devoted hospital chaplain is sometimes, somehow, in some way, still able to boost morale. Often when the end is near, it is he who represents the conviction that death is not a meaningless

cul-de-sac, and who, without a word ever having to be said, hints at a further and higher existence.

Suffering is an enigma. Is it a punishment for wrongdoing, a means of purification or simply a test of character? Varied reactions among seriously ill patients may provide a clue. On the one hand, there is self-pity and the resentment of those who ask "Why me?" (The American journalist Damon Runyon, who died of cancer, said he learnt to deal with this question by simply changing it to "Why not me?") On the other hand, there are those who are angry with frustration and impotence. And then there are those who display amazing courage.

Clarice was in her late seventies, had terminal cancer, and with about two months to go was admitted to the special care unit. Irrepressible in personality, she immediately took over the entire proceedings and to this hopeless ward — which no one left alive — she brought light and hope.

Surrounded by flowers, colourful pictures and copious photographs of her grandchildren, she filled the whole atmosphere with brightness. Whenever she had the strength, she went round all the other patients exuding optimism, dispensing kindness and chatting vivaciously away as if she and they did not have a care in the world. If she could not defeat the Angel of Death, at least she would clip his black wings.

When Benny from the East End was admitted, Jewish like Clarice, but only half her age — he was "too young to die" and he felt it — she sat with him for hours persuading, cajoling, bolstering his ego, restoring his equilibrium and alternately rambling on about everything under the sun, affording him precious moments to forget all about his condition.

She never gave up and when she herself died it was as if a light had gone out. Before they took her to the mortuary, I said Tehillim at her bedside. She looked very peaceful, this little lady who taught us that amidst pain and suffering there is room for grace and dignity and who gave us a glimpse of the triumph of the human spirit.

2.   The Long Day

Something always happens just before Yom Tov. Crises, which could easily blow over, suddenly come to a head or a congregant urgently requires the Rabbi. "I know it's your busy season, Rabbi," — the phrase sounds vaguely insulting as if rabbis do nothing for the rest of the year — "but I must see you for half-an-hour." Or there is an emergency that occurs punkt during the frantic hours of preparation for the festival.

When the hospital at which I was Jewish Chaplain telephoned on the morning before Yom Kippur, I knew, although I was already behind, that I would have to drop everything and go there immediately.

"Sister here, Rabbi, Ward 2. We have a problem with Mrs Levy. Could you please come right away?"

Specialising in diseases of the lower digestive system, the hospital, small but renowned for its pioneering work, was near the city. I raced there going through umpteen red lights and making a mental note to add my driving offences to the list of sins for which I would ask for forgiveness during Yom Kippur. The Sister was in her office.

"Good of you to come so soon," she said, rising to greet me.

"It's about your fast day, Rabbi. Starts this evening, doesn't it?"

I nodded.

"Well, Mrs Levy — you remember she came in last week, the lady in the corner bed?" I nodded again.

"She had to have a major operation yesterday. She's lucky to be alive, and the next few days will be really critical." She gave me a concerned look. "First thing this morning Mrs Levy asked for the ward doctor and told him she was going to fast from this evening till tomorrow evening. It's not really a question of food and drink at this early post-operative stage. Unfortunately she's also adamantly refusing the drip or any medication."

The Sister looked at me again. "She could easily die."

Walking along the corridor towards the ward, I frantically rehearsed what I would say to Mrs Levy. It was not going to be easy;

Mrs Levy, as I had noticed on the Chaplain's list, was over eighty, one of "the old school".

"Ours is a living religion," I was going to put to her. "If you're seriously ill you do not need to fast. Just the opposite; it's a mitzvah, a duty, to take everything you need to keep yourself going. In any event" — and here I would try a more sophisticated line of argument — "the drip does not count as food. It's normal eating through the mouth, not intravenous sustenance, that is forbidden by the Law. So you're fully allowed the drip and technically not really breaking the fast at all."

When I reached the bedside, she looked very weak and pale, but knew who I was and managed to greet me with a slow nod of recognition. We exchanged a few polite formalities and then I got to the point. As I cited chapter and verse from Jewish law absolutely forbidding her to fast, or even to attempt it, she heard me out with a pained expression on her old, lined face.

"Have you finished now, young man?" she asked, using the Yiddish term, yingl, for young man.

She then began explaining exactly why she was not going to listen to me or accept a word of what I had said.

She told me that she had fasted the whole of Yom Kippur since she was ten years old — "that's seventy-three years in a row, and I've never missed," she proudly stated. She explained that she had previously been caught in extraordinary circumstances yet had never violated the fast. During the Second World War she had been on the run with members of her family in southern Poland.

Although it was Yom Kippur, they had been forced to keep on the move. In the afternoon they had been offered food by friendly villagers, a rare occurrence in Poland, but had refused it and moved on. When the fast went out, they had no food at all and did not eat till late the next day.

Twice in the last stages of pregnancy she had managed to finish the fast. She had always fasted, she stressed, and this year would be no exception.

In a low but steady voice she went on to remind me that being a rabbi I should be aware, more than anyone, that Yom Kippur was a unique day, special in its great holiness. If she were indeed to pass away — and with this she clinched the argument - could I think of a better time than Yom Kippur on which to meet her Maker?

Further argument was futile, so with the traditional wish, somewhat pointed in the circumstances, that she "be sealed in the Book of Life", I took my leave. On the way out I told Sister I had failed.

Rushing back home to finish my preparations, I thought of all those who could but would not keep the fast. The borderline medical cases who, instead of discussing the situation with the rabbi, gave themselves the benefit of the doubt. Those who pampered themselves so that the minute a headache started, they slipped out of shul for a cup of tea and an aspirin. The self-indulgent who, unlike this old woman who would rather die than take any nourishment on Yom Kippur, had no staying power.

Throughout Kol Nidrei and the whole of Yom Kippur day, her old face kept coming back to me. At every lull in the proceedings I wondered how she was coping. I added a prayer that she should make it.

When the fast was over I shook hands as quickly as possible with the congregants, milling around, and dashed home. Gulping down a cup of hot coffee, I telephoned the hospital.

"It's something of a miracle, Rabbi," Sister told me. "Mrs Levy began to fast, she unplugged the drip herself, more than an hour before it was necessary, and she's refused absolutely everything today till it got really dark. The doctor, who knew all about her fasting, came in specially to examine her about twenty minutes ago. He says it's amazing. He's never seen anything like it before: there don't seem to be any ill effects at all. We're now giving her everything she needs and she's very comfortable."

"Thank G-d," I exclaimed in relief, "that's wonderful, now I can break my fast."

"Wait a minute, Rabbi. Sorry to keep you, but one more thing. The senior consultant wants to know: is it easy to become Jewish?"

3.   Happy Ever After?

The best moment of a woman's life is, or ought to be, when she holds out her hand under the chupah to receive the wedding ring from her groom.

The worst is when she is required to cup her hands to receive the get from the husband divorcing her, or more often than not from his deputed agent because he does not wish to have to drop it into her hands personally.

Four incidents, one after the other, jolted me into stark realisation of the magnitude and appalling consequence of marital breakdown.

Thursday afternoon

Answering a ring at the door, I found a young housewife I knew well standing in a flood of tears, her four-year old daughter clinging to one arm and her two-year old son to the other. It transpired her husband had run off with his secretary and abandoned her and their children without compunction. Somewhat unsuccessfully, I tried to calm her down.

Thursday evening

A couple in my community who had been married for thirty years contacted me to tell me they were separating. Could I possibly call round that evening as they needed help? I arrived to discover that they actually wished me to arbitrate on the division of their possessions. Their wrangling went on interminably and I was caught in the middle. How do you divide a music centre, a set of five books, the family dog? Gone midnight, they were still bickering over each item. When we came to a pair of Friday night silver candlesticks, a wedding present to both of them, I solemnly stood up, handed one to him and one to her and took my leave.

Shabbat midday

At a kiddush in honour of a bride and groom to be married the following day, a well-known estate agent came over to me, whisky in hand.

"I hope they'll be happy," he said in a wistful tone. On asking why on earth they should not be, he informed me the couple were going to live in a house he had sold no fewer than five times in two years, in each case to newly-weds, none of whose marriages had lasted more than a few months.

Sunday morning

Pandemonium. The father of one of the boys in cheder picked him up during the break, telling the teacher on playground duty they were going to visit grandma. When classes finished, the boy's mother arrived to fetch him and had hysterics when she discovered what had happened. The parents were divorced and the father was only allowed access on alternate weekends and this was not his turn. By a fluke, while the mother was insisting we contact the authorities, a cousin of his, aware of the custody arrangements, telephoned to say he knew where the boy was.

Of all the failings of contemporary society, few are as devastating as the plague of divorce. It knows no barriers and strikes anywhere, irrespective of social class, financial status, religious affiliation or length of marriage.

In Jewish circles the world over, the divorce rate is sadly so high that the local Beth Din scribe complains of sore fingers from writing gittin, while in Orthodox communities its prevalence tends to negate the age-old claim of the stability inherent in traditional Jewish home life. Rabbis, alarmed at the scarcity of stable homes, are contemplating adding to the seven benedictions of the wedding ceremony an eighth: a request to heaven that the marriage works.

Three generations are hurt by divorce: the couple themselves, their respective parents, and any children of the marriage, the last almost always innocent victims because they cannot comprehend the reason for their ruptured lives. Lawyers may speak of an "amicable divorce"; psychologists rarely do.

Of course the Torah permits divorce but it never recommends it. In the view of some rabbinic commentators, allowing a woman to marry more than one man legally formalises a degrading concept of wifehood, turning marriage into a game of "musical chairs". Indeed, the Essenes refused to allow a man to marry a second wife during the lifetime of his divorced first wife, as that would cheapen the marriage ideal.

Considering divorce a calamity, the Talmud tells us "the very altar weeps for one who divorces the wife of his youth". Maimonides in his code rules that a man must never marry a woman with the intention of divorcing her. Marriage is supposed to be for keeps.

Despite the high incidence of divorce in the Jewish community — the one-parent family is now commonplace and third marriages are becoming more frequent — and the fact that Judaism, being family centred, is acutely vulnerable on the home front, surprisingly few attempts have been made to determine specific Jewish factors, as distinct from general pressures, that might contribute to the malaise.

Perhaps it has something to do with materialism; couples who don't earn enough to emulate the neighbours' standard of living often seem to place their marriage in jeopardy. Perhaps the over protectiveness of Jewish parents, their refusal to cut the apron strings, causes damage, however well intentioned the meddling.

This aspect — JPI or Jewish Parental Interference — needs to be fully researched. So does the impact on the marital relationship of the dual role of today's female spouse. Often in full or part-time employment, she has also to carry domestic responsibilities, which are more weighty for the Jewish housewife. Success at being wife, mother and wage earner, all at the same time, is invariably expected by both herself and her husband.

Since we think we know a great deal more nowadays about human relationships (but do we?), much more could also be attempted in marriage preparation. The change from "me" to "we" is never easy, especially in a world which gives such weight to individual aspirations and the almost sacred right to self-satisfaction. Some help is required if the level of maturity for durable marriage is to be more regularly achieved.

No one venturing into marriage can possibly anticipate the areas of friction and engaged couples have much to learn from the experience of those who have gone before them. Crucially in education towards marriage, the husband and wife-to-be can be taught the essential role of staying power, so vital to their future well-being, and to recognise any danger signals.

Because the easy availability of divorce has marred the vision of marriage so that it is no longer thought of as a life-time partnership but rather as a hit-or-miss exercise, the aim must be to reinstate a sense of permanence in the younger generation's attitude.

When divorce again becomes a last resort and the words of the ketubah — "I will honour you and hold you precious" — are again held in high esteem, we may begin to stem the tide.

Under the chupah, for the first and hopefully the only time, the bride and groom must have before their eyes an example, provided by parents, an aunt and uncle, a married brother or sister, or close friends, of happy married life in a contented Jewish home, so that instead of falling victim to the prevailing trend they, too, may strive to remain united.

On the Biblical account of the formation of Eve from Adam's rib, the Midrash with customary curiosity asks: Which rib?

"From the rib over his heart," the answer is given, "that they might love each other forever."

4. No Way Out

A feeling of relief, mostly spontaneous, often accompanied by guilt, is liable to overtake those released from other people's dire predicaments.

Coming away from the intensive care unit where someone you know lies grievously ill, while obviously feeling truly sorry for the sick person, an inescapable feeling of paradoxical well-being can easily take hold.

Leaving the cemetery after officiating at a funeral, especially on a beautiful summer's afternoon, one seems to breathe with a greater sense of keenness.

All these are nothing compared with prison visitation. It takes years to shake off the sensation, almost tangible, of the main jail gates closing behind one, and again being free and out in the open.

For ten years I visited a maximum security jail. As a sensible precaution, visiting chaplains are never allowed to carry prison keys in case an inmate attacks them. As the long closed-in corridors are locked at both ends, you have to rattle the gates and call several times for a prison officer to let you through. Each time you leave the prison at the end of a visit and step out of the main gate, it is as if you have been there not just a few hours, but several years. Hence the feeling of relief.

"My" prison was a special psychiatric one, restricted to recidivists, who were treated by a team of psychiatrists and psychologists in addition to the welfare workers. At the time, it was the only prison in the country where the treatment took precedence over the manual work the inmates had to do. Because rehabilitation was taken seriously, and the professionals were of the highest quality, the success rate proved surprisingly high. About one in three of the inmates never got into trouble again.

A major component of the treatment was group therapy. All the inmates, including murderers, molesters, drug addicts and compulsive gamblers, were obliged to discuss in front of the others what crime they had committed, how they had done it and what effect it had on them.

Needless to say, this invariably proved a humiliating experience because all the others were only too eager to criticise anti-social action outside their own domain; the inmate who was the focus of attention nearly always had his personality pulled to pieces.

For the first time in their lives, many began to understand that all might not be right with their thinking and their actions. Placing a mirror in front of themselves to show up the flaws and distortions, the inmates came to see themselves as they really were, the first painful stage along the road to improvement. Indeed, the process has much in common with the Jewish concept of repentance, the essential first stage of which is the realisation that the sin against our better self has actually been committed and thus requires atonement.

When the medical superintendent (a fancy name for the Governor) left an urgent message for me to come to the prison immediately — it was nearly fifty miles outside London — I wondered what on earth was the trouble.

Ernie (not his real name) was in the psychiatric prison for fraud. All his life — he was in his late thirties — he had never been able to distinguish between honesty and dishonesty. Everyone was fair game for his deceptions, confidence tricks and downright cheating.

Having served three previous sentences, he had been sent to the psychiatric prison in the hope that the treatment might help him. It did, only too well. For the first time in his life, Ernie knew what made him tick, actually appreciated his motives and desires, and became acutely aware of his personal deviations from the acceptable norms of making a living.

And with that knowledge came fear. Instead of the eagerness to prove himself in normal life, which characterised fellow inmates who successfully went through the treatment, Ernie was scared to go back and face the world. He now knew himself so well, his every weakness, and he felt sure that in many situations he would succumb again.

So he refused to leave. In a statement rarely heard in prisons, Ernie said that although he was due to leave the following week, he did not wish to do so.

Meshuggah! The majority of prisoners count not just the years and months but the days and hours till their release, the precious moment when time returns to be their own. But not Ernie; he felt safer in jail. To be sure, there are some people to whom prison means security. There they have no responsibilities, the routine is set and despite the discomforts they at least have board and lodging.

But this was different; it was a cool, calculated turning away from freedom. He was saving everyone time: the police, the prison service, society at large. We would not have to bother to chase him down again next time. He would rather stay where he was.

As the taxpayer has enough of a burden providing for those already in jail and because it was obviously wrong in principle to keep Ernie in after his time had been served, and maybe also because the attempt at rehabilitation at least deserved the chance of validation, we all tried to make him change his mind.

When I arrived at the prison, I found Ernie with the key members of the team — the medical superintendent, chief psychologist (who happened to be Jewish), the resident chaplain and the psychiatrist assigned to him — and joined them in trying to persuade him to do the right thing and go.

For four hours we worked on him, trying to boost his confidence and make him see common sense. We offered the full support of after care and insisted that there was really no alternative. With a great deal of reluctance, he eventually agreed that he would, after all, leave the prison at the appointed hour.

I returned the same evening to London, worried about whether we had done the right thing.

About eighteen months later, I was negotiating the heavy traffic on the North Circular Road in suburban London when a car behind me hooted and began flashing its lights, urging me to stop.

I pulled on to the hard shoulder and so did the car following.

Out stepped Ernie. He looked immaculate: neat suit, white shirt, smart tie, polished shoes.

"How are things?" I asked when, after a moment, I recognised him.

"They're fine," he said, "couldn't be better," and he was obviously speaking the truth.

He told me he had a regular job as a commercial traveller, was earning good commission, had managed to keep himself on the straight and narrow from the day he got out and was planning to get married. We shook hands and I wished him well.

Resuming my place in the flow of traffic, I silently offered up a prayer that he would continue to make it, this rare human being who, contrary to the thousands who never learn from their mistakes, had actually won the victory over himself. No longer the prisoner of his own past, he deserved a decent future.

5.   Together With the Community

"I have never missed Kol Nidrei in my life."

Mrs Davis had come into hospital two days before Yom Kippur and she was inconsolable. She had protested to her doctor that she wanted to postpone coming into hospital until after the Yamim Tovim but he told her that in her condition she could not postpone it.

Oh dear, how on earth would she manage without shul on Yom Kippur? What sort of a day would it be ?

"Listen," I said trying to cheer her up a little, "you see that window" — we were in a narrow corner room in the private wing with one large window at right angles to the bed — "it overlooks the synagogue just across the road. So you see, you're not far from shul after all. Anyway, you'll be with us in spirit."

It took her five painful minutes on Kol Nidrei night to reach the window from her bed. She had wrapped a woollen shawl around her and clutched the Machzor she had included at the last minute with the belongings she had brought with her. Slowly she sank into the old easy-chair situated fortuitously near the window but it took her an age to manipulate it round the opposite way so that she could look out of the window.

A smile came to her lips. She could see the front entrance and the whole side of the shul and a large flow of people was already crowded into the entrance. An air of excitement surrounded the synagogue. Handshakes were exchanged. Friendly greetings filled the air — "Have an easy fast!" — "A Gut Yohr."

They should be starting very soon, she thought to herself. There was a last minute rush, the late-comers glancing guiltily at their watches and hurrying inside. Then all was quiet outside the shul, only the caretaker in his peaked cap on solitary duty.

Hoping the nurses would not disturb her — she had told them she wanted an early night — she opened her Machzor. Humming the tune of Kol Nidrei she followed the words with her eyes.

Of the many services of the Jewish year — she knew them all

intimately since she was a little girl — Kol Nidrei was one of her favourites. The lofty words, full of inspiration and yet so true to human nature, the traditional melodies, solemn yet somehow optimistic, never failed to have meaning for her. She turned the pages slowly, davening to herself and singing softly.

The rabbi would be speaking now. She always enjoyed the derashah, not because of the words, but because of the setting. Hearing without listening, she felt part of the congregation, the sheer warmth of belonging. It felt stronger on Yom Kippur somehow, this feeling of togetherness, as if there were no difference in time or place, as though all Jewish people everywhere, one big family, were praying together for a good New Year.

She closed her eyes and imagined she was in her own shul. Everything was wonderfully familiar and she looked down from her seat in the Ladies Gallery to where her late husband used to sit. She saw him in her mind's eye — in the last seat of the third row on the right hand side — interrupting his devotions during the long day to look up at her and silently question whether she was fasting alright.

She sighed. Ah, Yom Kippur with its very special power, a kind of spiritual magic, a feeling of the reality of holiness, a sublime day suspended in time. She felt close to her husband now. She wondered fleetingly how long it would be before she joined him.

They would be nearing the end of the service now. She finished the Al Chait of the Vidui, imagined the Ark open for Avinu Malkenu and hummed the special Yom Kippur tune for Anim Zmirot. Quietly to herself she sang Yigdal and Adon Olam.

They were coming out. Noisy and full of bonhomie, exuding the special partnership of the community of fasters, the congregants shouted infectious greetings to each other. The "Happy New Year"s wafted over to her window on the night air. "Gemar Tov," they called out to their friends and acquaintances.

It took her an age, step by difficult step, to shuffle back to her bed. It was worth it, every minute of it, she told herself, and was soon happily asleep.

Popping in to see her before Succot, I noticed she was looking much better.

"Pity you missed Yom Kippur," I said to her, "but G-d willing you'll catch up next year and for many more years."

She gave me no answer, and I wondered, on the way to the next ward, about the quizzical smile on her face.

6. The Open Hand

Israel was under threat again. Ominous clouds of war scudded across her borders, the fragile peace was liable to shatter at any moment and, no novelty in these situations, Jewish communities everywhere were asked to help.

We organised a meeting. It was good to be busy, to have something to do, to know we were trying in our own small way to lend a hand. Giving ourselves less than forty-eight hours to complete the arrangements, we managed to obtain the agreement of all the local synagogues to join together for one massive appeal meeting.

With frenzied zeal committee members spent hours on the telephone urging the community to turn up. "Not just an ordinary meeting ... an emergency ... a full-scale appeal ... must come along ... large shul hall ... bring your neighbours."

Arriving for the meeting, I was pleasantly surprised to find the hall almost full, and when our main speaker, a well-known Zionist personality, rose to speak there was standing room only. He spoke factually about the danger of war and movingly about the remarkable achievements of Israel, now at risk.

I had been invited to make the appeal. Sometimes this can be problematic, success or otherwise depending on a host of extraneous factors, and because, of course, the longest journey in the world is from the hand to the wallet. However, the situation for Israel was so critical that the large audience was in a genuinely receptive mood.

I opened with a direct plea to our sense of "Jewish togetherness". "If we do not feel we belong to one people, if we have no sense of responsibility towards our own flesh and blood, we need not contribute, it is not our concern. But if the House of Israel means anything to us, if we really care ..."

A middle-aged woman, smartly dressed, was sitting in the middle of the front row. Normally she would not have caught my eye, but the audience was very close to the platform. Perched on the edge of her seat, an anguished expression on her face, she was listening with avid attention to every word, and I could not help noticing her.

Half-way through my speech, she suddenly reached down to the hand-bag at her feet, took out a large silk scarf and, surprisingly, spread it out on her lap.

As I continued with my speech, I noticed that she took off a gold bracelet and, while concentrating on what I was saying, dropped it on to the scarf. A few minutes later she unfastened a brooch from the left shoulder of her dress and let it fall onto the scarf. Her necklace followed, and then at short intervals, as I was nearing the climax of my appeal, she took off her watch and a couple of rings from her fingers and added them to the collection.

I finished on a high and unashamedly emotional note. The audience applauded, in agreement with the sentiments I had expressed. Out of the corner of my eye, I saw the woman fold the ends of the scarf together and knot them firmly. As the stewards, strategically placed throughout the hall, began collecting the appeal cards, she came up to the platform and without a word placed the scarf and its contents in front of me and turned to leave.

"Wait a minute please ..." I said to her. But she merely waved her hand towards the jewellery. That was her donation, she gestured, and turned and was lost in the crowd.

We have always been a generous people. Persecuted so much throughout the centuries, we have come to understand the pain of suffering and want, and nearly always have been able to identify with it and do something about it.

Impoverished at most times and in most places, our ancestors retained an innate kindness. Even when they had next to nothing themselves they often insisted on sharing, and it took the rabbinic instruction not to give away more than twenty percent of what they had — double the ancient tithe — to save them from penury.

Never some kind of optional exercise but rather a matter of habitual duty, the extending of practical help at a time of need is engrained in the Jewish consciousness. The woman with the scarf was simply being true to centuries of Jewish practice.

"Was her husband with her?" the chairman of our local committee leaned over and asked me anxiously. He had untied the scarf and was looking down at the jewellery.

"No, not that I could see," I replied, "I don't think anyone was with her."

"Good quality stuff," he remarked. "We'll get a phone call."

Just after midnight, as the committee members, exhausted but exhilarated, had finished sorting out the hundreds of cheques and appeal cards and counting the total, the telephone rang. It was the woman's husband and he asked for me.

"Listen, Rabbi, let me explain something. You see my wife, well, let's say she gets very emotional. Her mother and sister live in Petach Tikvah and she is desperately worried about them. She's been in a real state since this started ... ." He paused.

"Please don't get me wrong, I won't go back on her donation, but I know her, we've been married nearly thirty years, all those items she gave you are of great sentimental value. In the morning she's going to regret handing them over to you."

I sensed he had some idea in mind so did not interrupt him.

"Look, I want to pay you their full value. Whatever they're worth, I mean it."

He paused again for a moment, then asked: "Have you got a jeweller there?" (On a Jewish committee, what a question: we had three!)

"Tell him to put a value on them. I'm coming round right now; whatever you say they're worth, I'll give you."

The sum was well into five figures. But the man was as good as his word. He turned up within ten minutes, came into the boardroom, checked all the items of jewellery, wrote out a cheque in full payment, handed it to us, put his wife's redeemed possessions in his attache case, smiled at us a little ruefully and left.

Tired but pleased with ourselves, we got up to go home. "She was not that generous," I said as we were locking up the front of the shul. Every head turned in query, wondering what on earth I was on about.

"I couldn't help noticing. She didn't — thank goodness — give us her wedding ring!"

7.   The Permanent Shadow

For weeks I'd had my eye on those baby roses in the nursery around the corner. The small front garden — we'd moved in six months previously and I hadn't yet got round to fixing it — had a neat little lawn and the roses would look so sweet with their pretty colours at just the right height. The soil was very good for roses. I would put them round three sides of the small lawn as a decorative border.

Gardening is a favourite pastime of spiritual leaders. It offers the opportunity of imitating the Divine — "Almighty G-d first planted a garden and indeed it is the purest of human pleasures" — and it is a quiet and restful pursuit. Unlike the old adage that farmers and gardeners need patience and have to wait upon nature, it really is an immediately satisfying exercise.

Mow the lawn and you can see the difference; weed a patch and the results are obvious; plant a few flowers and it gives everyone pleasure and, weather permitting, their growth is assured.

Dealing with so many intangible, difficult-to-pin-down areas, rabbis, ministers and priests find something joyously elemental in gardening and a refreshing relaxation from the world of the spiritual.

Mentally checking that the welfare of the community could wait a few hours — no funerals (thank goodness), up-to-date with hospital visits, and the shiur for later in the day already prepared — I hastened round to the nursery, selected the best of what I'd seen, came home and changed into old clothes. I went round to the front and began spacing the roses out, prior to clearing the border and bedding them in. I was on my hands and knees, trowel in hand. I was enjoying myself.

"Hello Rabbi, what in heaven's name are you doing?"

Jack, my next-door neighbour, was leaning over the hedge, a long cigarette in his mouth as always, staring at me with a look of amazement on his face. We had become friends with our neighbours as soon as we had moved in. Jack was a Polish Jew, his wife Inga German-Jewish, and they had lovely children. They were very active in the local Bnai Brith and were genuinely friendly and helpful. Jack was a survivor of the holocaust.

"You should not be doing that yourself," he exclaimed, coming round to stand over me, "gardening is not for you."

Something in his voice should have warned me this was more than casual conversation, but without waiting for me to ask him why, he told me.

"I don't garden at all. Not me," he said deliberately as I stood up to listen. "You see, we once had to garden at Ebensee."

He explained that in 1943 he was incarcerated together with a small group of fellow Jews at the concentration camp in northern Austria, Ebensee being a satellite of Mauthausen. His eyes narrowed and he turned slightly away as he recollected the details that he felt I must know.

"Listen," he said, with great intensity, "it was like this. The commandant and his wife lived some distance from the camp. They had moved into a new house but it was surrounded by an overgrown garden. That morning" — it sounded so clear as if this all had happened only yesterday — "the commandant's wife asked her husband to send over a dozen of the inmates to clear the garden and put it in order. He immediately sent a group of the Russians who were in the camp with us. They didn't do the job, apparently they were fooling around most of the morning, and they really annoyed the commandant's wife.

"So she phoned her husband to complain and he promptly sent guards to bring them back to the camp. It was lunch time, not that we had much for lunch. The commandant had the Russians lined up in front of all of us and they were shot — not together, but each separately — one after the other."

Jack took a long puff on his cigarette.

"In the afternoon they sent us to do the garden. We worked very hard, I can tell you, and we turned that rambling garden into a really nice sight. We didn't have many tools, so after a few hours our hands were bleeding and, because it was a hot day, we were really tired and thirsty. As I speak fluent German, the others asked me to approach the woman and ask her if we could have something to drink.

"She looked at what we had done and was very pleased with it, so she brought out some drinks for all of us. Late in the afternoon we finished the job and returned to the camp.

"So you see, Rabbi, I don't garden, not any more."

He gave me a look, patted me gently on the shoulder and smiled.

"Gardening," he said, without any bitterness in his voice or any hint of superiority, "gardening is for goyim."

He took another long puff at his long cigarette and with a short wave went back indoors.

All of us who fortunately never went through the horrors of the holocaust fail to realise the psychological impact and actual damage which living during those fateful years caused to everyone including the survivors.

Decades after the war, the trauma is re-lived — almost anything, however trivial, can trigger the unhappy memories — the anxiety surfaces once more and peace of mind and any sense of well-being is shattered. Like a dark and ugly stain, the black cloud of all that has happened seeps through to disturb the apparent normality. The shadow is permanent.

I had lost all desire for planting the baby roses, so I stopped gardening. It was many weeks before I summoned up the will to finish the job.

8.   Silence is Golden

Unit Number 2 of Westminister Social Services telephoned to say that a Miss Cohen, who lived off the Bayswater Road, requested a rabbi — other than her own. There are many valid reasons for bringing in an outside rabbi, sometimes due to embarrassment, or not wishing to bother one's own rabbi too often, or even sometimes for a second opinion. Would I oblige?

By the way I should know that Miss Cohen was terminally ill and also that she was totally deaf.

"And I just want to tell you," added the caller who was the social worker dealing with the case and who was not Jewish, "I'm also partially deaf."

We agreed to meet at Miss Cohen's flat the following morning. I got there five minutes late, due to heavy traffic, and they were already in the middle of an animated sign-language conversation. I felt like an intruder.

"It's all right, Rabbi," said the social worker reassuringly, "we can both lip read. So don't worry, we'll make out what you are saying."

We exchanged the usual pleasantries and the conversation was normal, except that if it be true that "in the country of the blind, the one-eyed man is king," it is patently not true that in the company of the deaf the one who can speak is at an advantage.

Far from it. They could communicate with each other with rapid sign language and unarticulated speech; I was the one who was left out.

"Are you scared of dying?" the social worker suddenly asked the sick woman out loud for my benefit and so that I would realise this wasn't just a routine visit but had a specific purpose. The question was asked as if we were discussing the weather, not a matter of great seriousness.

Miss Cohen nodded. "Yes," she said very quietly.

"Tell her about heaven, Rabbi," the social worker insisted, without looking at me but keeping her gaze fixed on the sick woman.

"Well ..." I hesitated, trying to think how best to reassure her and at the same time be true to traditional views. An other-worldly mystical holiness would not really appeal to her. Nor would an intellectual haven, nor the view that heaven is a special state of being, a higher form of experience, not a place at all.

Nor would the concept of moral progress — beautifully expressed by my saintly teacher Rabbi Isidore Epstein z'l, — that cooperation with the Divine is an unending ideal stretching beyond this earthly existence, so that life and after-life, the here and the hereafter, this world and the next, are bound together in a unity of service to G-d.

"We call it the Garden of Eden," I stated firmly, recovering a little from the initial shock of the question, and speaking slowly and deliberately so that they could lip-read. "It really is paradise. Think of the nicest garden you've ever been in. It's even more beautiful and pleasant than that."

I rambled on, trying to create an idyllic picture, describing the reward of eternal bliss for all people who have managed to be more good than bad on this earth.

"Death is not a cul-de-sac," I assured her. "This life with all its inconsistencies, fluctuations and incompleteness can't possibly be the only one. There is a deeply satisfying after-life. There must be an upstairs as well as a downstairs."

Miss Cohen was not impressed, a half-smile of incredulity covering her face at my description.

"Try again, Rabbi," the social worker said.

I took a deep breath and paused to gather my thoughts. I don't know precisely where it came from but I suppose I had been thinking about it subconsciously for many years.

"When you pass away, your soul, your inner being, the core of your individual personality, leaves your body shortly afterwards and ascends upwards. It travels a long way and eventually crosses over a long bridge. At the far end of the bridge, there's this house which looks very familiar. You could swear you have been there before. Just inside the front entrance, there is a big room."

Miss Cohen was now looking at me intently.

"And the souls of all the people you ever really loved on this earth, who meant so much to you, are there in that room to greet you — the ones you have really missed since they passed on — your parents and your favourite aunts and uncles and your big brother and sister and all the old friends you haven't seen for years ..."

I paused, but she was hanging on my every word and I went on.

"You feel very much at home there. There is a strong feeling of timelessness and a deep sense of contentment and well-being engulfs you. You have come home to eternity."

I stopped. There was a brief silence. Miss Cohen nodded her head in a gesture of approval.

"That's better," said the social worker. "Yes, that's better."

We chatted on amiably about more mundane matters, such as the rainy weather, for another quarter-of-an-hour or so. Miss Cohen thanked me for visiting her, and a few minutes later I took my leave.

The next afternoon I received an urgent telephone call from a cousin of Miss Cohen who somehow had learned about my visit. He had brought round her favourite ice-cream to the flat, but she was not there and he wanted to know if I knew where she was.

We checked up on all the usual places, eventually discovering that she had been admitted to St Charles Hospital in Ladbroke Grove late the previous evening and had died early in the morning.

That night I added to the Evening Service a special prayer for the repose of her sweet soul, and another silent prayer that my description of heaven was correct.

9. Old Bones

Visiting the old folk, especially those institutionalised in an old age home, is like trying to forecast the weather. You can never be sure how it will turn out.

The old folk, bless them, have evolved such a range of moods that it is almost impossible to predict their behaviour. Sometimes they are charming, and there is no charm like the charm of the old, as if all their years on earth have given them whenever they want the ability to relate better to fellow human beings.

But sometimes they are distant, remote, wrapped up in a world of their own. Be careful as you approach them because they may well not be in the same time zone as you — their eyes half-closed, deep in reverie, reliving an event of many years ago. Sometimes for whatever reason, or with no apparent cause at all, they are testy, grumpy and cantankerous. Sometimes impossible.

Easily remembering what happened over fifty years ago, they find it hard to remember what happened yesterday. They tend to forget, a few minutes after you have begun talking to them, who you are. Sometimes they forget who they are. It takes the patience of a saint, something I do not possess, to cope.

One of their many paradoxical and endearing characteristics is their categoric refusal to accept that the years have caught up with them, how old they actually are. When my wife's grandmother was eighty she refused to go to the Friendship Club because she was too young.

"Try it," we all begged her. "Come on Grandma. Just once. You may even enjoy it."

Drawing herself up to her full height — all of four foot eight, as we used to say — she gave us a withering glance.

"And what would I be doing," she demanded to know, "with all those old people?"

We experienced exactly the same problem with one of our syna-gogue programmes. Attempting special activities for the old people in the community who unfortunately lived on their own, my wife suggested we could begin with a tea party — "to break the ice" — in our own home.

Good idea. I told all the local organisations about it, publicised it in the shul newsletter and on the notice-board.

"Are you on your own?" the notice read. "Then this invitation is for you personally." And it gave details of the tea party "for elderly members of the congregation" on the Sunday afternoon of Chanukkah. Hoping to encourage maximum attendance, I also gave it pride of place in the announcements from the pulpit on Shabbat morning.

A woman member was waiting to pounce on me outside the synagogue.

"Rabbi," she accosted me, "I want you a minute."

"Shabbat Shalom," I said. "What can I do for you?"

"It's this tea. You know, the one you're holding soon. Well ...."

She hesitated as if trying to work out how best to explain an obvious point to someone of limited intelligence. "You've made a bad mistake. Upset a lot of people."

I looked and felt mystified.

"You invited 'elderly' people," she explained in an exasperated tone. "You mustn't use that word. It's hideous. Some people may mature but they never become elderly. After all, you are as young as you feel. You can't go around ..." she threw the words at me, her voice rising, "you can't go around calling old people elderly."

Sipping my whisky over kiddush, I wondered about the "mi she-berach" that would have come my way if I'd advertised "a geriatric tea for senile congregants" ...

The Jewish Welfare Board was unsympathetic. "You have to be careful what you call them, you know," the senior social worker scolded me. "Now she's telling me," I thought.

"They loathe 'old-age pensioners'. 'Senior citizens' is too American. "But," she went on, "why don't you try an 'age group'? Like 'tea for the 60 pluses'? Or the 'over 70s'?" She smiled. "Then they have to own up, you see. The onus is on them."

Brilliant, I thought. I altered all the subsequent publicity warmly inviting "those in the community aged 60 plus who live on their own".

It rained buckets the afternoon of the tea but a large number turned up. They sat round and chatted away and drank tea and nibbled at cakes and it was all very friendly and a huge success.

Next day a woman aged 59 telephoned to complain that she had been left out!

Recently I went to see a very old woman at hospital. Propped up against the pillows of the bed she lived in, the sole occupant of a small annexe off the main ward, she adamantly refused to be drawn into conversation.

"Hope I didn't wake you up," I began tentatively, approaching the bed. Silence.

"Are you feeling a bit better today?"

No response.

"Eating well?"

Not the flicker of an eyelid. "Oi vei iz mir," I thought, "how on earth can I break through? Nu, one more try she deserves at least." Leaning over I asked, "Tell me, how's the family?"

A sudden wave of understanding swept over her face. She sat bolt upright, her eyes open wide, arms flailing the air.

"I'd like to kill 'em!" she thundered.

Obviously the family had not been to see her for some considerable time, her children and grandchildren and erstwhile friends showing a total lack of consideration. And yet old folk are often very conscious of the needs of the young.

I recall visiting an old woman at my regular hospital, and before I reached her I could see she was distressed. I introduced myself and gently as possible asked if she was in pain.

"Oh no, Rabbi, it's not my illness, that's nothing." She clenched her wrinkled hands more tightly.

"It's ..." her old face went deathly pale, "it's my daughter-in-law. She's just been admitted to this hospital." She waved a hand helplessly in the direction of the medical block. "To one of the heart wards."

"Don't worry. I'm sure it will be alright. Really. She'll get the best of treatment, she'll get well soon." I rambled on, trying to placate her.

"You don't understand. With respect, Rabbi," she spoke in a low voice and pulled her shawl together as if in comfort, "I live with them."

There was an awkward silence. I now knew the reason for her distress.

"Don't get me wrong." She was eager I should not misunderstand. "They're wonderful to me. My son and daughter — yes, she's more like my own daughter — and the three children, my grandchildren, G-d bless them," she murmured a Yiddish phrase to protect them from harm, "they give me a lovely home. A good Jewish home," she added with a tinge of pride.

"But now ..." she stopped what she was going to say. She looked up. Every line on her face stood out and her eyes were full of great sorrow.

"It's no good being old," she said. As if I had not heard her, she repeated it.

"No good, you know, Rabbi. It's no good being old."

I told her she was wrong. Her family loved her, respected her. Everything would work out. She mustn't worry. She shrugged her shoulders and we began discussing something else. We chatted for a while and when the time came to go, I put both feet in it.

"I wish you a refuah shelemah, you should get well soon," I said to her, holding out my hand.

Her face froze.

"Rabbi, I thought you were a friend of mine. If you want to pray for me, pray I should never leave here alive."

Indeed, sometimes it is no good to be old.

Yet sometimes longevity is indeed a blessing. I recently attended the 100th birthday party of Lazer Abrahamson in Bulawayo. Not only did he sing the Haftara the day before with great gusto, he also delivered a fully articulate speech in a strong voice at the reception.

On being asked his recipe for a long life, he replied: "I take a brisk half-an-hour walk every day, I drink six glasses of water every day. And I go to shul once a day."

Not a bad recipe.

10. Defeating El Nino

Coming from Britain, an island which is swept by the rain and wind on an almost daily basis, I never really appreciated that rain was worth a second thought until South Africa taught me otherwise.

In August 1987 on my very first visit, the South African Union of Jewish Students asked me to speak to the Jewish students at Wits. There had not been any rain in Johannesburg for years and the lawn at Wits was not green; it was a whitish yellow. As we were walking from the student office to the hall, the students couldn't get over the fact that I paused to examine this so-called grass.

"Why on earth is it this colour?" I asked in astonishment.

"Because we haven't had rain for ages," the students chorused in reply.

It was then that the importance of regular amounts of rain, a pesky nuisance where I had come from, began to penetrate my consciousness.

The full force of the need was revealed to me the following year on Hoshana Rabbah. I was participating in the service at the Wolmarans Street Shul. It was early in the morning and there was not a large minyan — seventeen to be exact.

As we took out the seven Sifrei Torah to commence the circuits for the hoshanos, I noticed that two fairly elderly men looked visibly distressed. Then, when we completed the sixth circuit — "Adamah maierer, Save the earth from curse," I saw that while holding onto the lulav and etrog, they were both crying. When we took up the shaanos, the willow twigs, to beat them on the ground, tears streamed down their faces.

As soon as the service was finished I went over to them to find out what was wrong. I honestly thought that someone in the family had taken seriously ill or passed away.

"Can I help you?" I tentatively asked.

"We are mielie farmers in the eastern Transvaal," one said. "There has been no appreciable rain for a very long time. If we do not get rain soon, the ground will not be soft enough to plant, and we will be ruined. To us rain is everything."

Then I understood. Their tears were water, and they were asking for water from heaven.

A few days later the rain began to fall. Not the normal Johannesburg storms, thunder and lightning and sheets of rain bucketing down, but gentle, soaking rain which the ground could absorb. They both phoned me within a half hour of each other.

"See, Rabbi, we didn't cry for nothing."

In the special musaf prayer for rain, tefillat geshem, which we recite on Shemini Atzeret — we leave it until then so that hopefully we can have a dry week in the sukkah — the first piyyut refers to an angel called Af Bri.

The specific function of this angel is to supervise the rain clouds. But the name is a contradiction, af meaning anger and bri meaning health.

This paradoxical title alludes to the two main ways in which rain may fall. Sometimes it comes in harsh torrents and seems to be a sign of Divine anger. At other times it falls slowly and almost silently, bringing benefit to the soil and every thing that grows. The same angel, the same rain, but when you stand in it especially without an umbrella, you certainly know the difference.

Needless to say, generally, when one has set aside a day to watch a cricket test match, rain intervenes. In England, infuriatingly, the match can be held up by a fine drizzle that always appears to be stopping, but as soon as the umpires come out it starts up again, preventing any play. In England one usually goes to a cricket match with a good book in reserve.

South African rain can be altogether different. On the first occasion that we went to a day-night match at the Wanderers — it was a needle contest between the then Transvaal and Western Province — just as the match was coming to an exciting climax, it began to rain really heavily. My wife and I got up to go — it was 10 pm by then — and everyone asked why we were leaving when the game was so interesting and could go either way.

"But they will never be able to continue with the rain coming down like this," I insisted. They smiled at me.

"Sit down," they said, "and wait a moment."

Sure enough, after about twenty minutes the rain stopped completely and five minutes later the players resumed action. Richard Snell hit a couple of sixes and Transvaal won.

In September 1958 in my very first shul I got caught not in the rain but by the rain.

The beautiful Kenton Synagogue is situated in a park and has all "mod cons" including a little stream which flows by the side of the shul. On the first afternoon of Rosh Hashanah, after Mincha, I made the proud announcement that we would all go together to our brook and recite Tashlich. A large crowd of us promptly exited the shul and stood on the bank of the little stream, loudly reciting the traditional verses for Tashlich and the accompanying Psalms and petitions. We shook our garments, symbolically casting our sins from us into the water.

That night it began to rain. It rained for most of the Ten Days of Penitence and it bucketed down on erev Yom Kippur.

The little stream, which by now was not so little, became swollen and kept inching higher and higher. On Kol Nidrei night congregants who lived on the other side of the brook were just able to cross the little bridge over the stream to get to shul. But as we were finishing the service I received a message that the waters were now lapping the side wall of the shul and that the little foot bridge was impassable.

I was asked to announce that congregants who lived on that side should make a detour round safer and drier streets, which would take them another ten minutes.

You've guessed it. The congregants blamed me entirely for the flood. "You were the one who asked us to throw our sins into the brook and obviously since we had so many sins, look what's happened."

They ribbed me mercilessly, but it was all in good humour, and right after Succot the shul built a high brick wall adjacent to the stream.

But rain, especially in Africa which usually doesn't get enough of it, can nearly always be a blessing. A Jewish cattle farmer, who needed good pasture for his herd, once told me how he would search the sky at 5 am every morning looking for a puff of cloud which might indicate that rain was imminent.

Because the threat of drought in Africa is so prevalent, rain is indeed a blessing and we all need to pray with great kavanah that El Nino forecasts of skies bereft of rain clouds do not prove correct.

11. The Thread of Life — Thin and Thick

A colleague telephoned to say that a family whom he knew well were undergoing great trauma because their daughter, a girl called Evelyn who had been blind since birth, had contracted a tumour on the brain and it was malignant. He said she was being admitted to the hospital I regularly visited. Please would I do the family a favour.

"Of course," I said to him, "what do you want me to do?"

"She is a very intelligent girl," he said, "and she loves quizzes, so when you go to visit her when you are doing your rounds, ask her questions about Torah, Nach, Jewish History, Halachah, Shabbat and Yom Tov, and give her a good set of questions, she won't mind. She is very clever and that will at least keep her interest up."

I met her a few days later. She was about twelve, she had lovely black hair and the slight distortion about the eyes which the blind have, but there was absolutely nothing wrong with the way her brain was working.

I had thought up a few questions in advance and I put them to her. She answered with alacrity, her face beaming, and we got on very well indeed.

As the weeks went by, unfortunately but expectedly, her condition deteriorated and she found it more and more difficult to concentrate and more and more difficult to remember. The answers were not always forthcoming. So obviously I began to make the questions easier and easier, until the day came when I went to see her and she was not at all well.

We chatted a little and then she said, "Come on, Rabbi, ask me a question." So I asked her the easiest question I could think of.

"Tell me, Evelyn, what's the berachah over wine?"

She sat up in bed and began, "Baruch Atah Hashem ... ." Then there was a deep furrow on her forehead and I began to help her, "Elokainu ..."

"Yes, of course, Elokainu Melech Haolam ..." and then a long pause. She could not remember the end of the blessing for wine.

I leaned over: "Borei ...," I said. "Borei ...," she repeated.

"Pri ... ." "Pri, pri ... ." She could not finish it. "Hagafen," I said.

"Yes, of course, how silly of me. Fancy not even knowing the berachah over wine."

I felt utterly uncomfortable. One visits patients to cheer them up, not to upset them. This poor girl did not have long to go, and I felt I had upset her for no good reason.

So I said to her: "Listen, Evelyn, never mind, Hashem will understand."

She turned her head and looked at me, although she could not see me.

"I know," she said softly, and she took her hand out of the blankets and held it up in the air that I should take it.

"I can't remember the berachot today, but Hashem has always been good to me. Of course He understands, and He will forgive me."

About a week later she passed away.

The very next hospital visit I made which stuck in my mind, because of the tremendous difference, was to a man I had never met before, called Mr Lyons. He was in a private clinic in the West End of London, and some distant cousin who knew me asked me to pop in to see him because he had a request to make. So I duly turned up. He was a very pleasant man, in his mid-eighties. He was terminally ill and didn't have long to go.

He asked me if I would help him say the Vidui, the confession on the death bed. This is very rarely recited. Judaism has no last rites as such, and most people pass away in their sleep or while they are unconscious. Often they are too ill to say Vidui, or no one is with them when they slip into the next world. Death sometimes comes without warning. In more than forty years of hospital visiting I have only been asked three times to help Jewish patients say the Vidui.

"Of course, we will say it in a moment," I said to Mr Lyons, "but first tell me a little about yourself."

He looked at me, smiled and said, "Rabbi, I have had the most wonderful life. I was very lucky as a child. We were a rather poor family but I had wonderful parents and grandparents. I was the youngest of seven kids, and my big brothers and sisters all spoiled me. I am the last one left now, but my childhood was very happy."

I listened intently as he went on.

"I was okay at school, nothing brilliant, but I enjoyed it. I had a large number of friends in those days and some of us are still friends to this day. I missed out on the First World War, I was too young. During the Second World War I was one of the few who had an easy time. I was stationed in places where there was no upset. I married young. My wife was so wonderful." I thought I saw a tear appear in his eye. "We celebrated our golden wedding before she passed away, G-d bless her soul, a couple of years ago. It was a truly marvellous marriage. We have four kids and they are all really wonderful to me, and I have six grandchildren whom I adore. I really have been very lucky."

I looked at him. "And business?" I asked.

"Ah, that too. I suppose it's amazing, judging by all the stories you hear, but I was one of four partners and we never fell out. We weren't close friends, but we always respected each other. There was never any cheating, never any hassle. We talked everything over together. We were in the timber business which fortunately grew, and we all did very well out of it. I really don't have any complaints at all.

"I've enjoyed good health all my life, until a few weeks ago when I came in here, and really G-d has been very, very good to me. I just want to say Vidui because maybe I haven't been as frum, although I have kept quite a lot of mitzvot, as I should have been. I just want to set the record straight and ask for forgiveness, and more importantly, just to thank G-d for everything He has done for me."

I was elated by his account and at the way it was put over with such obvious sincerity. The sad fact is that so many people at the end of their lives have regrets and recriminations or there is a certain element of bitterness. Yet here was a man for whom everything had gone right, and instead of taking it all for granted he was genuinely grateful.

So together we slowly said the last modeh ani, not the one said every morning by observant Jews and Jewesses, but the last one.

"I acknowledge before You Hashem, my G-d and the G-d of my forefathers, that my recovery or death are in Your Hand ..."and it goes on to say that "if You do not give me a recovery and I die, may my death be an atonement for all the errors and iniquities and wilful sins that I have erred, sinned and transgressed before You".

And then a sweet ending — "May You grant my share in the Garden of Eden and may I be privileged for the World to Come that is stored up for the righteous."

So we said the words slowly, and then we said the Shema, and I said goodbye to him.

I checked up a couple of days later to see how he was getting on, and the sister whom I had met — she was rather cold, clinical and very efficient — said to me, "Oh, Mr Lyons, he passed away yesterday."

"I am sorry to hear that," I said.

"Funny thing," she added, "I was attending to him at the moment when he died. I could swear, when he left us, that he had a smile on his face."

III

COMMUNAL

1. The Ideal Rabbi

The qualities that make up "the ideal Rabbi" are favourite talking points among shul members and anyone and everyone who has anything to do with the Jewish community has decided opinions on the subject.

Ask any layman, and a long and detailed description of exactly what constitutes the good spiritual leader is likely to come tripping off his tongue.

The ideal rabbi must be a dynamic preacher, a conscientious teacher, a congregational manager, a regular visitor of the aged and infirm at home and in hospital, a tactful communal diplomat, an articulate Jewish spokesman, a skilled marriage and bereavement counsellor, a persuasive fund-raiser, a capable membership canvasser — and these are just a few of the requirements!

More subtle attributes include "a user-friendly attitude" towards everyone in the congregation. Approachability is the prevailing litmus test. Moreover, the ideal rabbi should be a man of G-d, yet human. "Our rabbi is human," one congregant says in amazement to another, "you can actually talk to him," as if rabbis were another species altogether.

Crucially, the ideal rabbi should always insist on the highest standards of Jewish observance but at the same time be possessed of Horatio Nelson's blind eye, a sort of religious Moshe Dayan, so as never to cause embarrassment or unease to congregants when they lapse. Further, he should be an effective and impressive leader while constantly remembering that it is not he, but the elected laymen — the president, chairman, treasurer and gabbaim — who actually run the congregation.

To identify properly with the younger generation, the ideal Rabbi should be under thirty while at the same time have twenty years' experience of handling teenage problems.

He should be gifted with powers of telepathy, so that five minutes after a congregant is admitted to hospital, without previous notification to the synagogue office or to the rabbi himself, the Rabbi should just happen to be in that ward to wish the person well. The ideal rabbi is ubiquitous: he can be presiding at a chupah and officiating at the cemetery and participating at a teachers' seminar, all on the same Sunday afternoon.

Of course the rabbi's shiurim and lectures must be of the highest quality, so that all shul members who do not attend know that what they are missing is nevertheless of the requisite standard. The rabbi should have the common courtesy to provide the congregation with a great deal of what they want and only a little of what they need.

Even if it were possible to find such a paragon of virtue, aptitude and all-round versatility, no rabbi could possibly live up to such an ideal for long.

To be realistic, it must be appreciated that rabbis are not by any means all cast in the same mould. While some have a penchant for the educational side of rabbinic work — preaching, teaching lecturing and writing — others prefer pastoral work, organising, visiting, counselling, and advising.

A long-standing debate in the Rabbinate itself is how long a rabbi should stay — assuming he is given the choice! — with the same congregation.

The vigour and impact of educational endeavours usually wane as time goes on. When the rabbi has served the same congregation for ten years or more, congregants are often able to anticipate in which direction the sermon is going to go before the rabbi himself gets there. The opposite is true of pastoral work. The longer the rabbi has been with the congregation, the more he can add to occasions of joy and the more help he can be in trying to solve personal problems and in times of trouble.

In this vein, a friend of mine once told me his test of the good rabbi. It is when one of the shul machers says to the rabbi at the morning minyan: "Oh, by the way, one of our members, Mr Goldstein, is in hospital," and the rabbi is able to reply, "I know. I saw him yesterday."

In answer to the question — "Why should anyone become a rabbi in the first place?" — a younger colleague of mine offers three short answers. Either he must be meshuggah - only those close to communal work realise the extent of the pressures and how awkward some Jewish people can be — or he's a shlemiel, unable to find useful employment in any other sphere, or he is a genuine idealist.

This last is a prerequisite for any measure of success. Any rabbi, who is stuck in the rut of "hatch, match and dispatch" without ever rising above the level of "officiating minister," is doomed to a very monotonous and weary professional life. Important as the rites of passage may be, and recognising that they sometimes provide the opportunity for spiritual elevation, they must be combined with a constant visionary role.

The rabbi must purposefully attempt to stimulate Jewish knowledge on the part of his congregants and gently encourage improved standards of Jewish observance.

Hence to hope to succeed in any way, the rabbi must be the functionary-cum-visionary. In addition to routine work, he needs to be sensitive to the spiritual development of the members of his flock and attempt to deal honestly with their questions, hesitations and doubts, and to strive relentlessly for the acceptance of higher religious standards.

While not necessarily disagreeing with the ideal model lay persons have in mind, rabbis themselves would probably describe their task as being three-fold.

As the word "rabbi" ("my teacher") indicates, the primary function of the spiritual leader is to educate his flock. This means conveying the eternal teachings with absolute conviction and endeavouring with young and old alike to win an appreciation and enhance the understanding of the treasures of Jewish sacred literature. Because of the multiple tensions that exist between transmitted wisdom and modern thought, it is an indispensable rabbinic function to attempt to validate the glories of Jewish tradition, Torah in its twenty-first century setting.

The second task is to care, whether it be for the congregant who is old and lonely, the divorced person who is anguished and insecure or the immature youngster who needs help. Only the rabbi who can share a little of the pain of an unhappy congregant can hope to be of some assistance and solace.

It is related of the saintly Rabbi Aryeh Levin z'l, of Jerusalem that his wife accidentally knocked her foot against a wall and was in great pain. The Rabbi accompanied her to the doctor and told him: "My wife has a sore foot and it is hurting us."

The third task is to inspire. Most shul members have a great liking for Judaism, no matter how much they have lapsed in their practice of it. Like an empty bottle of whisky, the aroma of Judaism — its ta'am — is still tantalisingly with them, however evaporated the substance. The devoted rabbi, the one who really believes in the beneficial influence of Torah and the impact for good it can have on one's life, can help to reawaken in the non-practising Jew the desire to reach up for a loftier range of spiritual experience, and by standing at their side encourage congregants to recapture that sense of uplifting joy invariably accompanying Jewish observance.

Of course the Rabbinate has its drawbacks. Because of the public nature of his activities, the rabbi is all too often prone to criticism and exposed to attack. One colleague has accurately pinpointed the acute vulnerability of the congregational rabbi at the mercy of congregants.

"Where can a person be really crazy and eccentric and get away with it?" he asks. "If you try it in business, you will lose money or your job. If you try it at home, your wife will box your ears. If you try it at the club, you will be asked to resign. But when it comes to shul, any and every trouble maker is allowed to get away with being meshuggah with impunity." He went on to suggest that it was a major task of lay leadership to provide protection for the rabbi against the idiosyncratic foibles of mischievous or malevolent congregants.

As with so many things in life, however, it is a question of balancing the undoubted satisfactions against the distinct disadvantages. Despite examples to the contrary, many rabbis do enjoy job satisfaction.

When a family decides to make the house kosher; when a young congregant tells the rabbi he is going to choose a career which will enable him to keep Shabbat; when, on a rainy evening, a good crowd turns up for the shiur; when a young housewife asks the whereabouts of the nearest mikveh; when the insights into Torah, which the rabbi has tried to communicate, are acknowledged to the extent that they become part of a congregant's life — these are sources of real satisfaction.

Moreover, there is no job which brings one closer to, or allows one to be more involved with, the people. The opportunity to capture the imagination of the young and channel it to good purpose, the ability to counsel wisely to the perplexed of our generation, to stir the Jewish heart and try to be of influence by personality and example — these can bring deep contentment.

Often the rabbi becomes involved in the individual congregant's life at a crucial moment. Because of the contact, sometimes, somehow, in some way, both come away the better for the experience. This is the reward of those who try to do G-d's work.

Not a job for a Yiddishe boy? Oh yes, it is!

2. The Ideal Gabbai

Just as laymen, particularly lay leaders, are experts on what constitutes good rabbinic leadership, so Rabbis, all rabbis without exception, cherish a picture of the ideal lay leader.

Because presidents, chairmen, treasurers and gabbaim give their services voluntarily to their congregation and spend many hours each week dealing with its needs, it may seem churlish to define the characteristics necessary for the job or dare to criticise their efforts on behalf of fellow congregants. Yet ...

I personally have been exceptionally fortunate (with one or two rare exceptions) regarding the personality, quality and sincerity of the lay leaders I have been privileged to work with, and am happy to confirm that without their warm support and honest endeavours I could not possibly have managed. Yet too many Rabbis have a somewhat different story to tell.

Friction between spiritual and lay leadership is regrettably a commonplace. Extremes which I have come across include the shul chairman who gave his dog the same name as the rabbi and, on the other hand, a famous cantor in Johannesburg who, whenever he was having an argument with his gabbaim, would conclude the Friday evening service by sorting them out.

The final hymn is Yigdal, and in the third last line it speaks of the Almighty "rewarding those who are good with goodness, and apportioning punishment to those who are wicked".

When he came to this latter phrase, he would emphasise it and point from the bimah to the three gabbaim sitting with their backs towards him in the wardens' box directly below. Naturally the gabbaim could not see his antics, but the rest of the congregation could.

Several essential qualities are necessary for the lay leader. The most basic is empathy; heaven help the rabbi whose chairman is unable to identify with him in any way or cannot or will not even try to comprehend his circumstances. Commenting on this short-sightedness, an elderly communal worker, with extensive experience of synagogue life, recently confided to me that he knew "many Rabbis whose lives had been systematically ruined by despotic shul chairmen".

Sometimes the relationship is so fraught and the mutual misunderstanding so profound, that fracture results. An acquaintance once told me with pain in his voice:"Our rabbi has just left the community of which I am a member. His parting words were 'I don't know if I failed you or if you failed me but together we failed'. What a terrible shame that was," he went on to say,"for both sides."

What is required is a measure of encouragement for the rabbi. Rabbis have feelings and emotions, too, and they, like all other professionals given a challenging a job to do, tend to blossom when their efforts are appreciated and to wilt when they are not.

Moreover, the good chairman will possess something precious called vision. He will feel dissatisfied if his shul is in a rut or simply marking time. He will yearn for a more dynamic communal programme; he will want his synagogue to become a power-house of Jewish activity. He will dream of better things for his congregation.

The biggest drawback as far as the rabbi is concerned, is when someone who is a failure in all other spheres of life is elected to synagogue office and immediately begins to throw his weight around. For some reason this congregational menace is prevalent. Those who are henpecked at home or mediocre at business are eager to misuse the power of congregational office to browbeat everyone around, especially the rabbi.

A London friend of mine once invented a new game, based on Monopoly, called Yichusopoly, in which all the artificial stimulants to synagogue egoists — your resolution is passed at the AGM, move forward three spaces — were given due prominence and allowed one to climb up the communal ladder.

Another common type which most rabbis readily recognise is the danger of the ba'al teshuvah who assumes office. This is a sad phenomenon, but it is quite often the experience of spiritual leaders who have succeeded in making a member really religious, that when that member is elected to the shul committee, he imagines that he knows the rabbi's job better than the Rabbi. With the ardent, often fanatical, zeal of the newly religious, this type can prove a persistent nuisance. There is all the difference in the world between offering sensible suggestions on how to improve the services or the educational activities of the congregation and constant unrealistic claims that the rabbi is not doing his best.

While it is always preferable, yet surprisingly rare even in these days of much-increased religious observance, that the gabbai be a practising Jew, a shomer mitzvot, there are many examples of gabbaim who, while not particularly observant themselves, nevertheless are able to make a positive contribution. Realizing the necessity of perpetuating Jewish tradition despite their own limitations, for which they blame themselves personally and not Judaism, they can achieve much for their congregation in the areas of sound organisation and financial health.

However, a senior colleague strongly recommends that all gabbaim, irrespective of their standards of observance, should at least attend the rabbi's adult education lectures. There must exist some positive Jewish religious link between the two parties.

Across the Jewish world, management committees of synagogues are subject to peculiar laws. It is amazing how often people who are successful in their careers — lawyers, professors, business magnates, physicians and scientists — are nevertheless unable to think straight and contribute cogently to the debate when put round a shul meeting table.

Problems which they would normally solve in a matter of minutes, by weighing up the pros and cons and coming to a satisfactory decision, are at a shul meeting discussed for hours — backwards and forwards — and then the committee usually comes to the wrong conclusion. It is called Jewish democracy.

By far the most successful recipe for lay and spiritual leadership is to enter into positive partnership together. As the conscientious rabbi worries about his congregation for 24 hours a day, it is nonsense to limit him to a category called "religion". Every rabbi worth his salt should be able to assert his talents and abilities and improve communal management across the board. Similarly, well-intentioned lay leaders should always be able to criticise constructively by suggesting ways of improving the spiritual and cultural programme of the congregation.

For over forty years I have observed congregations from the inside, and can honestly state that where this kind of partnership exists and there is a good rapport and mutual respect, the shul flourishes. Wherever it is absent, with hermetically sealed compartments between the two, there is either stagnation or hostility.

The usual bone of contention concerns the rabbi's salary and emoluments. While no-one enters the rabbinate to become wealthy, a rabbi is entitled to a decent standard of living. On the other hand, most shul chairmen and treasurers consider it their bounden duty to restrict the rabbi financially, as often and in as many ways as possible. Much scope in this direction is provided by expense arrangements for car and telephone, medical aid, repairs to the synagogue house in which the rabbi lives, and the terms of any pension.

It was once expressed to me by someone who should never have been elected to any shul committee, that "the rabbi must not earn more than the poorest wage earner in the congregation". On the contrary, cutting costs, especially where the rabbi is concerned, is an exercise in false economy. In too many instances the rabbi is beset with severe money problems, and due to these the quality of his work is adversely affected and a mood of resentment surrounds his relationship with the shul executive.

It has often been suggested, but never implemented, that training courses should be made available to all who aspire to synagogue office, a College of Lay Leadership. So many technicalities, not least of halachah when the presiding warden has to allocate aliyot on Shabbat mornings, have to be mastered, that a course of comprehensive instruction should be compulsory. Conflict resolution, or how to prevent disgruntled members leaving the congregation, needs to be included. Who would conduct such courses might well be a problem.

Staying too long in office also constitutes a source of regular and vehement argument. Sensible synagogues have a limitation, usually two to three years in the one position, that allows experience to be built up, prevents the same person occupying the same office for too long, and restricts the chances of dictatorship.

In Britain some years ago, the ministry of transport introduced yellow boxes at major junctions. Painted on the road was the instruction, "Do not enter this box until your exit is clear". Maybe the same advice should be written on the Wardens' box?

To persuade capable personalities of the younger generation to become gabbaim is a major headache. Unfortunately, voluntary work for a synagogue — unlike working selflessly for charities and other good causes, often non-Jewish — has an unsavoury reputation, not by any means always deserved, so that those who wish to be of service in some capacity do not seek election to synagogue committees.

Similarly, many professionals would rather work for non-Jewish organisations. Some years ago in London, vacancies were announced simultaneously for a senior teacher at a Jewish day school, for a youth director of a Jewish club, for an important welfare job at a Jewish old age home, and for a replacement at a top administrative post in a communal organisation.

Curious as to the cause of this spate of vacancies, I checked up as to why the previous occupants had left. In each case they told me that they had had enough of "Jewish committees". They were going to try to work for non-Jewish people, whom they felt sure would treat them in a better way.

While all this sounds very negative, there are indeed many lay leaders whose loyalty is an inspiration and whose dedicated efforts guarantee the well-being of their congregation and enhance its standards.

Remember: the rabbi is paid to be good but the lay leaders who do the job so conscientiously are good-for-nothing!

3.   Good Jewish Schools

It is often said that the answer to the problems of Jewish education is the establishment and availability of Jewish schools. One little
word is missing from the solution. It is not Jewish Day Schools which
are the answer — it is *good* Jewish Day Schools.

South African Jewry has succeeded in establishing a network of
Jewish Schools that are the pride and joy of the community. The community enjoys the highest percentage in the Jewish diaspora of Jewish
pupils attending Jewish schools; only Australia comes close in percentage terms, with American Jewry, Anglo-Jewry and French Jewry
trailing far behind.

A remarkable achievement of the rabbis, educators and lay leaders
of yesteryear, a Jewish community in which attending Jewish schools
is the norm and where every family requiring it receives a subsidy, has
been fully realized.

On the surface all appears well. The schools are happy and
bustling, the teachers skilled and effective, the facilities highly satisfactory. Most of the pupils do well at matric, sport and at getting on
with each other.

Below the surface, however, a variety of vexatious problems
undoubtedly exists. Our schools proudly boast a national/traditional
ethos. This means the entire system ought to be geared to producing
— to use the definition of one of the founders of the day school movement, the late Rabbi Isaac Goss z'l — "a completely integrated Jewish
personality," a person whose Jewish consciousness is rooted in the
spiritual heritage and historical experience of the Jewish people,
someone to whom Israel is a component of Jewish identity, and someone who feels comfortable with both.

Now it is certainly true that most of the pupils gain much from the
schools' Jewish atmosphere, that they are able to identify easily with
matters Jewish, that they have a genuine interest in Israel's well-being,
and that by and large they are proud of being Jewish.

But, apart from the Torah schools, such as the prize-winning Yeshiva College, with its unique campus developed by Rabbi Avraham Tanzer, there is an absence of ideology and personal obligation on the part of the pupils. Jewish schools should be about Jewish commitment, directly addressing not only *what* is a Jew or *how* to be a Jew but also *why* one should be Jewish. In this connection, a remarkable proof of failure is the lack of shul attendance on Shabbat by most Jewish day school pupils. Apparently they have had "enough of being Jewish" during the week.

Across the Jewish world, somewhat surprisingly, no official gauge to assess Jewish day school standards operates. Everything is gloriously subjective. The Reshut, the Joint Authority for Jewish Zionist Education in Jerusalem, tried a few years ago to establish the parameters of "basic Jewish literacy" and to fix proper indices to measure quality and progress, in place of the present self-assessment. Apart from an initial outline for Jewish primary schools, nothing was forthcoming.

The key failure rests with the motive of the parents. The axiom that Jewish parents send their Jewish children to Jewish schools to obtain a sound Jewish education is simply untrue. The real reasons for their choice revolve around ethnicity (to mix with fellow Jewish children), fear (to avoid anti-semitism) and secular educational ambitions (to attain university entrance). But not, please not, that their child be given a sound Jewish education!

Speaking more than thirty years ago at a Board of Jewish Education Conference, my predecessor Chief Rabbi Bernard Casper z'l, said:

"Jewish learning must surely be the most essential ingredient in a Jewish School. Without this element in the forefront, can there be a sufficient justification for the Jewish Day School at all? What, indeed, is the motivation of such a school? Can it be to provide schooling for Jewish boys and girls in comfortable surroundings free from anti-semitism? Or to ensure a good secular education with good chances for the matriculation? Or for good sports facilities? All of these are necessary and important. But they cannot in themselves be a sufficient reason for the large and permanent community invest-ment in a Jewish Day School. The only possible justification is the Jewish content in a degree, depth, scope and meaningfulness not otherwise attainable for some thousands of children. And it is to this aspect of our schools that we must apply ourselves in increasing measure."

As if to prove the point, the introduction in 1995 of Jewish Studies as a matric subject met with a lukewarm response. Hebrew at matric level is supposed to be compulsory (although an alarming proportion of the pupils, aided and abetted by their parents, manage to avoid it) and the additional burden of a Jewish Studies Matric initially proved something of an embarrassment.

Nor can the teachers, many of them highly qualified and dedicat-ed professionals, escape censure. Caught up in a paradoxical situation in which the school with its supposed "national/traditional" ethos is not on the same Jewish wave-length as the home, the role and poten-tial influence of the teacher becomes crucial.

Yet Israeli teachers in our schools, mostly yordim, are not in a posi-tion to advocate positive Zionism, let alone aliyah. Nor can a tradi-tional weltanschauung or Jewish religious lifestyle be transmitted by teachers with no personal predilection or association with them. To suggest, in the words of Herzl Fishman, that current Jewish educa-tional viability depends on "the dialectical interplay between religion and nationalism that expresses the authentic Jewish civilization" is to talk about gold to a teaching profession dealing in a lesser currency.

Furthermore, the synthesis promoted over a century ago by Rabbi Samson Raphael Hirsch, Torah im derech eretz (Torah together with secular wisdom), is largely ignored in a school system which hermet-ically seals off its Jewish from its routine academic activities.

Harmonizing Jewish tradition with modern thought is an essential exercise for the enlightened Jew, not only because of the multiple ten-sions which require resolution, but because claims for the validity of Torah wisdom can only be substantiated by informed comparison with secular wisdom.

Indeed in attempting to instil in the pupils an appreciation of Jewish values, an acute ideological battle ought to be waged against the values governing our society at the beginning of this new century. Because it now competes with such powerful alternatives, the informed Jewish view becomes more, not less, important.

If it be true that most teenagers live not so much by inherited rules and parental influence as by peer group behaviour patterns, it is even more essential for the school to become the forum for healthy debate on the relative merits of ancient and modern value systems.

Erroneous imbalance also affects the approach to teaching Jewish history. For understandable but somewhat regrettable reasons, the Holocaust predominates and has grown to occupy a cult-like status.

While it is essential for non-Jewish pupils to know about it, the inordinate emphasis as far as Jewish pupils are concerned is liable to instil a somewhat morbid view of Jewish history. Not only is the presentation of total suffering historically untrue, but the Holocaust, for all its undoubted importance, can never provide the younger generation with more than a warped motivating force towards positive Jewish identity.

The paucity of university students engaged in the whole range of Jewish studies is a further example of the demotion of Jewish learning. The post-emancipation era did not bring about any weakening of the primacy of education in Jewish circles. With regrettable consequences, however, it changed the emphasis from Jewish education to its secular counterpart.

As most of the churches in South Africa demand a knowledge of Biblical Hebrew in the training of clergymen, the paradoxical situation now exists in which hundreds of would-be dominees and ministers of religion study the Bible in the original Hebrew, by far outnumbering the handful of Jewish students engaged in the same exercise.

Hence a priority for our community is to reinstate a culture of Jewish learning, to endeavour to recapture that sense of esteem in which the learned Jew of yesteryear was invariably held. While a significant number of orthodox students has been attracted to study in yeshivot, precious few of the total Jewish student body have been attracted to Jewish studies at university.

On many campuses in the United States faculties of Jewish studies are flourishing and much interest prevails in investigating Jewish roots. Indeed there has been a renaissance in courses on Yiddish literature. No such resurgence is noticeable in our own community.

In the context of the developing new South Africa, a real sense of responsibility towards the society around them must be inculcated in the pupils.

Over a century ago Hirsch began an essay on the place of ethical training in education — that is, the concept that educational purpose is achieved not only in the advancement of technology but when intellectual power is directed to fulfilling the dictates of conscience — with the following, somewhat prophetic, words:

"Men who have the welfare of mankind truly at heart, in whose ears the cry of misery which goes up from human souls ... is not drowned by the songs of praise offered up to the brilliant intellectual achievements of modern times, are often haunted by the thought that the human genius must lower its head in mourning as long as the net result of our culture is not greater and more widely-diffused human happiness."

That the net result of *our* culture should be displayed in the alleviation of hardship and misery is the responsibility of the hour, to be jointly and severally borne. The South African predicament, however we choose to define it, will not be solved by living lives sealed off from the underprivileged, nor by the separation of intellectual acumen from social awareness. Rather our contribution will depend on the sensitivity of our social consciousness, finely honed by our intellectual appreciation of the human condition, and on the wise application of our resources.

Fortunately in this area there are rays of light in the darkness. A number of conscientious teachers are succeeding in transmitting sound Jewish ethical principles to their pupils and activating them towards involvement in a range and variety of much-needed social welfare programmes, especially those which help black students of their own age.

The generality of pupils, however, remains self-centred, their materialistic values mocking the impoverishment of the population as a whole. (The headmistress of a Jewish primary school recently had to forbid children aged nine to bring their cellular telephones to school.)

Improved Jewish standards can only come about if we are able to create more excitement about the issue. Professor Alvin Schiff, formerly of the New York Board of Jewish Education, suggests that the time has come to break down all barriers in Jewish education. The rabbi — the word means "my teacher" — should fulfil that function instead of being a general spiritual factotum; there should be no separation between school and shul, shul and school; and we should utilize every informal as well as formal avenue of Jewish instruction. Vitally, parents must participate with pupils in a family education experience promising better results than before.

The late Dr Harry Abt z'l, used to say that for a successful Barmitzvah there must be a Pa-mitzvah and a Ma-mitzvah as well, that is the parents must not concentrate only on the social aspects of the simchah, but participate with their son in his spiritual adventure of becoming Barmitzvah. Similarly, Shabbatonim should be organized with the whole family in mind, not merely a specific teenage group.

The excellent Encounter programmes at locations far removed from formal school surroundings, and during which many hundreds of teenagers have been enthused by informal Jewish tuition, is testimony to what can be achieved in transmitting essential Jewish knowledge in an enjoyable way. For the first time many Jewish pupils discover their living link to the Jewish people and to the treasures of Jewish civilisation.

The overall aim of Jewish education may be summarised by the ambiguity of the word *distinction*. In the Jewish educational context, this means teaching precisely those principles, values and practices through which Judaism asks Jewish people to be distinct, in the sense of being different from other peoples. And we need to impress the pupils with the distinction, that is the honour of adhering to those self-same principles, values and practices.

When everyone concerned — teachers, pupils, parents, rabbis, governors and well-wishers — join together to pursue this aim, the tide may turn for the better. And our Jewish schools, so admirable in many ways, can become really good Jewish schools.

4. The Power of Community

The most important entity in Judaism is the family circle. The kehilla comes a close second.

We have always been a community-conscious people, and if our survival can be attributed to the strength of the Jewish home, the intensity and power of the community has also played an undoubted part.

"Doing your own thing" is inexcusable in the Jewish tradition. The interdependence which bespeaks an acute sense of responsibility of each for the other is highlighted by the Talmudic teaching that the angels who accompany each person will condemn the individual, who in a time of trouble, goes off on his or her own and refuses to help the community. The angels will rest their wings on that person's head and say: "Since this person has refused to help the people in the time of trouble, they will not live to see the time of consolation and salvation."

Togetherness, an essential component of our Jewish lives, is evinced in a host of common concerns from worrying about the well-being of fellow congregants to sharing the problems of Klal Yisrael. No person is an island — we thrive thanks only to the viable relationship we enjoy with the community and affinity with the people of which we are a proud part.

It is not an accident that the Jewish dance is the horah, the inclusive circle with everyone moving shoulder to shoulder.

To pray correctly we require a minyan. True we can pray on our own, but Judaism encourages praying with the congregation. The Vilna Gaon suggests that the atmosphere of devotion created by the minyan is stronger then anything we can ever create individually, that each of us is elevated by the aggregate devotion to a higher standard than we could ever achieve on or own. The atmosphere generated by the gathering of worshippers, the genuine fellowship created by the collective expression of prayer, and the simple fact that it is difficult to be selfish in the company of the congregation — all these combine to make congregational prayer more praiseworthy.

The Talmud asks "when is it an acceptable time to approach the Almighty?" And the answer is given, not when we are on our own, but "at the hour when the congregation prays together".

As with prayer, so with the attempt to gain atonement: the congregation is in a more advantageous position then the individual. The Jewish confession is part of the public congregational worship on Yom Kippur, and not, as with some other religions, a hidden or private ritual. Such a degree of responsibility, each for the spiritual welfare of the other, is demonstrated by the fact that among Jews, the only way to confess is in the plural, "for the sin which we have sinned".

The great 16th century teacher and mystic, Rabbi Isaac Luria of Safed, asks: "Why was the Vidui arranged in the plural, so that we say, we are guilt laden, instead of I am guilt laden?" He gives the significant answer: "Because all Israel is one body, and every individual Israelite a member of that body. Hence follows mutual responsibility among all the members."

The consciousness that we are all there to help each other, that if someone has strayed from the straight and narrow, each of us shares the guilt because we should have tried to prevent it, carries dynamic potential for the eventual progress of our community. By associating ourselves as a collective in such dramatic manner, we are recognising society as a whole to be responsible for the standards (or lack of them) in current operation, and in a real way acknowledging our duty to do something jointly towards improvement.

In education, too, Judaism discourages isolation. The characteristic feature of traditional Jewish learning is the chavruta, the learning together with others. Visit any Yeshivah and you will see little groups of two or three bachurim heatedly exchanging views on the interpretation of the Talmudic passage under study.

Because knowledge is neutral and can be utilized for good or evil purposes — nuclear power, for example, can be a blessing or a curse — Jewish tradition has always insisted that learning be engaged in with one's fellows so as to obviate any possible anti-social tendencies.

The height of educational attainment is not to establish a new scientific formula at 3 o'clock in the morning, but to engage in study with one's fellows in order to strengthen the positive forces which make for social well-being. As the Talmud states, "the disciples of the wise increase peace in the world".

Practical help to the needy is very much part of the Jewish meaning of community. The Torah insists on the supply of help to the stranger, the orphan and the widow, and that the community shares its resources with the poor. So endemic is this characteristic, this long-established version of Ubuntu, that no visitor to the shtetl would ever go hungry.

Indeed the reason we recite kiddush in synagogue at the Friday evening service, when according to the Shulchan Aruch we are not allowed to eat or drink in shul and in any event kiddush may only be recited when food is about to be eaten, is that there was always a group of itinerant travellers, students and visitors to be fed. Those not receiving individual hospitality would be given a meal in the shul hall, and so the kiddush was originally recited for them and their meal.

Nowadays the concept of community is challenged. Automatically belonging to the community and affiliating with a particular congregation is no longer operative. Since the emancipation from the ghetto, the pressure to identify has been considerably weakened, so that belonging to a synagogue today is voluntary, and an option many Jewish families feel quite comfortable not taking up.

Cultural assimilation has also taken its toll, so that the community of today does not carry the same weight as yesteryear. A prime obligation thus rests on every congregation to attract membership.

The voluntary character of today's synagogal association carries awkward ramifications for the Jewish future. The realisation that synagogues will only prosper by the genuine friendliness of their welcome to newcomers, and by the quality of the services and cultural and social programmes they offer, has yet to be fully comprehended.

The raison d'etre of the house of worship as the embodiment of spiritual values is also under attack from the new scientists — physiologists, geneticists and the like — who combine to supposedly prove that human beings are products of random mutations and impersonal cosmic forces. Houses of worship can be mere decorative institutions with little influence on moral life, or they can accept the challenge of trying to combat the corrosive impact of trendy philosophies, to teach that human beings are not purposeless laboratory artifacts but moral and responsible beings.

A further key area is religious standards. In the past the transmission of Jewish values and the continuity of Jewish observance was largely a matter for the home. It was a vertical transmission — father to son, mother to daughter — and the sort of education which almost always had positive impact on the younger generation.

Nowadays for understandable reasons, the Jewish home in many instances is no longer capable of the task. To survive we must move to a horizontal transmission, so that the religiosity evinced by the synagogue rubs off on the individual members, whose family and personal Jewish conduct is raised because of the high example of the standards of the synagogue.

To achieve this, it is necessary for the synagogue to possess a core group of devoted Torah-observant men and women who deliberately set the tone for the congregation and provide a living example of the requisite standards. The rabbi on his own cannot do this since it is always assumed that it is his job anyway. But a group of like-minded devotees can do it and the remarkable return to stricter standards of Jewish observance is due mainly to such influential groups as much as to charismatic rabbis and outreach movements such as Lubavitch, Ohr Sameyach and Aish HaTorah.

A major additional obligation today is that the synagogue displays genuine kindness. The shul does not exist only for spiritual, religious, educational and communal activities but also for social welfare purposes — to alleviate, with great kindness, the personal problems of congregants, young and old, male and female. It is precisely at the moment of difficulty — of separation in a marriage, of the pain of divorce, of acute personal distress — that the individual needs the kehilla most; and it is exactly, precisely, at that moment that so many of our kehillot fail.

It is no longer true to say that our community is composed of happy families. Unfortunately there is a large and increasing number of broken homes.

A startling example of the incidence of breakdown in family life chanced my way. In 1965 I was obliged to take a medical examination for insurance purposes. Regarding my marital status, the only question on the form was: Are you married or single?

Twenty years later, I was again obliged to take a similar medical exam. There were no fewer than nine spaces for the answer on personal status. Was I a bachelor? Was I married — for the first time? Married — for the second time? Was I separated? Was I a widower? Was I divorced first time or second time? And then I was asked about cohabitation: Was I living with someone of the opposite sex? Was I living with someone of the same sex? Within two decades, the startling variety of social arrangements, the change from the stability of the family to the instability which is all too prevalent nowadays, is all too clearly displayed.

So the key question is: what can the shul do in terms of supportive policies and initiatives to help?

To try to make isolated members of the congregation less isolated, some worthy ideas have been put into practice. The first is the "big buddy" scheme. This is for children of one-parent families. Say a child is coming up to Barmitzvah and the parents are divorced, and he is living with his mother and daddy is not often around: somebody in the community, an older teenager aged 16 or 17, deliberately befriends this 12 year-old. He is there for him, helps him over little obstacles and psychologically is someone on whom that youngster can lean.

Loneliness is not only a problem with broken families. Especially in the South African context, we have widows and widowers in their eighties, their children and grandchildren live far away, and they are very lonely; nobody bothers with them. Some communities have an "Adopt a granny" project. You adopt a granny and regularly call on her, you do the shopping for her and help her to be part and parcel of the community.

Single parents must also be encouraged to become involved in communal activities. "Parents without Partners" — as single parents prefer to be called — have to be treated with great tact, somehow or other have to be made part of the social life of the shul. Some congregations hold monthly Friday night dinners for all of the above categories of people.

Every shul, in addition to its committee that deals with bikkur cholim, should have a special committee which deals with the individual problems of congregants who really need help. Let's call it a "Chesed" committee; its function would be to liaise with Jewish social welfare organisations; to be available for advice to all those in need; and to help with financial problems which are a very real issue for single parents. In some way or other, this chesed committee must become the conscience of the shul by its active willingness to alleviate the problems that individual members have, and that they cannot tackle on their own.

In this day and age they are entitled to turn to the shul and ask for help. A shul is not just there for davening — of course it's there for davening and for shiurim and for the hundred-and-one mitzvot which can be performed in the congregational arena — the shul is also there for deeds of kindness extended to the lonely and the miserable. We can never be spiritually healthy if we are ethically lacking.

In all these ways the power of the community can be asserted. Despite the enormous pressures towards fragmentation, the togetherness of the synagogal community can be maintained by standing shoulder-to-shoulder in heart-warming fellowship to fulfil the challenging obligations our changed circumstances force upon us.

5. Proper Prayer

Potentially the most inspiring of religious activities, prayer often turns out to be one of the least.

To capture the right mood, especially in our frenetic, distracting world is never easy, not only on weekdays when a strenuous effort to switch off from the outside world and concentrate on higher matters has to be made — but even on the holy Sabbath to attempt to reach up and communicate with the heavenly source can prove a formidable exercise.

Success depends on three separate components. The first concerns our motive in wanting to pray; the second relates to appropriate surroundings; and the third involves developing a proper technique of praying.

Our motives are usually pure when we are praising G-d or thanking Him. But they are often rather suspect when we are asking the Almighty to fulfil our personal requests.

The most selfish prayer on record is that of John Ward, member of parliament for Weymouth in 17th century England. He prayed as follows:

"Oh Lord, thou knowest that I have lately purchased an estate in fee simple in Essex. I beseech Thee to preserve the two counties of Middlesex and Essex from fire and earthquakes; and as I have also a mortgage at Hertfordshire, I beg of Thee also to have an eye of compassion on that county, and for the rest of the counties, Thou may deal with them as Thou art pleased. Oh Lord, enable the bank to answer all their bills and make all my debtors good men, give a prosperous voyage and safe return to the Mermaid sloop, because I have not insured it, and because Thou hast said, 'The days of the wicked are but short', I trust in Thee that Thou wilt not forget Thy promise, as I have an estate in reversion, which will be mine on the death of the profligate young man, Sir J L ... g. Keep my friends from sinking, preserve me from thieves and housebreakers, and make all my servants so honest and faithful that they may always attend to my interest and never cheat me out of my property night or day."

Directly opposed to this attitude is the advice of Rabbi Yaacov Emden, the 18th century Talmudist. In his Siddur commentary, he states that we should never make supplication for our needs with the intention of gratifying our own selfish desires, for that is not the worship of Hashem; it is self-worship. Our fixed aim, when asking for health, riches and peace of mind, should be that if Hashem does indeed grant them to us, we will utilise them in order the better to fulfil our responsibilities to Him, that our health and strength and material blessings will be utilised to good purpose.

Moreover, we require the right surroundings. This is not so much an aesthetic consideration, but rather one of familiarity. The Talmud lays down two rules regarding our place of prayer — that if there is a choice of several synagogues, we should settle on one in which to pray regularly, and that within that synagogue we should always pray in the same seat. Fully accustomed to our surroundings, we are not liable to be distracted and can concentrate properly on trying to make contact with our Maker.

The correct atmosphere can all too easily be disturbed. Coming late to synagogue, a disrespectful habit, is liable to disturb the service and often interferes with those who are really trying to daven. Punctuality is fundamental. With long services, especially on the sabbath and festivals, it is obviously absurd to expect every congregant to be in place at the very beginning, but the tendency is much the other way. Who, one may ask, deliberately misses the first half-hour of a film or goes to a concert in time for the interval, or starts a round of golf at hole number seven?

The exact opposite is recommended by the Mishnah, which informs us that we should come to synagogue before the service starts! "The pious men of early times," we are told, "used to wait a full hour before reciting tefillah, so that they might direct their heart towards Hashem."

The chattering brigade, incessantly using their tongues to communicate with those below instead of attempting to speak to Him on high, repeatedly intrude on the right frame of mind. The advice of Gluckel of Hamelin in her 17th century memoirs is apt: "Say your prayers with awe and devotion and do not stand about and talk of other things. While prayers are being offered to the Creator of the world, hold it a great sin to engage another person in talk about an entirely different matter — shall the Almighty be kept waiting until you have finished your business?"

A non-Jewish acquaintance told me that he once attended the services on Yom Kippur to see what they were like. Two men in the row in front of him were talking to each other about the stock market. "They got up for the main silent devotion — I believe you call it the Amidah - and as soon as they had finished they resumed their conversation on stocks-and-shares exactly where they had left off!"

All the difficulties concerning prayer are compounded on Rosh Hashanah and Yom Kippur, potentially the most inspiring services of the year. A sad paradox seems to operate — the more people, the less atmosphere for prayer; the longer the service, the less we are attuned to it.

The most irritating offenders, especially on Yom Tov, are the In-and-Out mob. Like little children who cannot keep still or concentrate, they spend as much time outside the synagogue than in it ("the service is the same as last year").

An old friend of mine, an educationist, once took a shtender to a raucous group of teenagers milling around outside the synagogue, and much to their astonishment delivered an impromptu sermon to them. A case of "If you can't beat 'em, join them!"

Another infuriating group are the clock watchers, especially prominent during the fast, who keep checking the time and wishing the hours away, instead of using it for its high purpose.

Many years ago, I seriously suggested that at the beginning of the Kol Nidrei service everyone should hand in their watch to the Shammas and that they would be returned at the end of the fast. It was not a popular suggestion.

No easy cure is available for widespread negative attitudes towards prayer. Nevertheless, a large step towards restoring meaning and a sense of purpose can be taken by worshippers themselves, if they adopt suggestions on prayer technique made by the great 16th century Rabbi of Prague, Isaiah Horovitz.

He wrote that prayer will spring to life when the person praying uses a little imagination to connect the words to present conditions either affecting him- or herself personally, to the needs of the local community, the Jewish people or humanity in general.

For example, instead of praying for health in the abstract, think during that prayer of someone you know who is unfortunately ill in hospital. The prayer immediately takes on vital meaning. Similarly, in place of asking for personal wealth to fulfil material ambitions, ask for it in the hope of being able to do some of the good deeds wealth can perform, and which you have always, one day, wanted to do.

In similar vein, and particularly relevant during the Days of Awe, sin is a neutral concept, unless we bring to mind our own failings, weaknesses and shortcomings and have the courage to seek forgiveness for them. Likewise, asking for blessings for the House of Israel is a lukewarm prayer. Pouring out one's heart on behalf of a Jewish community caught in some trouble, makes the same prayer altogether relevant.

To pray for peace in a sadly troubled world, one should have in mind the current war-ravaged countries of the world. "Shalom," the final request of every Amidah, must be accompanied by utterly sincere wishes for the dawn of a peaceful era, especially for the State of Israel.

Moreover, in expressing our most deeply-felt needs, our prayers can ascend from the selfish to the noble. To be of better service than we are now to the society around us, we can pray for qualitative blessings — more wisdom, greater strength of character and a reinvigorated will.

One of the most spiritually satisfying aspects of Judaism, the precious moments of prayer deserve our undivided attention, if possible our profound contemplation, and ideally our passionate exultation.

In Hamlet, King Claudius bemoans his inability to pray: "My words fly up, my thoughts remain below; words without thoughts never to Heaven go."

Instead of expecting automatic stimulus from synagogue services, we can endeavour to pray from the depths of our heart and so exert our conscious soul that our prayers may rise up on high.

6.   Seven Up!

Of all the areas of synagogue life, none is more liable to cause headaches to presiding wardens and none more likely to create friction among congregants than the vexed weekly problem of "dividing the honours" for the reading of the Law.

Moses, coming down the mountain, broke the tablets of the Law into small pieces. Every Shabbat morning many rabbis and gabbaim do likewise, cutting the Torah-reading to fragments to fit in a maximum number of call-ups.

A few important points of clarification may be in order because, firstly, there appears to be a competition among synagogues as to which can call up the most people on a given Shabbat — some of our large suburban synagogues never call less than double the statutory number and, when there are several simchas, often go over the 20-mark; and, secondly, because every synagogue experiences the pressure ("What? You won't give me six aliyas for my son's aufruf? Over thirty years I've been a member here and you can't give me a measly six aliyas?") and the threats ("I'll tell you what I'll do. If you don't give me an aliyah this Shabbos, I'll join the shul round the corner. That's what I'll do!").

The reading of the Sidra is an educational exercise — that is, we come to synagogue not only to pray but also to learn; our services are instructional as well as devotional. To follow the Keriat haTorah properly and listen to each and every word, it is obviously necessary to concentrate. Herein lies the problem. As the reading is chopped up more and more, and as an increasing number of congregants go up-and-down for their respective aliyot, concentration begins to wane and often tails off altogether before the Sidra is completed. The more people called up, the more satisfied customers. The educational purpose, however, has been defeated.

It is also not fully appreciated that the "stops" in the Sidra are subject to halachah. The person who has the privilege of reading the Torah for the congregation is not allowed to carve up the text in an arbitrary manner. He must abide by regulations which sometimes stipulate that the parashah at hand is to be recited without interruption. These also often preclude stopping due to the limited number of sentences in a paragraph and they always necessitate beginning and ending on a favourable note.

The time factor, moreover, is crucial. Should the leining take an hour or more, the whole balance of the service is ruined. Everyone starts to fidget, to look at the clock and to wonder how long they will have to wait before they can have a drink at the berochoh. Thus the calling-up of too many people is detrimental not merely to the reading itself but to the service as a whole, in that the derashah is delivered to a restless congregation and a cantorial item during Musaf to an impatient one. In addition, the fixed injunction to avoid tircha d'tzibura, unnecessarily troubling the congregation, is violated.

In the clamour for honours, three separate categories may be delineated. First and foremost come the chiyyuvim, those who are legitimately entitled to an aliyah. This category comprises a Barmitzvah boy, a bridegroom, a father to name his newly-born baby daughter, a person on the day of his yahrzeit, and so on.

Next comes the gantse mishpochoh, the family of the chiyyuvim. They are not really entitled to aliyot, but, after all, it is their simcha. The problem, which has troubled every lay leader who has ever stood segan, is where to draw the line, or rather, how to limit the family circle? The grandfathers of the Barmitzvah must be given kibbudim (who could be so mean as to deprive them?) but are the boy's uncles entitled to honours? The bridegroom is a chiyyuv, his father and future father-in-law are mishpochoh, but is his long-lost cousin, who has specially come from America for the wedding, to be included or not?

The third category are those with chutzpah. The nerve of some people is unbelievable and has been known to extend to requests for aliyot for business associates, old school friends, for the neighbours on either side, for a tsutsheppenish, and for Morry. (Morry? "Yes, I was called up at his son's Barmitzvah in Pretoria.")

To counter the current trend of maximising the number of aliyot, a deliberate attempt ought to be made to apply basic rules of procedure and so help alleviate the problem. For example, a person who has yahrzeit during the week is not automatically a chiyyuv, due to those celebrating a simchah coming before him in the order of precedence. Judaism is a living religion which almost always puts the happy before the sad, and because those commemorating a yahrzeit on Shabbat itself come before those who have yahrzeit during the week.

Some sensible synagogues, in the printed yahrzeit reminder, invite those with yahrzeit on a week-day to attend the morning service and be called up on the nearest Monday or Thursday, thereby lightening the load on the preceding Shabbat.

On the other hand, especially where young people are concerned, an aliyah can be given for no reason whatsoever except that of showing the young person that he counts as a member of the congregation. It is a fact that the Young Israel movement in the United States was begun by disillusioned young men who, given the plethora of yahrzeit aliyot claimed by older members of the congregation, never received an aliyah from the time of their Barmitzvah until the Shabbat before their marriage.

Much one-up-manship also exists regarding which aliyah is the best partially because many differences in custom exist. For Ashkenazim, the third aliyah is considered the most honoured as it is the first an ordinary Israelite can have, after the mandatory calling-up of the Cohen and Levi.

For Chassidim, the sixth aliyah is the best, as the kabbalah ascribes the sixth attribute of Hashem to righteousness. For Sephardim, the last one to be called up — mashlim — is the best as the "last is to be preferred". In some congregations the fourth aliyah has a degree of eminence, as we call up three on Monday and Thursday mornings and so it is the first to be added in honour of Shabbat.

All these degrees of priority are frowned on by leading authorities. The commentator Aruch Hashulchan states that since every sentence

and every single word of the Torah is holy, it is quite wrong to differentiate in the way that some of us do. It is invidious to discriminate
between one parashah and another in such an arbitrary manner.

This sentiment is blissfully ignored by gabbaim, who spend many
hours deliberating on who should get what aliyah. There is no quick-
er way to cause a faribbel than to give some Jewish personality what
he considers to be an inferior aliyah. To juggle that Shabbat morning's
call-up list to try to satisfy everybody is an exercise requiring great
dexterity and much diplomacy.

When my friend, Yehudah Avner, who was a Bnei Akiva leader in
my youth, was appointed Israel ambassador to the Court of St James,
he was invited, on his first visit to my synagogue in St John's Wood, to
choose between sitting in the wardens' box or occupying a prominent
front row seat.

As he is orthodox and a regular shulgoer, this was quite a
quandary. He decided to sit in the wardens' box. After a few weeks
he told me — he has a wonderful sense of humour — that the exercise of diplomacy in choosing who gets the aliyot was superior to anything at the United Nations or any of his problems with foreign affairs,
and that he was altogether fascinated by the negotiations backwards
and forwards as to who would be honoured with shelishi and who
would end up with maftir.

In any event, the whole purpose of having an aliyah is itself often
misconstrued. The gesture is not only to honour someone in the congregation, but to give that person the opportunity of honouring the
Torah, which is not quite the same thing! If this were to be properly
appreciated and widely publicised, we could perhaps move to a more
mature understanding which would allow us to give up our own
aliyah as readily as we now give up someone else's.

And maybe then we could all get home before the cholent is burnt
to a cinder.

7.   The Perils of Preaching

Many obstacles confront today's preacher. To begin with, we live in an audio-visual age; people really do have difficulty in simply listening. Unless they can see something, be it a television screen, slides or a video, listening at the beginning of the 21st century has become a difficult exercise.

So there is a premium on the dynamic delivery of the person giving the sermon. It has to be put over wherever possible in an exciting way, otherwise sleep is going to be the result of his efforts.

My first homiletics teacher used to remind us regularly that "If you don't put fire into the sermon, put the sermon into the fire". This is the recipe for some degree of success. The trouble is that, as we get older, it's not always so easy. I, for one, am so old I can sleep during my own sermons. Seriously, unless the presentation is lively, we are liable to make the entire congregation comatose.

Despite the difficulties of the subject, there are certain basic ingredients which, in most instances, make for success.

The first desideratum is a personal commitment to what we are saying; sincerity must suffuse it. If we ourselves are not absolutely convinced of the truth, virtue and value of what we are putting over, then how on earth can we expect our listeners to be convinced? The aim is to transmit a synthesis of intellectual conviction and personal credibility, accompanied by a degree of emotional appeal. That's an exhilarating challenge, but one that has to be met.

Conviction accompanied by passion — and even moderate views can be passionately espoused — usually wins a response. A mediocre message can be made appealing by the fervour with which it is put over. Conversely, a really good sermon may misfire because the speaker has been unable to communicate the message cogently. Just as a piece of sublime music can be made to sound ordinary or even discordant by a poor instrumentalist, so may an inspiring idea, couched in beautiful language, become a lifeless thing unless it be vitalised by a convincing delivery.

Next comes the love of words. The rabbi, no less than the journalist, author or broadcaster, must have an eager and abiding affinity to words. The late Malcolm Muggeridge, an immensely skilled and effective writer and television presenter, especially on the application of religious values to modern society, wrote in his autobiography:

"From the very beginning of my life I never doubted that words were my metier. There was nothing else I ever wanted to do except use them ... I have always loved words, and still love them for their own sake. For the power and beauty of them; for the wonderful things that can be done with them."

Hence in constructing the sermon, it is essential not to utilise the first words that come to mind but to find exactly the right words to suit the subject and to fit the audience.

Fundamental concepts and praiseworthy thoughts clothed in poor language will fail to have impact. While it may be true that the great orator is born and not made, it is equally true that by dint of hard work and constant practice, command of language can be raised so as to succeed in the sacred function of being an eloquent interpreter of the faith.

A major difficulty in our times is to avoid the vulgar and the colloquial, to try to be dignified and yet at the same time to be understood. The preacher stands on the moral high ground and therefore he is not allowed to put over his thoughts in anything other than a worthy way. So we have the great difficulty, it requires great dexterity, to be at one and the same time natural and comprehensible and yet dignified.

The Shakespearean critic, St John Irvine, translates Hamlet's famous soliloquy:
"To be or not to be: that is the question
Whether 'tis nobler in the mind to suffer
The slings and arrows of outrageous fortune,
Or take arms against a sea of troubles,
And by opposing end them?"
into: "For two pins I'd do myself in, only I haven't got the guts!"

Now the sense is very clear, but every vestige of dignity has gone.

Third, and very vital, is the illustration of the theme. Creating a verbal picture to add force to the plea, serves as a window shedding light on the subject at hand.

I was once asked to speak about Joseph's coat of many colours. The problem for the modern mind is why such enmity, indeed murderous jealousy, should have been aroused in Joseph's brothers by him having received a technicolour coat. Surely the brothers were not short of clothes? So what was the real significance of Jacob's gesture of favouritism?

Egyptologists have discovered from the painted tombs of early Egypt that Semitic chiefs wore a coat of many colours as the insignia of leadership. Thus Jacob, in giving Joseph a coat of many colours, had marked him out for chieftainship.

Purely by coincidence, a few days before I spoke on this theme, I read in the daily newspaper about the latest winner of the Masters Golf Tournament in Augusta, Georgia. The report included an account of the handing over of the famous Green Jacket by the previous winner. Aha, I thought, leadership in golf is indicated by the handing over of a brightly coloured coat, and in South Africa — where many would proclaim sport the most popular religion — a sporting illustration is invariably appreciated.

So I began with one golfer acknowledging the expertise and leadership in the game of another by handing over the Green Jacket and then went on to explain the real significance of Jacob giving his son Joseph a coat of many colours.

It is absolutely essential in the structured development of a sermon, which must of course carry one — and only one — single theme, that the greatest care is taken with the beginning and the end. The preacher must be able to grip his audience from the outset. A weak opening may well create the impression that what is going to follow is not worth concentrating on.

A colleague of mine, who was a good preacher and who is now retired, ministered for many years to an elderly and wealthy congregation in central London. Many of the old people were deaf, but some of them had procured up-to-date and sophisticated hearing aids, which allowed them to switch to a radio station, which was built into the hearing system.

My friend swears that if he did not begin his weekly sermon with a compelling introduction, he could see many of these old congregants, after the first few minutes of his peroration, fumble with the controls and deliberately switch their hearing aids to the radio channel.

Likewise, the concluding and decisive moments of the sermon must endeavour to impress the full weight of the moral argument upon the minds and hearts of the listeners.

In a sermon on continuity, delivered in South Africa on Yom Kippur, I ended with a story which had been communicated to me by a friend in England.

He is a Levite and he has an only daughter who by chance married a Cohen. He wrote to me about his grandson, who had celebrated becoming Barmitzvah before Rosh Hashanah, to tell me that the family had spent Yom Tov with him.

When they were all in shul on the first day of Rosh Hashanah, at the relevant point during Musaf, because my friend was a Levite he went outside the synagogue to wash the hands of the Cohanim prior to the priestly benediction. He looked up and saw that his grandson — who of course was a Cohen, as his daughter had married one — was also in the queue waiting for the washing of the hands.

When his grandson eventually reached him, the young man looked at his grandfather and said: "Listen grandpa, this isn't fair. I'm a Cohen and you are a Levi, and you are going to wash my hands. But you are my grandpa, so please will you bless me before I go into the congregation with the other Cohanim to bless you and all the others?"

My friend described to me the great joy, almost ecstasy, he felt in blessing his grandson with the traditional priestly benediction which, of course, fathers and grandfathers are also allowed to use for their own flesh and blood. Then, a few minutes later, he had gone back into the congregation and his grandson had blessed him with the priestly benediction.

This was the great reason for joy, the feeling of unity and the bonding of the generations. Continuity is guaranteed when grandfathers bless their grandchildren, and the grandchildren reciprocate.

Purely because an airmail letter had been received at the right time, I had been provided with an emotional and very appropriate ending to a Yom Kippur sermon.

Choosing the right theme is also vital. Here, too, it is advisable to remember the four major categories into which themes may be placed. Firstly and obviously, there is guidance, that is offering Torah insights on contemporary issues. There are a huge number of these, especially concerning business and medical ethics, and congregants are often interested in the Jewish view on a given topical problem.

Secondly, but sparingly, there is musar. This is literally "moral instruction" to the congregation about their failings; their failings to observe the commandments, their failings to live up to Torah, their failings to live a life consonant with the beliefs to which they claim to subscribe.

This category should not be indulged in too often. If the preacher lambasts his congregants every Shabbat, or even once a month, the congregation is liable to be upset or irritated or, even worse, to pay no attention, because no one likes a ticking off on a regular basis.

The late Reverend Dr Abraham Cohen z'l, a brilliant lecturer in homiletics, used to remind his pupils that the Torah itself berates the children of Israel at length only twice. Likewise, the wise preacher will castigate his congregation sparingly.

Then, of course, the pulpit can be used for information. It is a good idea to take a specific prayer from the Siddur, ask the congregation to turn to it in the prayer book, and to explain it — who wrote it, its theme, its message, differences between one ritual and another, its place in the liturgy, the music to which it is set, and any other interesting items about it.

Similarly, one can take a Jewish religious custom and explain the origins of that custom and the proper way to carry it out. This never fails to hold the attention of most congregants who appreciate being informed about the interesting customs of Judaism.

Lastly, the category of inspiration — to recognise from time to time that congregants have legitimate fears and doubts and to offer them hopes and dreams; to try to put over, in a sympathetic way, all that Jewish spirituality has to offer. This, of course, cannot be done every week, but for example at yizkor, not in a mawkishly sentimental way, to point out the validity of the lessons which have been handed down to us by our forebears.

One can also be inspirational about tefillah, often with its deeply moving power; and try to be inspirational about the value of observances, such as the holiness of Shabbat. In the final analysis the preacher's task is to articulate the beauty and truth of the teachings of the faith.

How long — or rather how short — the average sermon should be is a matter of much debate. Clearly, we live in an age in which the concentration span of most people is relatively short. It is possible that the average concentration span is little more than ten minutes.

Now while it is true that a ten minute sermon is many times better than a twenty minute one because most people's attention will wander halfway through the latter, it is, of course, also true that to deal adequately with a major theme, one does require a little more time. For routine preaching, most rabbis stick to the golden rule of never exceeding fifteen minutes, and, whenever possible, to be a little shorter than that.

How long the impact of a sermon lasts is a moot point. All rabbis would like to think that the impact of their sermon lasts for ages, that the Friday night derashah is discussed at the Friday night table, the Shabbat morning sermon at the Shabbat lunch table, and that it merits a mention during the following week. But experience teaches otherwise.

People very rarely remember a sermon unless it is repeated — and then everyone seems to remember it! Of course, controversial sermons are remembered and discussed, and often the subject of much heated debate. But, generally, the influence of a sermon cannot be said to last for any length of time.

In this, as in everything, there are surprises. I recall visiting a twenty-year-old student in a university on the east coast of Scotland and to my utter surprise and delight he repeated to me, almost verbatim, the Barmitzvah address I had given him some seven years earlier.

Similarly, but not too often, a captivating idea, moving story or telling phrase are recalled years later, and one's actual words affectionately cast up decades after they were first spoken. One never knows whether what one says will bear fruit, but the greatest compliment any preacher can be paid is when the words have struck home and beneficially affected the listener.

A lot of hard work goes into preparing a fitting sermon and it is good to know that, albeit rarely, the words have been taken to heart.

8. Unions of Synagogues

The axiom that a group of synagogues can do more good than a synagogue on its own, which should be self-evident, does unfortunately require some justification in the Jewish world.

Most Jewish communities have national unions, federations or synagogue groups, joined together for common purpose. But there are vast differences among them. Some, like the Consistoire in France, owe their origin to the country's government; others are a communal effort at establishing a collective religious benefit. With the United Synagogue of Greater London, each synagogue is "locked in" to the union legally, financially and administratively, and the costs of running the head office are deeply resented by the constituent synagogues. But, when it comes to the Union of Orthodox Jewish Congregations of America, each congregation retains its full independence — the Americans would not have it any other way — yet looks to the joint organisation for a variety of cultural, religious and spiritual benefits.

The most obvious advantage of a union lies in the provision of kosher food. In the United States and South Africa, a huge range of supervised kosher items carrying the logo of a recognised Beth Din or Rabbinate is available to the consumer, in America primarily in urban areas of Jewish domicile, in South Africa throughout the country. In recent years, an increasing number of non-Jews is buying and eating kosher; they recognise that it is healthy and pure (a message still to be put over to many Jewish families).

Although the availability has improved of late, Anglo-Jewry has lagged behind in this regard. Due to ridiculous personality clashes and selfish rivalry among the diverse orthodox groups, a multiplicity of kashrut authorities has resulted, and the poor customer has been made to suffer. Whereas in other countries, kashrut is a major source of income for the union of synagogues, in Britain due to the rumpus over shechita the United Synagogue actually managed a few years ago to incur a loss of more than a million pounds.

Moreover, in Britain the Jewish housewife is obliged to shop with a list informing her of "approved" items rather than the goods themselves carrying the kosher mark. Some time ago, a friend of my wife was stopped by the store detective in a large supermarket: he could not understand why she kept picking up packets and tins and then diving into her handbag to check these against the list. Fortunately, a call to the Kashrus Commission was sufficient to have her released.

The main point is that a single synagogue could never arrange for the supply of kosher foodstuffs on its own. It is easy enough for the kosher person to reach out for the items needed and put them into a supermarket trolley but he or she sometimes forgets that a huge amount of skilled work goes into guaranteeing that the items are satisfactory from the Jewish religious point of view. Halachic and scientific knowledge, protracted negotiations, supervision, fail-safe systems to prevent any change in ingredients — these are some of the more obvious elements of the whole operation. In the South African context, thanks to the quality of the current lay leadership, the expertise of the Beth Din and the hard work of the kashrut department, provision of kashrut is at a very high level.

Because there is such diversity in the range and quality of services offered by unions of synagogues, the key question which ought always to be asked by an individual congregant is simply: "What advantage do I get out of being a member of the group that I would not get by being a member of an independent synagogue?"

Frequently the answer can be positive, although it is surprising that the advantages some unions provide are not supplied by others. In London, the synagogue building was probably built thanks to a reasonable United Synagogue loan. Likewise, the Jewish education at the shul cheder or at the local Jewish day school will have been subsidised by the union. An Anglo-Jew also enjoys the services of the Chief Rabbinate and Beth Din; in America where the former does not exist and the latter's control is spasmodic, basic policies and the issue of Jewish status, so crucial to orthodox life, are at best unclear and at worst chaotic.

On the other hand, in the United States every member of the

union will have on offer comprehensive levels of adult education; in London these failed because there was such apathy that congregants refused to go up the road to the neighbouring synagogue to participate in a superior programme. At regular intervals the American Jew will receive from head office in New York publications of popular appeal but containing solid Torah content and items of Jewish communal interest.

The Union of Orthodox Congregations in the United States also boasts its own youth movement, the National Conference of Synagogue Youth, which has an attractive programme throughout North America; in 1970, with a hundred teenagers from New York, I participated in a Shabbaton hosted by a synagogue in an outer suburb of Montreal. The United Synagogue in London has failed lamentably in this vital area.

Because it is able to generate collective impact, a union of synagogues is also ideally positioned to advance a spiritual agenda. In South Africa, for example, the union has held successful "Taste of Shabbat" campaigns. As a result of educational pamphlets, communal meetings on the theme of how best to overcome problems of sabbath observance in today's world, and with all the rabbis focusing simultaneously in addresses and lectures on the joyous celebration of Shabbat, many — particularly young married couples — have been attracted to try to keep Shabbat. No synagogue on its own could have had this impact.

A weekly pamphlet, called Shabbat Talk, pioneered by my colleague Rabbi Ron Hendler, and containing moral problems for all the family to discuss together, as well as current news items and fascinating insights into the Sidra, is circulated to Johannesburg homes and has proved a delightful addition to the Friday night table.

In asking the same question as the layman — what advantage do I enjoy by being part of the union rather than independent? — the average rabbi would probably experience some difficulty in pinpointing the answer.

To be sure, in-service training is a bonus. Subsidised by the union and organised by the Yeshivah or Rabbinical Training College in association with experts in the field, the courses cover an impressive range, from time management to counselling skills, and are invariably of help.

In common with university lecturers, rabbis imagine that because they know something about a subject they are able automatically to transmit that knowledge. Not so. I recall attending a long course on "becoming a better communicator," conducted by an expert who taught professors how to teach, and it really was an eye opener.

Assistance with the congregation's programme is likewise forthcoming. Particularly in the United States, and especially with the non-Orthodox unions, a constant stream of useful ideas, practical suggestions and educational material is available to the rabbi for easy incorporation to his synagogue programmes for Festivals and Shabbatonim.

Concerning specific professional requirements, however, the rabbi within the union is usually no better off than the rabbi of an independent congregation.

Security of tenure is a major bone of contention. Despite the fact that the halachah states that after a successful trial period, any Jewish functionary — rabbi, cantor, synagogue secretary, teacher in a day school, or official in a communal organisation — is fully entitled to security of tenure, this law is abused.

Heaven help the American rabbi on a short-term contract who forgets, or mistakes, the names of his congregants' children. The United Synagogue in London utilises "rolling contracts," that are also against the rules of halachah.

Surprisingly, no proper career structure for the rabbinate has evolved in any part of the Jewish world. The situation is totally hit or miss, dependent on who happens to leave and who happens to be available at the time. No business corporation in the world would utilise its personnel in such an arbitrary way.

A simple test shows how ludicrous this situation is. If someone who had extensive personal knowledge of the rabbis and the synagogues of London, New York, Johannesburg, or Sydney were asked to ignore current incumbencies and — waving a magic wand

— to draw up his own list, matching a given rabbi with a given congregation, hardly any rabbi would be occupying his present position!

Great unhappiness has resulted for too many rabbis, demoralized due to the often unsatisfactory operation of placement bureaux and the absence of an overall career structure. Having served a community faithfully for years, they repeatedly see themselves bypassed in favour of younger colleagues who have no proven track record but who dazzle with a scintillating sermon or thought-provoking address.

If the lay leaders of synagogue unions were to exert some imagination, a fairer system could be introduced. Once the basic ability of a young rabbi has been ascertained, he should be given tenure for life, but not with the same congregation. Every seven years or so, he should be moved to another pulpit, in keeping with his ability and the overall requirements of the union. The Methodist Church, lehavdil, has been doing this with a great measure of success for decades. The clear advantages — security of employment, fresh stimulus to prevent being in a rut, and the ability to place candidates in an incumbency best suited to their personal talents — far outweigh the disadvantages, such as having to "break oneself in" at a new congregation and one's children having to change school more than is advisable.

Another intrinsic difficulty with unions of synagogues is their sheer lack of emotional appeal. Allegiance is owed by the congregant to his own local shul, to which he is often deeply attached, and the notion of a "supra-loyalty" to a remote union of which his synagogue happens to be a part is hard to develop.

Despite the criticism that they are all too often lumbering dinosaurs, despite their obvious vulnerability to augmented "shul politics," and the accusation that they fail to influence Jewish communal life as well as they ought to do, it is high time that we all recognised the power for good that unions of synagogues possess.

At a time of rampant assimilation across the Jewish world, we should try to maximise their potential as a force solidifying the spiritual cohesion essential to a viable Jewish future.

9. Of Commas and Baritones

Because the work is supposed to be l'shem shamayim, "for the sake of Heaven," one would imagine that the way a synagogue is run would be above board and strictly beyond reproach. Everyone involved would be motivated and devoted, the highest principles would operate. There would be no petty politics. Behaviour would be exemplary, in keeping with the sublime ideals for which Judaism stands and befitting the sacred nature of congregational activity.

Oi, would one be wrong!

There may well be some places where all concerned, lay and spiritual leaders, voluntary and salaried workers, are worthy of the task. But synagogue members and Jewish religious organisations are as prone to human foible and fault as any secular group and establishment and indeed have been known on occasions to outdo them when it comes to petty squabbling, self-aggrandisement, inefficiency, bitter infighting and downright cheating.

Examples? One is spoilt for choice but here is a random selection.

The United Synagogue of London, the overall body of a group of some sixty synagogues, periodically elects honorary officers from among the lay leaders of its constituents to serve as president, vice-president, treasurer, and so on. Twenty years ago there were nine of them — I do not know how many there are nowadays — and one of them was repeatedly leaking confidential information to the Jewish press.

The capable secretary at head office, the late Nat Rubin z'l — a large man who chain-smoked and, under his burly exterior, had a quick mind — was instructed by the then president to circulate a strictly confidential document to his colleagues. Suspecting that the contents might be revealed to the press, Rubin asked the typist to prepare eight copies of the text, all with the same wording but each different from the others in the placing of the commas.

This was a brilliant stratagem. Commas are optional in the punctuation of many sentences and most readers hardly notice their presence or omission. The confidential document was duly leaked to the London Jewish Chronicle, the printer faithfully copied the commas of the unique original, the honorary officer concerned was confronted and had no option but to resign.

On the East Side of Manhattan there is a small shul that is popular for weddings. But there is a snag. As you know, towards the end of every wedding ceremony a glass is shattered in commemoration of the sad fact that the Temple in Jerusalem no longer stands.

But the formidable Shammas of this synagogue, if he does not like the look of the groom, deliberately places an unbreakable glass beneath the groom's right foot. Anxious to display his prowess to everyone, especially his new bride, the newly married man keeps trying to smash it — but to no avail.

A chazan, well known in the provinces, once applied for a position in a large shul in north-west London. He was admirably suited to the job, with a lovely voice and deep knowledge of the liturgy and he conducted the services with great dignity.

But he was a baritone and all the choral music of that synagogue happened to be arranged for a cantor who was a tenor. So on the Shabbat of his trial, his Musaf kedushah was deliberately sabotaged by the choirmaster and choir who sang their usual accompaniment for a tenor, making the applicant sound out of tune. Catch them changing all the arrangements to suit the newcomer!

Fortunately the chazan was able to obtain another appointment in a shul with not such a lazy choir, and he spent many happy years there.

Just before I came to Edgware, the ladies' guild had a furious row with the wardens. They had redecorated the bride's room at the shul and had lavished a great deal of time and care on it, sparing no expense. The decor was beautiful, and included pleasing paintings and tapestry chair seats. They locked the room and instructed the caretaker it was only to be used by the happy brides.

But the honorary officers obtained a key and began using it every Shabbat as a repository for their top hats, which they plonked down on the plush chairs.

The ladies found out and were furious. When the honorary officers persisted, the entire guild resigned en masse. The row ensued for months and developed into a major crisis: contrary to the view of spiritual and lay leaders, the most important people by far in any shul are the caretaker and the ladies who organise the kiddush. Where would any self-respecting synagogue be without "the kichel and herring brigade"?

Fortuitously a member of the management board with a practical approach to matters quietly arranged for plastic fitted covers to be made for the tapestry chairs and, following this sensible compromise, peace was restored.

A recurring difficulty in all synagogues concerns who should be called up to the Torah for the reading of the tochachah. These verses of dire warning about the punishment to be meted out to the Israelites for disobedience to the Divine will are found towards the end of Leviticus and in Deuteronomy. For the official reading of these curses, it is customary in some shuls to call up the Shammas; in others the officiant who is reading the Torah that day himself takes that portion.

In one of my synagogues, the presiding warden always used to give this "honour" to the person on the board of management who had most recently argued with him over a congregational matter. Shortly after he had been called up and the curses were being chanted in a low voice, it would dawn on the recipient exactly what portion of the Torah he was being given, and the warden would chuckle mischievously throughout. It was a unique way of preventing people picking future quarrels with him!

During my tenure of office at the resplendent St John's Wood Synagogue, I was hoisted by my own mechitsah. The ladies' gallery can only be reached by several flights of stairs, so a very old congregant called Mrs Rafer, who was truly devout and loved to attend the Shabbat morning service, would sit quietly downstairs at the very back.

As she was more than 90, we tactfully ignored this technical breach of synagogue seating that requires the separation of men and women. However, there were one or two young men studying at Yeshivah who came home during the vacation to be with their parents, and they began to voice their objections to the old lady's choice of seat.

I held out for a long time, but eventually arranged for a mechitsah to be constructed directly in front of the back row of seats, so that any old or infirm women could sit there in conformity with the halachah. It was a pretty mechitsah of above requisite height, with a Magen David design and delicate filigree work in gold. It blended perfectly with the interior decoration of the synagogue. It was see-through so that the women could observe what was taking place as well as follow the service. I was very pleased with it.

On the first Shabbat morning after its installation, we all watched surreptitiously for Mrs Rafer's arrival, wondering what her reaction would be. She came in at the usual time, took one look at the new mechitsah and, instead of sitting in the back row behind it, walked slowly and proudly past it and took up a seat in front of it!

After the Reading of the Law, when we were parading the Sefer Torah round the synagogue prior to replacing it in the Ark, our procession passed near to where she was standing in her new seat. She gave me a withering glance, as if to say, "You can do whatever you want — and so can I."

She occupied the new position every Shabbat without fail for several months but unfortunately then passed away. The other old women dutifully occupied the seats behind the partition, but her valiant spirit seemed to hover in front of the mechitsah long after she had gone.

In one of the towns of Southern Africa, a place with only a few dozen Jewish inhabitants, there was a furious row between leading personalities which resulted in a breakaway from the one main shul. The small community then divided according to loyalties, so that a town — which found it difficult to keep one synagogue going with the requisite quorum of ten males — now had two shuls.

The national president of the Jewish Board of Deputies telephoned me in anguish.

"You're not going to believe this," he told me. "They now have two shuls and for the last four Friday nights, there were nine people in one and nine in the other — eighteen men but no minyan."

We decided to fly there and try to make peace. A few weeks later, the president and chairman of the Board of Deputies, the genial spiritual leader of the country communities, Moshe Silberhaft, and my wife and I, descended on the community, who turned out in force at the local hotel for the meeting.

I addressed the small congregation and appealed to them passionately to restore unity.

"All Jewish people are responsible for one another," I quoted from the Talmud and regaled them with Midrashic lore about all of us being "in the same boat." I reminded them that we would never have survived as a people for so long if internal divisions had been permitted to damage us. I asked them to rise above their quarrels and allow harmony to reign.

Miraculously, not only did they hear me out, they decided there and then to take whatever steps were necessary to heal the rift. We were thrilled at the outcome — by no means usual in these circumstances — and several weeks later learned that they had kept to their promise. Peace had been restored, they had re-united in the one synagogue, and they had a minyan.

I have always been an admirer of the Sephardim. The dignified and courteous manner in which their synagogue services are conducted — having obtained an honour they bow politely to each other rather than shake hands like the Ashkenazim — and the warmth of their congregational esprit de corps are very appealing.

South Africa rejoices in several Sephardi congregations in Johannesburg and Cape Town, the majority of the members having originated from Rhodes, the most easterly island of the Aegean Sea. After emigrating to the Belgian Congo, now the Democratic Republic of Congo, they moved to Rhodesia, now Zimbabwe, and from there to

South Africa. Immensely proud of their heritage, they have retained their customs intact.

So when I was asked by one of the Sephardi synagogues in Johannesburg to help heal a rift which had brought about an unhealthy split among the membership, some of whom had broken away to form their own congregation, I was genuinely distressed but determined to try and bring them together again.

I was invited to address a special meeting with all the members present. I told them that one of my saintly teachers, Rabbi Dr HJ Zimmels z'l, had published a study on the relations of, and differences between, the Ashkenazim and Sephardim. Because there are certain peripheral differences in their decisions regarding kosher meat, the Sephardim being strict in some instances and the Ashkenazim in others, the question arises — may a Sephardi partake of a meat meal prepared by an Ashkenazi, and vice versa?

In reply, he produces documentary evidence that in Amsterdam in the 18th century, the Ashkenazim used to partake of meals prepared by the Sephardim at their homes and at weddings and circumcisions, and vice versa, and both ignored the differences.

"If Sephardim can get along with Ashkenazim, and Ashkenazim with Sephardim, do you not think it is high time for Sephardim to get along with Sephardim?" I asked.

There was silence for a minute, and then they all applauded, and amicable relations, which unfortunately proved to be somewhat temporary, were restored.

The most serious organisational mix-up in synagogal history, hilarious in hindsight, occurred many years ago in my native Glasgow. There used to be a small shtiebl in Dixon Avenue in a district called Crosshill. There were not many members but what the establishment lacked in quantity it made up in quality, and it was always a privilege to join them and their rabbi in prayer.

As with most congregations, when it came to Rosh Hashanah a large number of additional local Jewish residents wished to be accommodated for the services. The regular premises were too small, so the synagogue hired a dance hall, the Dixon Hall, at the end of the street for the duration of the high holy days. The hall was transformed into a synagogue, with a portable Ark, a movable bimah, and suitable seating for men and women.

Everything went smoothly for a number of years, but then Yom Kippur fell on a Shabbat and the shul committee completely forgot that as they were occupying a dance hall and it was a Saturday, the hall would be needed for the "Saturday night hop".

The fast may end early in other climes but in Glasgow it usually does not go out until after half-past seven. At six o'clock that evening, the caretaker of the Dixon Hall duly turned up for work, so that he could dismantle the temporary synagogue and make the hall ready for the dance that evening.

But the Jews were still praying. In fact they had not yet started Ne'ilah. Undaunted, the caretaker pushed his way to the front, interrupted the service and asked all the worshippers to leave.

"Ye'se have been prayin' a' day," he shouted at them in a broad Scots accent and in exasperation. "If the guid Lord hasne listened to ye yet, He's no goin' to listen to you the noo!"

And with that piece of great Scottish wisdom, he sent the bewildered congregants packing. The men retreated to the shtiebl and crowded in to finish the service; the women were left standing in the street.

Who ever said shul life was dull?

10. What Makes Synagogue Services Effective?

Too often the shul service is simply taken for granted and nobody bothers to question to what degree, if any, it is effective.

As one who has the opportunity and privilege of attending different synagogues throughout Southern Africa, from Bulawayo to George and from Maputo to Windhoek, I am able to appreciate the immense variety our shuls offer, the vast array of local differences, and to attempt to assess the active components of an effective service.

Each shul has its peculiarities, some delightful, some idiosyncratic. All succeed in some measure, or the minyan would just disappear, but a number of obvious variables affects the degree to which services are effective.

The music is crucial; if the chazan or ba'al tefillah has no voice, or if the choir sings out of tune, the congregation is in for an uncomfortable few hours. By far the most enjoyable services are those in which the congregation participates by singing together. No matter how good the choir is — and there are some superb synagogue choirs in South Africa, which proudly maintains the tradition of full choral services — the thrill of everyone joining in and singing to Hashem cannot be surpassed. In those shuls where the chazan and choir lead the entire congregation in the singing, rather than excluding them, the congregants feel they really belong. They are uplifted on the wings of song.

Comfort is also a major consideration, although the seating should not be too comfortable or it will aid sleep during the derashah. If the seats are old and wooden, if the shul is badly ventilated and its acoustics are poor, the uncomfortable congregants cannot wait for the service to be over soon enough. This is particularly true of the ladies' gallery, which in some shuls is so high up as to cause dizziness, and in others so steeply sloped that the women need mountaineering experience to negotiate the perilous journey to their seat.

Taking proper advantage of architectural support mechanisms, modern synagogues usually allow everyone a view of the Aron

Kodesh, but old shuls usually have pillars which often obstruct the view. A relative of mine had a front row seat in a large Glasgow synagogue, but when he sat down he could only see half the Ark because of the pillar. Accordingly, he only paid half of his membership subscription.

Whereas in the rest of the Jewish world the bimah is invariably situated in the middle of the shul with rows of seating behind, for some reason throughout South Africa the bimah is located at the end of the shul with a large expanse of carpet between the bimah and the Aron Kodesh.

Despite numerous requests for a satisfactory explanation for this phenomenon, no one has given me one. Either it must be an architectural quirk or maybe it is simply that no one wants to sit behind the bimah. Certainly the seating arrangements are a vital factor in engendering a sense of togetherness and a feeling of belonging to one entity. In the properly designed synagogue, no part of the congregation is physically cut off or isolated and thus everyone feels part of the proceedings. Much ingenuity in this direction has been exerted in recent times to give the women a real sense of joining in, while at the same time doing justice to halachic norms.

Clearly it is easier to pray in a beautiful synagogue than an ordinary one. What precisely constitutes ideal aesthetic surroundings is of course a matter of taste. There are some beautiful old shuls in which it is very easy to pray, while indeed there are a number of inspiring modern ones. But sometimes the old shuls are just too old for modern tastes, and sometimes the new shuls are so outrageously modern as to offend tradition.

Effective services require a degree of professionalism. The cantor ought to be a qualified musician and well trained in nusach, and the rabbi ought to prepare his sermons rather than speaking off the cuff. The flow of the service is also important and gabbaim who indulge in long stoppages during the Reading of the Torah are often guilty of spoiling the service.

The atmosphere which the congregants themselves create can be the major component of an effective service. Contrary to popular opinion, decorum does not mean an absence of noise — witness the high-decibel volume of any Chassidic minyan in which everyone is joyously or tearfully shouting out prayerful pleas. A similar intensity of devotion can be experienced in a hushed synagogue when the chazan is softly singing a solo piece and everyone is listening intently to him. Hence decorum means an atmosphere conducive to prayer.

A sense of occasion helps enormously. The feeling that what is going on is not mundane is basic to the good service. Not taking the proceedings for granted, but being imbued with a sense of privilege at participating in the exalted mitzvah of prayer is the hallmark of the dignified shul. This means the correct balance must be sustained; no one part of the service should be rushed while another is of inordinate length. It also means introducing a little variety into the service from time to time to avoid over-familiarity and boredom.

Dress befitting the holiness of the synagogue also helps. Due to the glorious climate in South Africa, standards of synagogue attire have fallen to what many rabbis consider an unacceptable level. No one, except perhaps a journalist, would dream of going to an appointment with an important client without being suitably dressed, but it has become the practice in our shuls that "anything goes".

In most shuls in the Jewish world men are expected to wear a jacket and tie and married women must wear a hat, otherwise their appearance is considered disrespectful. It is worth mentioning that no Afrikaner woman ever goes to church on Sunday morning without wearing a hat. Some of our teenagers, more suitably dressed for a work-out at the gym, would actually be refused entry to some shuls in other countries.

The length of the service is a hotly debated issue. Whereas some shuls manage to complete the Shabbat morning service in two hours, some shuls, especially when a Barmitzvah is being celebrated, take 4 hours. It may sound illogical, but undoubtedly there is more actual davening in the shorter service than the longer one!

An acute generation gap is evident throughout the Jewish world regarding the length of our services. Most of the old school — those over the age of fifty — prefer a "proper service" with chazan, choir and all the trimmings. The youngsters, considering the service not to be a spectator sport but a participatory exercise, prefer a good short service.

This dichotomy is at the root of the current battle raging between shul and shtiebl. Many young adults, particularly those who belong to one or another of the ba'al teshuvah movements, want to pray personally — raise their own voice in prayer — in the congregational context and feel more at home in the shtiebl's intimate atmosphere. They also want to utilize the time "saved" by a short service to be spent studying in a shiur.

Among the casualties of this division is chazzanut as a profession, the number of full-time synagogue positions in the Jewish world having been cut by some seventy percent since the Second World War.

Another emerging difficulty is that while no one doubts the genuine spirituality and kavanah of the shtieblach, the large congregations are becoming increasingly short of members of the younger generation. Sensible indeed are those synagogues who consciously allow an "alternative" minyan within their premises, rather than drive the youngsters away.

The effective synagogue service?

Pleasant congregational singing in a comfortable shul in congenial surroundings, in which most of the congregation actually wants to daven, a qualified rav and trained chazan conducting a not-too-long service: these appear to be the successful ingredients.

A gratifying number of congregations aim for it. For those who do not, this analysis may be worthwhile.

IV

NATIONAL

1.   The First Elections

Months of preparation went into the first ever democratic elections held in South Africa.

As the vast majority of the population had never before had the opportunity of voting, a huge educational exercise was undertaken, including media publicity and special adult classes. These included state-funded plays that showed the potential pitfalls and stressing that everyone was free to vote his or her their choice and that people should not allow themselves to be unduly influenced.

Likewise, mammoth preparations involving many thousands of volunteers were undertaken to ensure the smooth running of the electoral process. My wife and I attended all day seminars to acquaint monitors and stewards with the detailed plans to prevent mayhem and to ensure safety and peace.

The three days of voting at the end of April 1994 proved to be exhilarating. The real winner in these elections was the electorate. Standing in line for anything can be an exasperating exercise but, with amazing patience and tenacity, millions of people stood for hours in the sun waiting to cast their votes.

Everywhere there was a wonderful spirit of hope. Almost as if apartheid had never existed, whites, browns and blacks mingled easily in good-humoured togetherness, waiting for the chance to seal their joint destiny.

The excitement had begun for us the evening before, when, at midnight, the old flag came down and the new one was unfurled at civic centres throughout the country. With the Israeli ambassador, Alon Liel, who had been instrumental in forging close ties with the ANC, and Natan Sharansky, part of the Israeli observer team, whose presence seemed somehow to symbolise the success of the fight for freedom, we stood in the square outside the Johannesburg civic centre and watched the historic moment.

A few hours later, at 5 am, my wife and a stoic band of women from the Jewish Board of Deputies started duty as peace monitors at Joubert

Park, one of the potentially more volatile districts in the centre of the city. Jewish student monitors were everywhere to be seen at the voting stations and in the largely Jewish suburb of Houghton residents provided buckets of orange juice that were passed up and down the long lines of black domestics and gardeners standing in the sunshine.

As I was being driven from Berea to Yeoville and Rosebank, I marvelled at the miracle which had brought us thus far. The negotiations at Codesa 1 and 2 had proved unsatisfactory and it was only Joe Slovo's brilliant stratagem at the summit meeting in September 1992 that saved the day. His suggestion of "sunset clauses," providing for initial power-sharing proved acceptable to the Nationalists as it meant they would not have to surrender everything at one go, and acceptable to the ANC both because they did not have any experience of running a country and because after the initial period they would not have to share power.

It was miraculous also that the extremists on the right and the left were marginalised. The right-wing Afrikaaner movement, the AWB, tried in vain to "rescue" President Lucas Mangope, the puppet head of Bophuthatswana when, following demonstrations, they "invaded" the homeland in March. Not only did the exercise end in ignominy for them but the amateur soldiers of the AWB discovered that bullets can kill. Any notion of military insurrection throughout South Africa in an endeavour to thwart the elections was destroyed.

White racists had also made desperate attempts to dissuade the electorate from voting with a series of bomb blasts. The first, in the centre of Johannesburg on the Sunday before the elections, killed nine people and injured ninety-two. On Monday, at a taxi-rank in Germiston, east of Johannesburg, a bomb blast killed ten, and early on Tuesday morning, as voting was starting, an explosion ripped through the international arrivals terminal at what was then Jan Smuts Airport, but fortunately no one was killed. It says a great deal for the electorate that no one seems to have been put off voting by these outrageous attempts.

The Pan Africanist Congress did not attempt to disrupt the elections in any way. Its leaders seemed to believe that they would be voted in as a major player in the new parliament. In the event, the PAC achieved less than two percent of the vote.

Another disruption was almost caused by Chief Mangosuthu Buthelezi's perceived intransigence. He had refused for months to be part of the election process and it was not until Professor Washington Okumu of Kenya pointed out to him that Inkatha risked being side-lined by its non-participation, and Arnold Zulman of Durban was for-tuitously able to arrange an eleventh hour meeting between Buthelezi and Nelson Mandela, that the chief agreed to take part.

He announced this momentous decision with only a week to go to the first of the three election days and the printers had literally to work all day and night to produce millions of stickers to attach to the already printed ballot papers.

Thus "miracle" is not too strong a word to describe the chain of events, the timing and the happy outcome.

The mood of euphoria evinced by the thousands who patiently wended their way towards the voting stations was wonderful to expe-rience. There were many deeply moving incidents. A teenager in the Northern Province carried his crippled 85-year-old great-grandfather on his shoulders for thirteen kilometres from their shack to the near-est polling booth so that both could vote for the first time in their lives. A very old woman was propelled to her voting station in a wheelbarrow. Hundreds began queueing in the early hours of the morning for the "privilege" of being able to vote.

At the fifth station I was monitoring, some kind person shoved a glass of mineral water into my hand, pushed me into an empty seat and instructed me firmly "to take five minutes off".

It was all going so surprisingly well that I began to think about some of the problems that were bound to surface when the elections were over. Apart from the concern that the standard of living of the huge black population would not suddenly improve — it was going to take ages and so much would depend on how much patience would be exercised — there was the concomitant problem of the increasing crime and violence.

Of specific Jewish concern was the likelihood that government subsidies to Jewish day schools and old age homes were unlikely to continue; the funds would be needed to help the grossly underprivileged.

There was anxiety, too, over the relationship between the future black-dominated government and Israel. The possibility of a wedge being driven by government between Judaism and Zionism could not be discounted; the Palestinians would almost certainly be given diplomatic status as soon as the new regime took office.

I wondered also about bridge building. The colossal task of reconstruction — of hearts and minds no less than of social and economic structures — was an awesome challenge that could be met only with the full cooperation of all communities. In the middle of the elections I felt the weight of the responsibility on my Jewish community, which would have to reach out positively, offering its skills and resources to help defeat the conditions that perpetuate poverty.

As I finished my rounds — and it was a marvellously stimulating day — I wondered how Jewish people had voted. It was possible that some, or perhaps even many, had supported the National Party to strengthen the opposition bloc against black dominance. Traditional Jewish support for the Democratic Party would also no doubt have been displayed.

When the results eventually came, most people recognised that the ANC deserved its win but were relieved that it did not gain the two-thirds majority that would have allowed it to monopolize the formulation of the new constitution. There was also public sympathy for Buthelezi's party, whose victory in Kwazulu Natal probably averted civil war in that province.

For months previously I had sat on the Panel of Religious Leaders for Electoral Justice — among its members were Archbishop Desmond Tutu and Yasmin Sooka, both later to be forceful personalities on the Truth and Reconciliation Commission — and we had done our level best to encourage our own faith communities to support the electoral process in every way.

When we met for the last time, just after the results had been announced, much uneasiness was expressed at blatant irregularities, including the disappearance of ballot papers, the illegal opening of ballot boxes, mistakes in the counting of votes and, unbelievably, the setting up of a few bogus voting stations. Sheena Duncan of the South African Council of Churches, a doughty member of our committee, solemnly went through the long list of democratic flaws.

An ecumenical delegation of leading religious figures from abroad was present at the meeting as they wished to hear our verdict as to the fairness of the elections, which they were obliged to transmit to their home countries.

When Sheena had finished, there was an awesome hush while everyone digested the negative information. Then, probably because I had been outspoken on several key aspects of the process which we had heatedly debated prior to the elections, every head in the room turned towards me.

"Look," I said quite calmly, "these were our first elections. Millions of people had never voted before and thousands were inexperienced in supervising the procedure. Of course there were problems, that was only to be expected, but I firmly believe that the results truly reflect the will of the people."

My colleagues let out an audible sigh of relief and one by one hastened to endorse my conclusion. So our very first elections went off remarkably well and engendered a mood of optimism. In no small measure, the success was due to the gracious behaviour of former state president, FW de Klerk, especially in defeat, and to the powerful inspiration of Nelson Mandela's personality, including his magnanimity in victory.

Towards the end of a long but exhilarating day, as I was making my way past the still long queue to the entrance of one of the voting stations, an elderly Jewish acquaintance at the front of the crowd caught hold of my arm.

"What berachah shall I make?" he challenged me.

"Shehecheyanu, the blessing over new things," I replied.

After more than three hundred years of white domination, the new South Africa had been born.

2.   Communist Friends

I nearly lost my job when my wife went to the conference for enlightened academics, mayors and businessmen, organised by the Five Freedoms Forum with the African National Congress in Lusaka, Zambia, in July 1989 to discuss the role of whites in a changing society. Ann simply wanted to find out more about the situation at first hand and also about the aims of the ANC, directly from its leaders, the National Executive Committee being based in Lusaka.

"But they're communists," remonstrated my management when they found out and had summoned me to an emergency meeting, "and the ANC is a banned organisation. How can the Chief Rabbi's wife even think of mixing with such people?"

Fortunately for me an acquaintance from Reuters had tipped me off the previous day that Nelson Mandela was going to be being taken from Pollsmoor to meet with the then state president, PW Botha, that very afternoon. I kept my cool.

"I don't know why you're getting so excited," I replied quite calmly. "At the moment the state president is having tea with Nelson Mandela."

They looked at me as if I were meshuggah but one of the committee members slipped out to contact the South African Press Association and check my facts. After an embarrassing hiatus which lasted about ten minutes, he returned and nodded confirmation to the chairman. They changed the subject.

My wife has no interest whatsoever in politics and has never been involved with any political party, but she was genuinely curious to find out as much as possible about South Africa's problems and to learn some of the proposed solutions to them. She enjoyed the proceedings at Lusaka and met a host of personalities including Oliver Tambo. Joe Slovo and Ronnie Kasrils were there, and she invited them any Friday evening they might be in Johannesburg to join us for the traditional chicken soup and kneidlach.

When the South African delegation returned to Johannesburg, it was met by the press, not by the police, a significant sign that the situation was changing for the better.

Some months later, Ronnie Kasrils took us up on the Friday night invitation and because he is such an ebullient and likeable personality we had a highly entertaining evening. The next morning on the front page of the Saturday Star, there was an item that the police were looking for Ronnie in connection with Operation Vula. Our sons, who were visiting us from England at the time, were very much amused that our guest of the previous evening had been illicit.

At the "third seder" in our home the following Pesach, at which tribute was paid to the concept of freedom and to all those from Moses to Mandela who had struggled to achieve it, and which included heart-rending accounts of overcoming tribulation such as Masha Greenbaum's famous description of the make-do seder in her concentration camp, I presented the "boykie from Yeoville" with a red kippah.

I inscribed it "to my communist friend" and he was tickled pink, or rather red, to receive it. Since then — nothing, of course, to do with my gift — he has distinguished himself in government.

First-hand acquaintance with Cosatu House has come my way through participation in seminars and as a trustee of the Job Creation Trust. The only rabbi ever to have been invited there to participate in debate, I found the treatment meted out to me genuinely respectful — I was once called "Comrade Rabbi" — and the proceedings absorbing and high level.

On one occasion when we were discussing "Marxism and Religion — Alternatives to Globalising Capitalism," which was an attempt to build bridges between socialist thinking and religious morality, I recall spelling out the welfare state prescribed by the Torah, while cautioning that the conditions and frame of reference could not   really be equated with the society of today.

I quoted Dostoevsky's *The Brothers Karamazov* to the effect that "Christianity missed the boat, when in bringing the message of eternal hope to humanity, it forgot man's need for bread," whereas "Marxist Socialism missed the boat when, in its zeal to assure bread for men, it forgot that man lives by more than bread alone". With some justification, the participants wanted to know what liberation theology was doing to improve the current situation.

At the briefings that Nelson Mandela was thoughtful enough to hold from time to time with religious leadership during the protracted negotiations with government, I met Joe Slovo. At Codesa 1, we had a long and friendly argument about the effectiveness of communism, Joe citing China as an example of success. I prophesied that when the ANC came to power, despite the alliance with the SACP and Cosatu, reality would force a continuation of free market policies. He gave me his big smile.

Due in a large measure to his formidable negotiating skills — his "Sunset clauses," which enabled the Nationalists initially to share power but then required them to surrender it to the majority, were a stroke of genius — the new dispensation came into being. Six weeks before the first elections, he addressed a Jewish gathering at the Albow Centre in Cape Town.

The hall was absolutely packed and I recall that before dealing with political issues he spoke at length on his Lithuanian Jewish origins. He told the audience that he had visited his native village and tried to locate the home he lived in as a child. But the little synagogue had been destroyed, he could not find out where it had been, and he only knew where his house was in relation to the shul. I teased him afterwards that all true Jews only knew where they were if they also knew where their synagogue was. He gave me his big smile.

When he died — he was already making a success of the difficult job of Minister of Housing — I was not surprised that the government, the ANC and the family asked me to participate in the memorial gathering at Orlando Stadium on January 15, 1995, prior to his interment. I did not attend the funeral itself.

I have never experienced such difficulty in preparing a speech. On the one hand, Joe was a humanist socialist, the last person a conscientious rabbi could be expected to eulogize. On the other hand, he deserved great adulation for his championship of the oppressed.

So I decided quite simply to quote the two motivations — one religious, the other humanitarian — towards helping fellow human beings.

The speech was well received by all those in the stadium, Archbishop Desmond Tutu giving me a big hug, but I was subjected to hate mail, most of it unsigned, from some members of the Jewish community who felt strongly that it was wrong of me to have taken part. They were of course entitled to their view. My supposed offence was compounded by a rather strange misunderstanding of a sentiment I expressed in the course of the eulogy.

My exact words were: "Let not those religious people who acquiesced, passively or wrongly, with the inequalities of yesteryear, let not those religious people dare to condemn Joe Slovo, a humanist socialist, who fought all his life for basic decency, to reinstate the dignity to which all human beings are entitled."

When I said "religious people," I actually had in mind members of the Dutch Reformed Church and its allies, but many — including Joe's own daughters who subsequently wrote about it — interpreted my words as referring specifically to members of the Jewish community. With hindsight — it's always easier with hindsight — I can see how the impression arose, but it was caused as much by a guilty conscience on the part of those who complained as by my lack of foresight.

The truth is that Slovo's death had prompted awkward reminders of the fact that most of the Jewish activists against apartheid were either agnostic or atheist. The popular columnist of the London Jewish Chronicle, the late Chaim Bermant, made the point in no uncertain terms when he wrote that " ... the voice of conscience was, in the main, expressed by Jews who had renounced their faith. It was almost as if one had to stop being a Jew before one could start being a mensh."

Now that the new South Africa was a reality, there was a kind of ambivalence — a hate/love relationship — displayed by most of the Jewish community towards the Jewish heroes of the struggle. "Yet morally speaking," as Professor Arnold Abramovitz, formerly of the psychology department at the University of Cape Town, correctly asserts, when pointing to the dividends which accrued vicariously to the general Jewish community due to the behaviour of the 'renegades', "they saved our bacon" [sic].

The verdict of history will favour Joe Slovo, whom I was privileged to know. This was my Jewish tribute to him:

"We gather together today to mourn the passing of Joe Slovo and to give thanks for his great life. We give thanks for the quality of his character. He possessed a wondrous mixture of contradictory traits — he was an intellectual who had his feet very much on the ground; a theorist who always put the needs of the people first; a man who faced the turbulence of volatile times with gentleness and good humour; a white man who with every fibre of his being fought to improve the lot of his black brothers and sisters.

We give thanks for his humanity. There are two major motivations towards helping fellow human beings. One is religious. The fatherhood of Almighty G-d betokens the brotherhood and sisterhood of humankind. We are all G-d's children, responsible for the well-being of everyone on earth, commanded to reach out the hand of help each to the other.

Social justice and benevolent action are as old as the Bible. The prophet Amos, for example, stoutly defended the oppressed, thundered with indignation against the idle rich for their ill-treatment of the poor: "Let justice well up as the waters, and righteousness as a mighty stream" (Amos 5:24).

The second motivation is humanitarian — it springs from a deep sense of identification with the oppressed, the ability to hear their cry, an acute awareness of the realities of poverty, a personal anguish at the suffering of fellow human beings. This was Joe Slovo's way. His humanity was boundless and inspirational; he became the true champion of the oppressed. Let not those religious people who acquiesced, passively or wrongly, with the inequalities of yesteryear, let not those religious people dare to condemn Joe Slovo, a humanist socialist, who fought all his life for basic decency, to reinstate the dignity to which all human beings are entitled.

He was proud to acknowledge the Jewish roots of his compassion. Brought up as a child in a Lithuanian ghetto, he experienced at first hand the degradation and misery of being unfairly treated for no proper reason. So in the South Africa he grew to love, he determined that no one should be singled out for unfair treatment for no proper reason. It was not enough to avoid harming others — positively and purposefully one had to strive to ameliorate widespread poverty and hardship, to build a society based on harmony and equality, in which every single individual would be respected. This was the driving force of his life's work: to achieve in an egalitarian, non-racial society the betterment of the living conditions of the entire population.

Another great freedom fighter, the Reverend Martin Luther King, once said, "We are all inextricably bound together in a single garment of destiny." Joe Slovo brought the fulfilment of that dream, that we are all part of one big caring human family, so much closer.

We should appreciate that it is not genius, nor glory, nor even love which truly reflect the human soul — it is kindness. Countless millions of people, touched by the humanity and kindness of Joe Slovo, will forever cherish him in their hearts.

We give thanks for his bravery. Unflinching throughout the struggle, he never gave up in the darkest hours but soldiered on to tackle seemingly insurmountable difficulties. Thank goodness he witnessed in great joy the deserved success of the founding of the new democratic South Africa, with all the promise it carries for our future.

And he was so brave in his terminal illness. Not for a moment did he give up his arduous task at the Ministry of Housing; he summoned reserves of energy when he had no strength left. He showed us all the triumph of the human spirit over sickness, fatigue and adversity.

There is an old Rabbinic teaching, a beautiful one, that just before a person dies, an angel comes to him from heaven and asks the vital question: "Tell me, is the world a better place because of your life which is about to end? Is the world a better place because of the efforts you exerted? Is the world a better place because you were around?"

For Joe Slovo, we give the answer Yes, a resounding Yes. The world is a better place, thanks to you, Joe, and your remarkable life.

Joe, we say farewell to you. We will always remember you with pride and affection. Shalom, dear brother, Shalom. Rest in eternal peace."

3. Inauguration Day

Even the weather smiled on this most auspicious day.

Security officers arrived to pick us up at 6 am and a feeling of excitement began percolating inside my wife and me. As we progressed along the highway to Pretoria, abundant precautions were in evidence — we noticed police cars and armoured vehicles parked every hundred metres or so — and our convoy was then directed to a bypass where we joined a queue of VIP vehicles going to the Presidency for the official breakfast.

As we drove through the suburbs of Pretoria, whole families were taking breakfast outside the front door of their house to see who was passing by and to join in the fun. They smiled and waved, many of the children with flags, and added a tremendous air of joyousness to the proceedings.

It was hard to believe we had come through the elections relatively unscathed. Only some two weeks before there had been ominous signs that a happy day might not be the outcome. Few people, especially those abroad, expected South Africa to overcome the huge hurdles.

It was not just the bombs in central Johannesburg, Germiston and at the airport, but an apprehension that the elections would be chaotic, an opportunity for mayhem and violence. There was fear that Inkatha would lose in its own back yard in Kwazulu Natal, with the subsequent danger of civil war. There was the distinct possibility that the ANC would gain more than two-thirds of the vote, so that power-sharing would not be a meaningful exercise and the Government on National Unity would not be able to live up to its name.

As we approached the Presidency on that sunny morning, all the fears seemed to have vanished. Here we were about to witness the installing into office of the first president of the new South Africa. Here we were witnessing one of the greatest vindications in world history, that the person unfairly jailed for so many years, who had come out of prison utterly devoid of bitterness and somehow full of hope, was now becoming the ruler of a true democracy.

As if to emphasise the feeling of harmony, the guard of honour lining the streets to the Presidency was composed of personnel of all three branches of the defence forces plus members of Umkhonto we Sizwe, the ANC's military wing, plus soldiers of the National Peacekeeping Force. They stood side by side in good humour, proud to be part of the same force.

Not everyone thinks the new flag is pretty. There are too many colours — red, white and blue, black, gold and green, all in the same design. Yet it grows on one, and when you see half a dozen of them bunched together, flying in the breeze, somehow they combine to give a delightful splash of colour, pleasing to the eye.

We parked at the end of a golf course and walked through to the Presidency, a most beautiful building with huge reception rooms and glorious marbled terraces.

The world's leaders may be divided quite simply into "those who are nice" and "those who are not so nice". The whole world was present to applaud South Africa's achievement and wish her well for the future, but some royal representatives and national rulers with their huge bullet-proof limousines, multiple security guards and air of personal importance, seemed to think they were doing South Africa a favour by being there.

Fortunately, however, most joined in the general euphoria and were in relaxed party mood. Only Nelson Mandela would be able to attract to his inauguration such disparate elements as Benazir Bhutto and the vice-president of India, President Ezer Weizman and Yassar Arafat, and a host of African, Asian and South American leaders who would normally prefer not to be seen in each other's company. Amazingly, Fidel Castro, a most impressive figure, was to be seen laughing with the South African generals his Cuban troops fought against in Angola.

For well over an hour in this exalted crowd we played "spot the celebrity," an exercise which was to continue throughout the morning and at lunch.

The atmosphere was informal and relaxed at the Presidency and you could walk up to anyone and say "hullo". Mrs Hilary Clinton and Mrs Tipper Gore gave my wife a big hug. We discussed British politics with Lord Callaghan and Douglas Hurd, the European community with Crown Prince Willem of the Netherlands and President Soares of Portugal, and the future of South Africa with Joe Slovo and members of the new cabinet. We had photographs taken with Prince Philip, Sheik Mohammed of the Muslim Judicial Council and his entourage, and a group of laughing women from Malawi in multi-coloured national dress.

The inauguration ceremony was timed to begin at 11 am and shortly before 10 we were ushered into coaches with the ecclesiastical contingent, including a lively Archbishop Desmond Tutu and my Hindu colleague, PA Lakhani, for the short ride to the Union Buildings. We were taken up the historic, narrow stairways to the main podium and began to realise that as most of the crowd had not yet arrived, there was going to be a long, though pleasant, wait.

Although the ceremony began more than an hour late, this was due to the very elaborate security arrangements surrounding the hundreds of world leaders.

So we sat on the podium for about two hours watching the high and mighty being seated below us. Arafat sat at the back, with Mendel Kaplan, then chairman of the governors of Israel's Jewish Agency and a local philanthropist, in the middle. There was musical entertainment, in English, Afrikaans and Zulu. "Anchors Away" greeted Vice-President Al Gore. Winnie Mandela, looking quite magnificent, took her seat behind us.

We got up to greet the De Klerks, the Sisulus and Adelaide Tambo. By now, the air of excitement was very powerful. The Mbekis then entered in highly joyous mood and finally President Mandela, solemn but relaxed, accompanied by his eldest daughter.

The official proceedings were short, simple and dignified. Chief Justice Corbett was in full command and the deputy presidents and president took their respective oaths of office.

The four religious leaders had been allocated ten minutes; two-

and- a-half minutes each. I had been asked to give a Biblical reading, and had decided days before to choose verses from Isaiah. Rather than take one continuous section, I deliberately selected a verse here and a verse there, which would allow me to mention the key ideas of justice, righteousness, peace and confidence in the future. To get it exactly right, I also consulted the rabbinic commentators and looked at half-a-dozen different English translations, including the recent Revised English Version which utilises modern idiom without sacrificing beauty of language.

Amazingly, this selection succeeded in bamboozling dozens and dozens of religious denominations, government schools and individuals, all of whom bombarded my secretary with telephone calls for weeks afterwards to have a copy of the exact text.

As we went up to participate, President Mandela hugged each of us in turn. He was very warm towards me as we had been together only a few days before at the Sea Point Shul in Cape Town. As we hugged, he said to me, "Rabbi, I want you to know that I saw President Weizman of Israel yesterday".

Of course we already knew about that meeting, but I thought it was most considerate of the new president on "his great day," when the whole world was watching him, to bother to make the connection between the South African Jewish community and Israel, and to let me know that he understood how vital that connection was to us.

Any nervousness I may have had evaporated with the long wait, so I was quite calm during the Isaiah recitation. About halfway through I realised that the huge crowd in front of me was following each word, and that somehow they were appreciating the appropriateness of the text. As we learned later, the cameramen of two of the international TV networks covering the ceremony focused during the reading on President Mandela. It showed him listening intently and visibly moved by the reading, especially at the words "for though the mountains shall depart and the hills be removed, My love shall never depart from thee ...".

The air force fly-by was quite magnificent. President Mandela stood with hand over heart in salute to the forces of which he was now commander-in-chief. The massed military bands played both national anthems, Die Stem with its great dignity and Nkosi Sikelel'i Afrika with its hauntingly beautiful tune. The guns fired their salute.

All was sight and sound, elation and triumph.

The fly-past was superbly arranged with tracer colour ribbons from the military jets painting the national flag in the sky and huge army helicopters flying slowly with reverse flag masts suspending the flags beneath them. It was unbelievably enthralling and the huge crowd, especially the thousands and thousands on the lawns below, cheered and cheered. The new South Africa had become a reality.

No single word can describe the feeling of those precious moments. South Africa, formerly the world's outcast, had now come back to the fold. A wave of relief and pride and hope engulfed us all.

If we were delayed getting there, there was an even longer wait for the coach to take us back to the Presidency for lunch. When we got off the coaches we walked down the path towards the huge marquee, lined with black, white, Indian, and Chinese school children, dancing and singing.

At lunch we were seated with Minister of Finance Derek Keyes and the mayor of Cape Town, and next to the new cabinet ministers Pallo Jordan and Mac Maharaj. There was total informality with much good will running from table to table.

Thanks to the expertise and personal attention of our kashrut department, we had an almost identical meal to the main menu, Derek Keyes commenting favourably on such expert provision.

We again indulged in "spot the celebrity" and this time spoke to Robert Mugabe and Joshua Nkomo of Zimbabwe, and the Archbishop of Canterbury. The speeches were short and to the point, FW de Klerk introducing Boutros Boutros Ghali, the secretary-general of the United Nations, who welcomed South Africa back to the family of nations.

Altogether a memorable occasion. Confidence in the future abounded; that in defiance of its political extremes and despite its contradictory mixture of languages, races, cultures and religions,

South Africa would indeed fuse together to realise its potential. Such optimism was founded not on wishful thinking but on the solid achievement of the first democratic elections in which the people counted simply because they were people.

Indeed, a day of great emotion and of joyous tears. A day of humble prayer, that the Almighty in whose hands are the destinies of individuals and of nations alike, would bless President Nelson Mandela and the new South Africa with peace and prosperity.

Selected verses from the Prophet Isaiah:

54: 7-8 Thus saith the Lord: for a small moment have I forsaken thee; but with great compassion will I gather thee together. In a little anger I turned My face from thee for a moment; but with everlasting kindness will I have compassion on thee.

54: 14 In righteousness shalt thou be established; thou shalt be far from oppression, for thou shalt not fear; and from terror, for it shall not come nigh unto thee.

60: 18 Violence shall no more be heard in the land, nor ruin and devastation within they borders; but thou shalt call thy ramparts Salvation and thy gates Glory.

32: 16-20 Justice shall make its home even in the wilderness and righteousness shall dwell in the grassland; and the work of righteousness shall be peace and the fruit thereof quietness and confidence for ever.

Then shall my people live in a peaceful habitation, and in safe dwellings and tranquil resting places.
It shall be cool on the slopes of the forest then, and cities will lie peaceful in the plain. Happy shalt thou be, sowing every man by the waterside, and letting his ox and ass run free.

54: 10   For though the mountains shall depart and the hills be removed, My love shall never depart from thee, neither shall the covenant of My peace be removed from thee.

57: 19   Shalom, shalom, la-rachok v'la-karov, amar Hashem u'refa-tiv. Peace, peace unto everyone, whether near or far away, for I shall heal you all, saith the Lord.

10 MAY 1994
PRETORIA

INAUGURATION DAY

Inauguration of Nelson Mandela, 10 May 1994; the new President embraces the Chief Rabbi.

(photo: courtesy Pretoria News)

Induction as Chief Rabbi of South Africa, 10 March 1988 – 3 Chief Rabbis; the late Chief Rabbi B.M. Casper z'l, Chief Rabbi Harris, Lord Jakobovits z'l. *(photo: Isaac Reznik)*

10th Anniversary Banquet, Cape Town, 6 November 1997; the Chief Rabbi, President Mandela, Rabbi Michael Harris and Mrs. Ann Harris. *(photo: Shawn Benjamin)*

A cricket fanatic all his life, the Rabbi is still willing to don a pair of pads. On this occasion he retired injured soon after going in to bat. (photo: David Rabinowitz)

Jewish delegation with Nelson Mandela, June 1990. Front row: Helen Suzman, Nelson Mandela, Rabbi Cyril Harris, the late Isie Maisels Q.C. z'l. Back row: Solly Sacks, the Hon. Abe Abrahamson, Prof. Michael Katz, Thabo Mbeki, Yusuf Surtees. (photo: courtesy Zionist Record)

Chief Rabbi Harris in conversation with the late Cardinal Basil Hume, head of the Roman Catholic Church in Great Britain, at a British Board of Deputies function. President of the United Synagogue, Victor Lucas, is in the background. The Chief Rabbi looks younger because the year is 1981.

(photo: Peter Fisher)

The Chief Rabbi appeared with legendary Goon, Harry Secombe, on the famous Goon's television show Highway. The Rabbi (as he was then) is explaining the meaning of Chanukkah to Secombe (and an audience of eight million). In the background is a Christmas tree.

(photo: courtesy London Weekend Television)

From left to right: Former Israeli Ambassador to South Africa, Alon Liel, with the late mayor of Johannesburg, Les Dishy, Chief Rabbi Yisrael Meir Lau, Ashkenazi Chief Rabbi of Israel with Chief Rabbi Harris – May 1993.   (photo: courtesy SA Jewish Times)

South Africa's Chief Rabbi with Dr Jonathan Sacks, Chief Rabbi of Great Britain, at a charity banquet in Johannesburg – August 1997.   (photo: courtesy SA Jewish Times)

The physical Rabbi, playing tug-of-war with children from the Selwyn Segal Home for the Handicapped. (photo: Jack Shapiro)

President Thabo Mbeki receives the Jewish Prayer for the Republic from the Chief Rabbi at UOS Banquet, Cape Town, 27 January 1999. (photo: Herby Rosenberg)

4. Constitutional Tensions

Much praise is rightly given to the South African constitution for being an excellent guiding document for a truly democratic society.

Yet a number of worrying tensions are to be found between the constitution and the principles and values enunciated by most of the religions of the country. Obviously one would like to be in the position of being both a good citizen and a devout member of one's faith, so these tensions are real.

A crucial difference in emphasis exists between the two. The provisions of the constitution can be challenged and are subject to change whereas religion, claiming to deal with absolute values and perpetual injunctions, does not alter fundamentally. One could of course argue that religions are also prone to development. This is historically correct but the core principles of religion are in normal circumstances inviolable.

Moreover, in that most religions claim their legitimacy from a higher authority, the sanction against doing wrong is more severe. By offending civil law, one is hurting society; by breaking religious law, one is offending against both humanity and G-d.

Further, the realm of activity of each is quite different. It is axiomatic that the law of the state serves to foster, protect and enhance human rights; divine law, on the other hand, is composed of injunctions and obligations. Professor Haim Cohn of the Hebrew University points out that when any system of law imposes an obligation or forbids one to perform a certain action, by implication a right is simultaneously being granted; for example, the prohibition "you shall not murder" implies that every person has a right to live. Nevertheless, the religious prerogative is to insist on the fulfilment of duties, the rights being secondary to them.

Furthermore, religion will often expect a person to forgo a legal right when the circumstances demand it, in order that a more equitable result can be achieved. During its debate on negligence, the Talmud provides this remarkable example.

Rabba bar Bar Chana, who was wealthy (unusual for a rabbi!), hired some porters to bring up barrels of wine from his cellar to the banqueting hall. Fooling around, they broke a barrel. Thereupon Rabba confiscated their jackets which they had hung up before commencing work.

The porters were aghast at this means of exacting compensation so they summoned him before Rav, head of the academy at Sura and the local magistrate. When he heard what had transpired, Rav immediately ordered Rabba to give them back their jackets.

"Is this the law?" Rabba demanded to know. "

"For you, yes," answered Rav.

The porters then said to Rav that they had worked all day and that Rabba, who had hired them, had not paid them. Rabba was furious at their impertinent request because they had already caused him financial loss, but Rav again ruled against him and ordered him to pay their wages.

"Is this the law?" Rabba expostulated.

"For you, yes," replied Rav.

In other words, wherever possible, religious law will not insist only on the dictates of civil law, but will also appeal to our higher instincts. In Rav's opinion, Rabba, being a rabbi and wealthy to boot, had to be, as it were, ultra holy; it was unfair for him, notwithstanding his legal rights, to confiscate the clothes of poor men and not to pay them.

Another moral difficulty with the constitution is that it tends to give preference to the rights of the individual over those of society as a whole. A controversial example, and the subject of much heated debate since the abolition of capital punishment, is the simple statement in the bill of rights that "everyone has the right to life."The Bible recognises no such overall right: anyone who consciously commits murder may forfeit his or her life.

A famous Talmudic dispute of the second century informs us that the leading rabbinic authorities agreed with abolition, the death penalty having ceased to be operative after the Sanhedrin, the highest Jewish court, no longer existed. Rabbi Simeon ben Gamaliel opposed this view, being of the firm opinion that if one did not punish murderers effectively, there would be nothing to deter others from killing. He stated: "If capital punishment were to be done away with for good, there would be an increase in the number of murderers in Israel."

In the strident debate for the reintroduction of the death penalty in South Africa, compelling arguments are often overlooked by both sides.

In favour of bringing back capital punishment, one could emphasise the very point that not only the individual has rights but so does society in general. Is it not wrong to care more about the life of a murderer than the lives of ordinary people? Should society protect the perpetrators or its citizens?

The deterrent value of capital punishment is often unfairly dismissed because no one can quantify its value. Comparisons between states in the United States of America which carry out the death penalty and those which do not, are not by any means conclusive. Texas may well execute higher numbers and still have a higher crime rate. That does not necessarily discount the value of deterrence; maybe without the death penalty, the crime rate in Texas would be even higher. Furthermore, there have been many cases in Europe and America of murderers who, having served a term in prison, commit another murder.

In a situation where the taking of life is gratuitous — so many hijack victims in South Africa are needlessly slain — it can be maintained that the restoration of the death penalty would, paradoxically, enhance the value of life, while its absence cheapens it.

Against all this, the arguments to maintain abolition also carry validity. The clinical procedure of carrying out the death sentence is brutal and chilling and demeans civilisation. Abolitionists insist it does not achieve anything, other than another death. In addition, the danger that the wrong person has been hanged is ever present; there are notorious instances of the official killing by society of innocent persons. Of much weight in our South African situation is the argument — much loved by sociologists, but also unquantifiable — that much crime is caused by social and economic deprivation. That is not to condone crime in any way but to suggest that to some degree society itself is guilty, not just the malefactor.

So the answer suggested by the Talmud — to keep the death penalty on the statute book but to carry it out rarely — may have some merit. True, it is related that a Sanhedrin that was responsible for one execution in seven years — a variant tradition maintains one in seventy years — went down in history as a "harmful" court, but some workable solution must be found.

Tension also exists regarding the relationship between Church — I refer here to all religions — and the State. While no one expects the country to become a theocracy, and nor does anyone foresee a totalitarian regime under which religions are repressed, there is much debate as to precisely what constitutes the middle ground. Clearly a healthy collaboration and interaction should exist between the state and religious organisations. But, especially in a country in which the vast majority belongs to one religious denomination or another, exactly in which areas and to what degree the state should concede some power to religion is a matter worthy of serious discourse.

Unfortunately no good model of the church/state relationship is available. The United States, with its much vaunted separation of church and state, despite which it remains a highly religious country, even carrying G-d's name on its coinage, spends an inordinate amount of time arguing over prayers in public schools. In Israel there is open conflict on vital matters of religion and state between the Orthodox and the Supreme Court. Both India and Ireland, where religion is a way of life, should have come up with an effective formula, but have not.

It is noteworthy that both Nelson Mandela and Thabo Mbeki understand religion to be a substantial driving force in helping to influence the transformation process beneficially. More than this, the head of government has repeatedly urged religious leadership to fulfil the role of watchdog by crying out against corruption and wastefulness in government itself, to strive to ensure the application to society of the principles and values contained in the constitution, and to exercise religion's prophetic function to hold out promise for the future.

The most controversial area of conflict between the constitution and most of our religious movements centres around the difference between freedom and licence.

Homosexual partnerships, for example, which on the basis of the constitution last year received legal recognition in the Cape High Court, are considered anathema by most religions. No discrimination in matters of sex is countenanced by the bill of rights but a different ethic permeates religious reasoning which sees such relationships as frustrating the procreative nature of sex, as damaging to the respective roles of male and female and destructive to the fundamental purpose of family life.

Lord Winston, in his adventurous research at London's Hammersmith Hospital, tells us that males will soon be able to give birth by attaching the foetus to the wall of the abdomen, implanting a placenta, and by undergoing a caesarian section at the time of delivery. If successful, this will enable gays to have "their own children" but religion is not likely to give up its objection. As Rabbi Lord Jakobovits z'l, has stated: "'Love' between consenting adults of the same sex cannot justify the morality of homosexuality any more than it can legitimise adultery, however sincerely such acts may be performed out of genuine emotions and by mutual consent."

If by its insistence on "no discrimination in matters of sex" the bill of rights is seeking tolerance for other people's lifestyle, that is one thing, but if it means granting equality to relationships considered deviationist by most religious codes, that is another.

A further instance is the limitation on freedom of expression, which — after a vociferous debate in the constitutional assembly — was incorporated in the constitution. While in the United States the First Amendment guarantees freedom of expression — this has allowed organisations such as the Ku Klux Klan to "perform" publicly — our constitution restricts freedom of expression by not extending it to the "advocacy of hatred that is based on race, ethnicity, gender or religion, and that constitutes incitement to cause harm".

A significant moral victory was achieved here against those who were of the opinion that freedom of speech is sacrosanct. Most religionists feel that in a heterogeneous society such as ours, with such a long history of racial abuse, and where the possibility of friction between one group and another is always present, the constitution itself must provide the requisite protection.

The crux of the matter is whether it is preferable for pernicious beliefs to be publicly aired so that they can be challenged openly, or whether poisonous views should be forbidden to pollute the atmosphere in the first place. If the experience of the last century — from Nazi propaganda to the apartheid South Africa of yesteryear — is anything to go by, incitement to hatred can all too easily triumph over free speech.

An additional anxiety for religious people is that religious practice does not appear to be properly safeguarded. Obviously, since the constitution is still new, the meaning of a considerable number of its clauses still requires elucidation, and many legal cases will ensue in the years ahead to clarify the issues and to determine which interpretations are legitimate.

The section on cultural, religious and linguistic communities is a case in point. How they are to be promoted and protected has already been the subject of umpteen official seminars, but the precise nature of these rights is still quite vague. Two examples of the failure to protect religious practice are the persistent setting of examinations on holy days, a situation compounded by the refusal of some universities to make satisfactory alternative arrangements, and the current failure of the health department to ensure that religiously observant doctors are able to fulfil their year of community service without having to compromise their religious practice.

A more subtle consideration is the creation of a climate conducive to religious observance. Constitutional Court Judge Albie Sachs has stated: "If there are Muslims who wish to attend mosque on Fridays, and Jews who refuse to ride on a bus on Saturdays, or Christians who believe it is sinful to catch fish on Sundays, that is their business and their right. They cannot impose their beliefs on others, nor can anyone take their beliefs from them."

In similar vein, Buti Tlhagale, the Catholic Bishop of Bloemfontein, has declared that "religious influence needs to be removed from the fundamental law of the country. It is believers who ought to keep the Sabbath holy, not the state imposing it on everybody else."

Quite so, but both have missed the psychological importance of the correct atmosphere that should surround the fulfilment of religious observance. Religious people do not live in a vacuum and — this is the flip side of religious coercion — non-religious people can so easily spoil everything for the religious.

I recall Sundays in the Scotland of my youth, when it was "the Lord's Day". People refrained from washing their cars, all the shops and cinemas were closed, and even those who were not churchgoers helped to create a tangible atmosphere of holiness. I am told that in the South Africa of yesteryear, despite all its glaring faults, similar conditions prevailed.

Hence the interaction between religion and general society depends not only on constitutional dictates but very much on the spirit in which they are applied. This incorporates the willingness of people in general to cooperate — not such a great sacrifice — in helping to foster the conditions amenable to the proper fulfilment of religious practice.

Despite the above reservations, nothing can detract from the positive advantages which accrue as a result of the constitution. It provides for plurality and freedom of religion and, despite the tensions that require resolution, has delineated the framework within which all of us may flourish.

5.   Getting the Get Bill

Since the Ghetto walls came tumbling down some two hundred years ago, an apparently intractable problem has existed in many countries of the Jewish world, a problem caused by the wedge between civil and religious divorce.

Time and again a Jewish husband has divorced his wife according to the law of the land, and then often spitefully, and usually in the hope of financial gain, has refused to give her a Get. Sometimes the situation is reversed: the husband has been willing to give his civilly divorced wife the Get but she has refused to accept it.

To overcome this major stumbling block in our own community, many interested parties engaged in a number of activities and processes that started in the middle of 1989 and reached a happy conclusion towards the end of 1996 and that I want to describe.

Several noble attempts preceded ours. Such worthy personalities as Judge Leslie Lawrence, a past chairman of the Union of Orthodox Synagogues, and Harry Schwarz, former ambassador to the United States, who submitted a Private Member's Bill, had suggested a variety of legal remedies. Many rabbis, especially those with a knowledge of South African law as well as halachah, also tried to solve the problem.

The redoubtable Ros Rosenberg, a divorce advocate and close friend, has been known to resort to the Talmudic argument that if the civilly divorced couple die without the Get having been given or received, they will, since they are still married in Jewish law, remain forever intertwined in heaven. This argument has been known to work occasionally with orthodox and superstitious people.

The credit for initiating the new process, guiding it with great wisdom and seeing it through until it became law, goes primarily to Judge PJJ Olivier, formerly vice-chairman of the South African Law Commission, leader of the special project on Jewish Divorces, and now of the Appellate Division.

Highly knowledgeable on the subject, Judge Olivier rightly claimed that "as long as the couple were still considered to be married in the eyes of their religion, the civil divorce was rendered virtually ineffective. South African law is saying 'this couple is divorced' but the Jewish community is saying 'this couple is still married'. Hence it is the duty of civil law to try to resolve the contradiction".

And so it all began in May 1989, when the Minister of Justice required the Law Commission to undertake an investigation of Jewish ecclesiastical divorces and to consider appointing a committee of experts to assist the commission.

A few months later, the commission approved the inclusion in its programme of an investigation entitled "Jewish Divorces," and in August 1989 the commission's working committee approved the establishment of a project committee under the chairmanship of Judge Olivier.

In January 1990, the Minister of Justice appointed the members of the Project Committee: Rabbi MA Kurtstag and Rabbi Dr D Isaacs (of the Beth Din), Professor J Sinclair (at that time deputy Vice-Chancellor of Wits), Advocate N Segal, D Shapiro (an attorney), Mrs Ann Harris (my wife, then at the Wits Law Clinic), Rabbi Adi Assabi (formerly of the Union for Progressive Judaism) who was succeeded in 1994 by Rabbi Michael Standfield (chairman of the SA Association of Progressive Rabbis), and myself.

After several exploratory meetings, a draft working paper, Committee Paper 169, was considered. This ran to 138 pages, and after giving a clear summary of the problem, went on to describe attempts to solve the predicament in other countries and finished with our initial recommendation.

Our new angle concentrated on avoiding the separation of the religious and civil divorce by insisting on them being "two sides of the same coin". Thus we recommended that whenever a couple had been married under religious auspices, and that religion required a religious divorce, the civil divorce be made contingent on the granting of the religious divorce. Of all the attempts made to solve the problem, we considered with justification that ours was the simplest and the best.

Because the Law Commission, for constitutional reasons, did not wish to restrict the provisions to one religion, it became necessary to examine problems similar to those of the Jewish Get. For example, Islamic religious tribunals are sometimes powerless to dissolve a marriage of parties adhering to the Muslim faith. In Islam, when a marriage ends, the wife has to offer to repay some, if not all, of the dowry that the husband originally paid to the wife's family. Should the husband refuse to accept the return of the dowry, or part of it, the tribunal's hands may be tied, thus necessitating a legal solution similar to that of the Get.

After due consideration, a further draft, Committee Paper 224, was sent to the working committee for approval, and in January 1993, Working Paper 45, a thorough, comprehensive and commendable document, setting forth the present legal position and containing recommendations for legal reform, was distributed for general comment.

Much publicity was given to the matter by the general and Jewish media and much apposite comment was proffered. Conscious of the need to solve the problem, the South African Jewish Board of Deputies and the Coordinating Council of National Jewish Women's Organisations of South Africa, representing thousands of Jewish women, officially supported the proposed amendment.

The Reform movement was among the few to oppose the proposal, as it considered it unacceptable that the Beth Din be given the right to exercise authority over the entire Jewish community. They also endorsed an earlier observation by Professor Sinclair that civil authorities should have no jurisdiction, and certainly not meddle, in religious affairs.

In addition to helpful suggestions by Dayan Berel Berkovits of the Beth Din of the Federation of Synagogues in London, the remarks of Mr Justice DA Melamet to the effect that "it is difficult to see how a person can claim ... that the civil marriage has irretrievably broken down [yet] persists [in claiming] that the religious marriage still exists" were of significant value.

As usually happens when any subject comes before the public, there was the view that the provisional proposal went too far and the view that the proposal did not go far enough.

After all the observations had been duly considered, the commission approved the report, and submitted it to the Justice Minister in October 1994 for the consideration of parliament. Although the matter was now out of our hands, the then Minister, Dullah Omar, was kind enough to see us some six months later to assure us that there were no party political objections to the proposed amendment and that likewise none of the religious communities had voiced objections to it.

After the bill had received its preliminary approval by parliament, it went to the relevant portfolio committee for consideration. A few last minute hiccups occurred; some members of the portfolio committee objected to the proposals on the grounds that it was not clear how other religions, such as Islam, would be affected. Moreover, the constitutionality of the amendment was challenged in that it appeared to take away the right of a Jewish husband to deny the Get. To this latter argument, the reply was given that it can hardly be considered discriminatory if the person who is demanding a civil decree of divorce is at the same time refusing to grant a Get.

During the second reading debate in the old Senate, virtually unanimous approval for the amendment was expressed. Senator Moosa mentioned that in his own case his Islamic religious marriage was followed only two years later by a civil marriage in court. Much to the amusement of the senators, the Minister of Justice commented: "I hope to the same woman on both occasions."

Although one senator criticised "how conservative some orthodox religious practices are" and looked forward to the time when there was "no longer a patriarchal system of dominance in our society," the bill was not opposed, and it was assented to on November 12, 1996 before parliament rose. President Mandela signed it, and the Divorce Amendment Act 1996 was published in the Government Gazette of November 22, 1996.

In many ways it was revolutionary because secular courts are generally averse to becoming entangled in doctrinal matters. But in the words of Ashraf Mahomed, a Cape Town attorney, "the Divorce Amendment Act is a significant piece of social legislation geared towards creating a harmonious coexistence between our secular laws and various religions and cultural affiliations."

When we received the actual text, a surprise awaited us. Despite our carefully worded amendment, the Law Committee of parliament apparently wished to strengthen it. So they added a further clause to the effect that any barrier to the remarriage of either spouse also had to be removed.

At any rate, after hundreds of hours of meetings, after six years of promoting a change often accompanied by aggravation and heartache, after the arduous efforts of the Law Commission who employed a research lawyer to study Jewish divorce, after the due processes of parliamentary law, after all the earnest debate and not a little controversy, after all the undeserved tears of agunot, the amendment was the law of the land.

The task of informing judges, advocates and attorneys lay before us. The amendment was not retrospective and, furthermore, might also only apply when both parties conceded that the marriage had irretrievably broken down. Where one party contested the civil divorce itself, our amendment might not be able to overcome the resistance to giving or receiving the Get.

Yet we heaved a collective sigh of relief. A stream of congratulations reached us from across the Jewish world. Describing it as "an extraordinary achievement," Rabbi Rafael Grossman, the then president of the Rabbinical Council of America, wrote to us "what you have accomplished is a great Kiddush Hashem".

1. The Divorce Act, 1979 (Act No. 70 of 1979), is hereby amended by the insertion after section 5 of the following section:
Refusal to grant divorce
5A. If it appears to a court in divorce proceedings that despite the granting of a decree of divorce by the court the spouses or either one of them will, by reason of the prescripts of their religion or the religion of either one of them, not be free to remarry unless the marriage is also dissolved in accordance with such prescripts or

unless a barrier to the remarriage of the spouse concerned is removed, the court may refuse to grant a decree of divorce unless the court is satisfied that the spouse within whose power it is to have the marriage so dissolved or the said barrier so removed, has taken all the necessary steps to have the marriage so dissolved or the barrier to the remarriage of the other spouse removed or the court may make any other order that it finds just.

Short title

2. This Act shall be called the Divorce Amendment Act, 1996.

6.   The Lovely and the Hideous

There was a body in the middle of the street.

We were in the car in the early evening on the way to a function at the Carlton Hotel, now closed, and just past the taxi ranks in Von Wielligh Street, our driver swerved to avoid the body.

Sleeping? Comatose? Drunk? Dead? All these were possible, especially the last, as the figure, dressed in the shabbiest of clothes, was lying face down, immobile, and out for the count.

"Stop a minute," I suggested. Our security guard gave me a withering look, as if to say it was the last thing to do in downtown Johannesburg when it was getting dark. So we did not stop to see if we could be of any help and maybe he was beyond it anyway.

*   *   *

A few kilometres outside Hazyview, close to the Kruger National Park, on the road going northwards there is a breath-takingly beautiful display of bougainvillaea.

Just as you negotiate a slight bend in the road, you come across a sight so delightful that most motorists turn round and traverse the same stretch of road again to feast their eyes on the profusion of glorious colour.

On the side of the road, cascading down a six metre wall is a range of gorgeous bougainvillaea — some are mauve, some cerise, some a vivid magenta, some white, some bronze and some a delicate, dusty pink. Whether by accident or design, the tinctures complement each other perfectly so that the multi-coloured vision forms a magnificent and utterly dazzling botanical treat. Like William Wordsworth's famous daffodils, years later these bougainvillaea may be joyously recollected by the "inner eye".

*   *   *

A five-star hotel was launching its new kosher cuisine at a glittering black-tie banquet and we were treated to a seven-course meal. Dish after succulent dish was consumed with great relish, and we were engaged in eating this gourmet repast for more than three hours. We all ate and drank far too much and the event was a great success for the hotel and the more than 300 guests.

Five minutes after I returned home there was a ring at the outside gate. It was the young black couple who lived somewhere nearby and who came from time to time for food. My wife gave me bread, cheese, fruit and milk and I took it to them at the gate. They thanked me profusely. They seemed to me not to have eaten anything at all that day.

*   *   *

On my first visit to South Africa in August 1987, I was taken by my colleague Rabbi Selwyn Franklyn, then rabbi of the prestigious Sea Point Synagogue and always an outspoken critic of apartheid, to see Crossroads. He felt I should know about "the real South Africa" so that if I were to be offered the Chief Rabbinate, I should at least be aware of the pivotal problems of the country.

I have never seen such squalour in my life. In the most deplorable living conditions imaginable, the teeming hordes eked out a pitiful existence. Anywhere else in the civilised world these dilapidated, ramshackle "living quarters" would have been condemned outright and demolished.

But this was home to thousands, with broken planks of wood, empty tins, bits of wire, black plastic bags and the odd brick put to constructive use. Rain was pouring down that morning and the whole settlement was a miserable, soggy mess.

*   *   *

The southernmost point of the African continent is Cape Agulhas, not Cape Point as is commonly thought by those who have never visited these parts, and nearby is the fishing village of Arniston. Looking out to sea from the quaint harbour — the Atlantic has become the Indian Ocean —one is immediately struck by the stunning colour of the water.

It is a beautiful translucent shade of turquoise. Here, at the end of the world, the huge expanse of water is neither sombre nor murky but serene and placid, a warm and pleasurable tint of greenish blue. The first time I saw it, I remember reciting two benedictions: on seeing the ocean, I said the blessing thanking G-d "Who has made the great sea," and then my favourite one when I see beautiful things, "Who has such as these in His world".

*   *   *

I was shot at in Boipatong. Following the terrible massacre in June 1992, arrangements were made to hold a memorial meeting in the local football stadium prior to the funerals of the slain. Accompanied by a group from the Black Sash, we arrived early from Johannesburg and there was already a huge crowd. We could hear the hubbub of 20 000 people crammed in the small stadium, and thousands more — the number increasing by the minute — were milling around outside.

Our small contingent from the Jewish Board of Deputies consisted of Selwyn Zwick, then a vice-chairman, Seymour Kopelowitz, the national director at the time, our driver Girvis and me. Four students from the South African Union of Jewish Students were our security team at the venue.

We took the decision to park our car on the periphery and walk about one kilometre to the stadium. Already the whole area was ringed with police Casspirs — trying and failing to be inconspicuous — and there were pockets of policemen at regular intervals. We felt it would be easier and safer to go on foot as the car might get caught up in the huge crowds later in the day and it would be difficult to find a clear way out.

As we walked along the mud track which passed for a road, the hearses were still moving slowly along towards the stadium. It was a harrowing sight, especially the little bodies of the murdered children in silver-coloured coffins behind the glass of the sleek limousines — a regular irony in this country is that, poor all their lives, the dead are given a luxurious send-off.

As we entered the stadium, Archbishop Wilfred Napier was chanting appropriate prayers. "We cry out from the depths unto Thee, O Lord," and we managed with some difficulty to negotiate the way to our seats near the platform on the far side. An array of political speeches followed — Jay Naidoo was passionate in his condemnation of the atrocities — and even Archbishop Trevor Huddleston, normally cool and detached, thundered against the Government:"Christianity is not a religion of love only," he averred, and quoted Psalm 97,"Ye, who love the Lord, hate evil". There was nothing more hateful than apartheid, he went on to emphasise, and it was thus meritorious to hate the current regime.

It was a surprisingly hot day for June, and as the crowd inside and out grew larger and larger, the atmosphere became more and more intense. After listening to more than four hours of speeches, we realised they were going to continue for most of the day. It was now unbearably stifling, so feeling rather guilty we slipped out of the stadium.

We pushed through the enormous crowd and somehow made it back to the mud road. Seymour and Girvis were a hundred metres or so ahead of us, and Selwyn and I were walking and talking and wending our way through the mass of humanity. Just as we passed a small group of policemen, someone in the crowd, which apparently had been taunting the officers for some time, picked up a boulder and threw it at them.

The police opened fire. One moment Selwyn and I were talking to each other and the next there was pandemonium, everyone crouching down and running, and bullets whistling in the air.

"I'm going to throw myself in that ditch," Selwyn shouted to me, pointing to a hollow in the side of the road.

Knowing he did not enjoy the best of health, I shouted back that it was not a good idea, and gesticulated to him that we should follow the crowd by crouching down and running as quickly as possible.

Which is what we did, and after what seemed like an age, the firing stopped. Next day we gave to charity, and recited the benediction Hagomel, which one does on being delivered from danger: "Blessed art Thou, King of the Universe, Who bestows favours on the undeserving ...".

*   *   *

The Blyde River Canyon is a spiritual experience. One looks down, deep down the rocky, creviced gorge to the river below, and then up and up, each tier of mountains soaring higher than the next. Here in the Northern Drakensberg, the patterns of earth and sky give a new dimension to beauty.

*   *   *

Ah, lovable, ugly, impossible country. Country of violent hijackings and jacarandas, of the Garden Route and Soweto's squalour, of necklacing and flame trees, of gorgeous Plettenberg Bay and restless patients sleeping in the corridors of Baragwanath Hospital, of the exquisite side-by-side with the unacceptable, of such widespread frustration and such inextinguishable hope.

Lovable, ugly, impossible country.

7. Inter-faith Concord

An admirable feature of the religious life of South Africa is the extent of the co-operation among its faith communities.

In an impressive range of vital areas — whether urging religious education in government schools or lobbying against euthanasia, whether joining together against crime or striving for more hours for religious broadcasting, whether battling poverty or promoting community development, whether encouraging improved standards of behaviour or engaging in the struggle against Aids — the collective religious voice is heard across the land and it has proved an immense force for good.

Not every denomination, and by no means every cleric, was initially enthusiastic. The accusation that religious togetherness would lead to the danger of syncretism, a merging of differing beliefs and diverse rituals into one common faith, had to be countered for the nonsense that it was.

Likewise the fear had to be allayed that joining together with other religious denominations to try to effect the betterment of general society might somehow lead to a watering down of one's own commitment. There are those who firmly believe that because their own religion contains the truth — the whole, revealed truth — there is no room to show respect to other religions, let alone participate with them in any venture. If they did, they feel they would be somehow letting their own side down.

The contrary view, that if one wishes respect to be shown to one's own religion it is only proper that one respects the religion of others, required from the outset to be promoted actively. We had to emphasise that in the search for acceptable common denominators of religious tradition, the distinctiveness of one's own faith need never be compromised nor allegiance in any sense weakened. Without giving up one iota of one's own faith, one may indeed overcome separateness in an affirmation of the positive good which mutual respect and joint co-operation can bring.

So despite the hundreds and hundreds of different denominations active in this country, despite the old animosities generated by the Dutch Reformed Church, despite political differences between various groupings — not least Muslims and Jews regarding the situation in the Middle East — the inspired insistence of Archbishop Desmond Tutu and the impelling arguments of the South African Chapter of the World Conference on Religion and Peace succeeded in bringing us all together.

In many other countries inter-faith relationships are polite and the wishy-washy agenda concentrates on "safe" subjects such as the parameters of tolerance. In South Africa, where the issues are weighty and real, the very success of the transformation process depends at least in part on the ability of the religious communities to pool their collective strength and fulfil a historic role.

A congenial climate fortunately prevailed from the beginning, and the inter-faith movement has developed in recent years, evincing an unparalleled degree of mutual trust.

Our first major task was the drawing up of "The Religious Charter," or, to give it its full title, "The Declaration on the Rights and Responsibilities of Religious People". This was a necessary, if mammoth, task because we felt it absolutely vital to the new dispensation and to the drawing up of the new constitution, that we enunciate the values essential to the creation of a just social order and that our collective strength be added to the promotion of reconciliation and reconstruction.

Over a period of some eighteen months during 1991 and 1992, we held numerous meetings and seminars, consulted far and wide, and eventually finalised, at a two-day conference in Pretoria, a draft to be approved by all the faith communities in the country.

While a large measure of unanimity prevailed throughout the deliberations, some areas proved contentious and much heated argument was ventilated before satisfactory compromises could be reached. It was not so easy, for example, to define "religion" in the first place. After considerable debate, we managed to achieve consensus on a rather long definition: "We understand a religion to mean a group of people who, in their quest for ultimate meaning, hold common beliefs in transcendent and sacred reality, expressed in forms of worship, veneration, ethical norms, social structures and customs."

Missionary activity — particularly in view of the prevalence of evangelical faiths — was a thorny issue. To prohibit any religion to propagate its beliefs freely would in many instances rob it of its principal function, yet to exert no measure of control whatsoever was considered by most representatives to be undesirable.

Hence we listed a number of safeguards. Propagation of one's own faith should be done "with respect for the beliefs of others, without malice, slander or the denigration of any person or religion, avoiding the dissemination of malicious falsehoods and promotion of racial hatred." Crucially, missionary activities should not be "directed at children under the age of eighteen, except with the permission of their parents," and no coercion could be exerted nor material inducements offered.

Polygamy was another controversial complication. Due to the preponderance of customary marriages and the approbation of the practice by religions such as Islam — although only a small minority was married to more than one wife — it was clearly advisable to include our recommendation as to how to alleviate the hardships caused by unrecognised marriages and disputed succession.

An enormous row ensued, but despite some of the monogamous religions insisting that at the end of the 20th century it was not feasible for the proper running of society to allow both monogamy and polygamy, the conference nevertheless suggested that "the state should recognise personal and private law systems of religions where these are in conflict with existing civil law".

All in all, the declaration was a commendable effort. It certainly solidified the notion of a collective religious approach and created an atmosphere conducive to further joint campaigns. Sadly some of its simplest proposals are still in abeyance. University examinations on holy days, for instance, are still frequent, although the declaration calls for respect to be shown to the holy days of all religions and asks the authorities to do whatever is necessary to meet people's religious needs.

While our new constitution safeguards religious practice, precisely what this means has not yet been clarified and many test cases will be brought in the years ahead to determine the parameters of religious rights and where these are being infringed.

The reformation, after 1994, of the South African Broadcasting Corporation provided another quite fascinating avenue for religious co-operation. After long deliberations with the many different faith communities in the country, a Religious Broadcasting Panel was appointed early in 1995 to help implement the official religious policy of the SABC. I had the privilege of being nominated by the Jewish community and, after public interview, of being selected to serve for three years on the RBP, a committee of fifteen different religious personalities.

It was a wonderful and yet frustrating experience. We got on so well with each other — African traditionalists, Muslims, Catholics, African Independents, evangelists, Dutch Reformed, Anglicans, Hindus and Jews — that we were able to develop genuine mutual respect and profound understanding of our respective spiritual aims. I made new friends, particularly the Reverend Bernard Spong of the South African Council of Churches, a truly knowledgable communicator. The sense of fellowship was genuine, and if ever the politicians at the United Nations should summon such a spirit of amity among diverse groups, the world would be guaranteed progress and peace.

Our arguments were with the SABC. Our role had not been precisely defined, so that whereas we felt we had a real say in religious programming, as regards aims, style and content, the staff members responsible for production considered we were there in an advisory capacity only. Many of our proposals were ignored. Our own effective chairman was Archbishop Njongonkulu Ndungane, who subsequently succeeded Archbishop Tutu in Cape Town, but this did not prevent friction over the exact relationship of the RBP with the religious sub-committee of the SABC board, and with the board of governors, on both of which our chairman also sat.

Needless to say, the most monumental row was over budgeting. Having made the praiseworthy ruling that religion was far too important for broadcasting time to be sold to those independent enterprises who possessed the funds, and that there must be a free and equitable allocation based on the membership size of the various denominations, after an initial period of eighteen months during which religious programmes flourished, the SABC reneged on its own policy for religious broadcasting and proceeded to cut left, right and centre.

This was a great pity. The specific faith programmes on TV — especially L'Chaim, produced by Helen Heldenmuth with great flair — attracted audiences far wider than the religious community for which they were primarily designed. The weekly inter-faith discussion panel, Credo, presented by the Reverend Cedric Mayson of the Commission on Religious Affairs of the ANC also proved very popular.

Hence the SABC's decision in May 1997 to make severe cuts came as a bombshell, and we almost immediately lost all the specific faith programmes. The promise was given that, should the financial position of the SABC improve, the budget for religious broadcasting would be restored. Because the programmes are not only valuable in themselves but do so much towards deepening understanding of other faiths and in building bridges so essential to the future, one hopes they will return soon.

A further desideratum is that religion should never be restricted to a separate compartment of its own, isolated from "real life." Throughout the world of broadcasting, prime time magazine programmes on issues of public concern — capital punishment, for example — feature prominent politicians, lawyers, psychiatrists and clergymen, but all too often in South Africa the religious viewpoint on matters of great moral import is not given the opportunity of being aired.

Religious leadership has also joined hands to combat crime. The Gun Free South Africa campaign was wholeheartedly endorsed at its inception by all high profile clergymen and the pressure to fulfil its vision has not abated. No one can logically propound that the proliferation of firearms is making the country in any sense safer, so the demand for stringent legislative measures to restrict the allocation of gun licences is a crucial factor in the fight against crime.

Research into police dockets on robbery and hijackings in Johannesburg proves that if you carry a gun you are far more likely to end up being shot. The myth that the gun is a friend that will help you, and that it will guarantee your safety, is nonsense. The fact is your gun exposes you to higher risk.

Those of us urging much tighter controls are fully aware of the opposition to curtailing individual rights and of all the self-protection arguments. Against them is the greater right of society as a whole. A direct correlation exists between the number of firearms and the extent of injury and, paradoxical as it may appear, the truth is that the fewer the quantity of firearms in private hands, the safer our homes and streets become.

Infringement of human rights also came to the fore in the anguished debate as to how best to counter the fearful situation on the Cape flats. The Inter-Religious Commission against Crime and Violence in the Western Cape came together early in 1998 in response to the wave of bombings and indiscriminate attacks afflicting the region. Among our proposals — which we put directly to President Mandela when he gave us the opportunity of expressing our concern — was the imposition of curfews in the most troublesome areas.

The idea was that the army and the police working in tandem would announce the curfew and shortly afterwards proceed with a house-to-house search for illegal weapons. Despite the urgency of taking such steps, some politicians and some senior personnel at safety and security were vehemently opposed to any action reminiscent of the apartheid era and so the proposal was rejected.

In vain did we protest that the comparison was spurious and that the invasion of privacy this time round would be in a good cause, but to no effect. Similar proposals, such as granting the authorities the power to detain suspects for as long as questioning them required, were also viewed askance. Clearly individual rights predominate to the detriment of society in general.

By far our most significant achievement to date was the Moral Summit.

Initiated by President Mandela himself, who in June 1997 called on the leaders of major religious communities to apply their collective spiritual strength to deal with the country's moral crisis, a new group, the National Religious Leaders' Forum, was convened. Clearly if there was too much crime, violence, corruption and unacceptable behaviour around, the religious communities, especially their leaders, had to accept some of the responsibility. The correct values were somehow not coming across.

The inspired new angle the president formulated was that the transformation of South Africa required positive relations between religion and politics, that the moral qualities of the former should permeate the latter and together develop a process of moral renewal involving all the citizens of the country.

After much deliberation and heart searching, and following honest analyses of the reasons for the spiritual malaise, it was decided to issue two major appeals for improved behaviour. The Code of Conduct for "persons in positions of responsibility" concentrated on virtues such as integrity, incorruptibility and accountability.

The Ubuntu Pledge for all citizens asked everyone to strive to be good and do good; to live honestly and positively; to respect all people's rights; and to promote peace, harmony and non-violence.

The Moral Summit was launched with great fanfare and ceremony in the Mayor's Chamber at the Johannesburg Civic Centre in October, 1998. Almost all the political leaders were present to sign the pledge, and their speeches were even more religious than those of the religious leaders assembled for the event.

The cynics could scoff that given the monumental levels of crime and misbehaviour the whole exercise would prove futile. Most people, however, accepted the call as being long overdue, and were genuinely impressed with the partnership of religion and politics, which had succeeded in evaluating the reasons for moral failure and pointing the way towards moral renewal.

Nowhere else in the world would the top politicians come together with religious leaders to jointly endorse a programme promising so much. It deserves to succeed.

8.   Madiba

Of all the friendships I have been fortunate to enjoy, the most special is with Nelson Mandela.

The first time I had the privilege of meeting him personally — I had been present at briefings he thoughtfully gave to religious leadership soon after his release from Pollsmoor Prison but these were rather formal occasions — he was recovering from minor surgery in the Park Lane Clinic. In the company of Helen Suzman, the late Isie Maisels, who had successfully defended Mandela in the Treason Trial, the eminent economist, Professor Michael Katz, and two stalwarts of the South African Zionist Federation, Abe Abrahamson and Solly Sacks, we spent an amicable hour chatting with him. A young-looking Thabo Mbeki was in attendance.

The atmosphere was very relaxed and Mandela reminisced with Suzman about the old days of the struggle. He chided her gently about her views against economic sanctions, but she was her usual forthright self and defended her stance firmly and cogently.

Meanwhile, Maisels, a doughty and life-long supporter of Israel, berated Mandela for his close friendship with Yasir Arafat which had been so publicly displayed at the Namibian independence celebrations.

"I did not help to save your life at the Treason Trial so that you could associate with Israel's enemies," Maisels robustly declared. Mandela smiled, and shrugged off the attack with his customary good nature.

A few weeks later at a rumbustious musical evening at the home of the late Clive Menell, who was an ardent supporter of African culture in all its varied forms, we sat together at the back of the large lounge. It was jam-packed, altogether lively and stimulating, and Mandela, casually dressed in a deep green polo-neck, sat on the floor and hugely enjoyed the concert. An intrinsic component of his charm, one of his most admirable characteristics, is that he is never out of place — no matter the company, occasion or circumstances.

There was such a large crowd that our hostess, Irene Menell, kept sending trays of assorted food, drinks and fruit through the open

windows from the garden into the lounge. My wife and I kept passing the trays on to Madiba, but he was not hungry and kept waving
them away with a smile.

After the dramatic first elections, he decided that during the weekend before his inauguration the president-designate would embrace
all the major religious communities by visiting them on their respective holy days: the Muslims at a mosque on Friday midday, the Jewish
community at synagogue on Shabbat morning, the Hindus at temple
and the Christians in church on Sunday.

It was an imaginative and deeply appreciated gesture — to the
best of my knowledge no political leader of any other state has ever
engaged in a similar exercise — and it symbolised in a tangible manner the new regime's desire for harmonious relationships and was a
magnanimous way of including everyone.

We chose the Marais Road Synagogue in Sea Point as the ideal
venue for the occasion, and for halachic reasons, which include the
banning of cameras and tape recorders inside the synagogue, decided
it would be preferable if the distinguished guest arrived towards the
end of the statutory service.

A large contingent, including Albie Sachs and Carl Niehaus, accompanied Mandela and needless to say the synagogue was packed. After
an appropriate special prayer by the local rabbi, Dr Jack Steinhorn, the
National Chairman of the Jewish Board of Deputies, Mervyn Smith,
welcomed the distinguished visitor. He referred movingly to Robben
Island — clearly visible on that memorable Shabbat — and to the
great exultation experienced by everyone at the extraordinary change
of circumstance that enabled the former prisoner to be saluted by us
as our future president.

In my short address, I wished the new government every success
in its efforts to establish real democracy in the country, called for the
reconstruction of hearts and minds no less than social and economic
structures, and pledged the support of the Jewish community in the
historic task of nation building.

In praising the "massive dignity, obvious sincerity and absolute integrity" of the president-designate, I used a Xhosa phrase, learned from our domestic worker, Constance, "Sonke sixinga ukuthi, uyindoda elungileyo kakhulu" ("All of us think you are a really exceptional man").

Mandela replied with considerable grace. We then went into the berochoh, where he declined the wine in favour of a cup of hot water and shortly afterwards he addressed the press corps and the huge crowd outside who had been waiting patiently but excitedly for his appearance. He spoke at length on his hopes for the new democracy.

After the magnificently impressive inauguration ceremony, we met quite frequently on diverse occasions from the Gun-Free South Africa's patrons appeal to him for support, to the opening of the Jewish National Fund Park at Mamelodi, from the launch of his book Long Walk To Freedom to the state banquet in honour of Queen Elizabeth.

I especially recall his speech in praise of Archbishop Tutu at Lenasia on the occasion of the Peace Lecture organised by the World Conference on Religion and Peace. Mandela was recovering from a delicate eye operation — the damage had been caused by years of work in the lime quarries while a prisoner on Robben Island — and every few minutes he had to stop and press a handkerchief to his eyes to dry them.

He did this slowly and deliberately in a thoroughly regal manner. He stopped his discourse, stretched out for the handkerchief on the podium in front of him, dabbed his eyes, then returned the handkerchief to its place. With anyone else the repeated gesture would have been awkward and cumbersome, but he carried it off with truly royal panache.

One has noticed the same nobility during his parliamentary speeches whenever he has stopped for a sip of water. The ordinary and mundane is carried out with majestic grace.

At Lenasia I was given the honour of proposing the vote of thanks, and having expressed wholehearted gratitude to Archbishop Tutu for his insightful lecture, I turned to the president.

"We are all so sorry, sir, that you are having trouble with your eyes,"

I said, "but we want you to know there is nothing wrong with your vision."

When Yitzhak Rabin was cruelly assassinated, the government sent Thabo Mbeki to represent South Africa at the funeral in Jerusalem. But Nelson Mandela made known his wish to be present and to speak at the memorial service organised by the Jewish community.

So on that sad Tuesday evening following the Saturday night murder, a large congregation gathered in the Oxford Synagogue in Johannesburg to pay tribute to the slain Israeli Prime Minister. President Mandela came to show his respects and he was accompanied by a large contingent of government and ANC personalities, including Walter Sisulu and Tokyo Sexwale. In his address, the president highlighted Yitzhak Rabin's great courage, expressed heartfelt admiration for his quest for peace and voiced his hope that the process would not be derailed by his tragic death.

At the end of the moving service, it was announced that the congregation should remain in their places until the president and his entourage had left the synagogue.

Because he is so considerate, Mandela did not go straight out but paused to have a word with the teenagers from the youth movements who had been standing patiently in the aisle throughout the service, holding the flags of South Africa and Israel. As he was going down the line, he was interrupted by a young boy aged about ten, wearing a large black hat, who pushed his way through and stuck out his hand in greeting.

The president took it — he never ignores anyone, however small — and there ensued the following hilarious conversation, overheard by my colleague Rabbi Ivan Lerner of Claremont Shul.

"Tell me, young man, what's your name?" the president asked.

The boy told him.

"And which school do you go to?"

"The Torah Academy," the boy answered with pride.

The president had never heard of this Lubavitch school, but nodded as if he had.

"Very good," he continued. "Tell me, do you study hard?"

The boy's face shone.

"Oh sir," he replied, "I study really hard, morning, afternoon and evening."

"That's fine," said the President, encouragingly. "I want you to know that if you continue studying really hard, one day you may become the president of South Africa."

There was a pause.

"What? Me? Become president?" the startled boy uttered, looking up from beneath his big black hat. "I can't become president. I'm not black."

The president looked down at him.

"Young man," he declared with great seriousness, "this is a democracy. If you study hard, one day you can become the president."

The test of friendship, even with a head of state, hinges on mutual trust. Also on respect — that any differences of opinion will be understood and appreciated — and, of course, that you can tease each other.

At a recent formal function, when everyone else was wearing a suit and tie, Madiba was wearing one of his famous multi-coloured shirts, not with a staid and dignified pattern as he often wears and which are really quite smart, but a garish combination of yellow and purple blotches.

"I wish I had a shirt like that," I joked.

He gave me a wry smile and changed the subject.

When the SABC launched the "Don't Do Crime" campaign at its headquarters in Auckland Park, the president, who is almost always punctual, arrived twenty minutes late. Addressing the invited audience, he explained that his helicopter could not take off from Pretoria due to very heavy thunder and lightning.

"So I apologise for being late," he went on, "and if you want an explanation why heaven sends us such weather" — he waved a hand towards where my wife and I were sitting — "just ask Cyril."

Bishop Peter Storey turned and smiled at me, no doubt somewhat relieved that a rabbi had been asked to account for the quirks of the weather.

On his 79th birthday, Madiba telephoned me early in the morning.

"I need to discuss a serious development with you," he said.

I wished him a happy birthday and told him he should take the day off, but he told me he'd just returned the day before from a state visit to Indonesia and that he had received information that the American members of the International Olympic Committee were likely to vote against Cape Town's bid for the 2004 Games due to fears about safety.

Apparently the news of the recent fire-bomb at the Marin household at Claremont in the Cape had reached the United States, and the "American Jewish lobby" was urging their fellow countrymen on the IOC to spread the word that Cape Town was a dangerous place.

President Mandela was very keen for reasons of morale that Cape Town should succeed in its bid, and as a member of the genial Raymond Ackerman's Olympic Bid Committee I had participated in numerous promotions to give the efforts a boost. We kept reminding everyone that although there were five Olympic rings symbolising the five continents, Africa had never hosted the Games and that our turn was overdue. I even had a specially-knitted kippah, displaying our Cape Town Olympic logo.

So I understood Madiba's concern, and we discussed various solutions including publicising in the United States that the fire-bomb was an isolated incident that should not be exaggerated. We were not to know at the time that the Cape bid was doomed in any event. From the results of the ballot, it was clear that most of the African representatives, for reasons which may not have been altogether praiseworthy, voted against South Africa.

Purely by chance some two weeks later, on a completely different issue, I approached him for help. On a matter which could have affected the safety of our Jewish community (but which subsequently turned out to be harmless), I was asked by the Jewish Board of Deputies to seek the president's intervention so that the truth could be discovered. He proved altogether helpful in smoothing the way, so that within a matter of hours the deputies' anxieties were allayed.

Several months before it happened, I was privileged to know the best kept secret in the country: the marriage of Nelson Mandela to Graca Machel.

Madiba telephoned me towards the end of March, 1998 and after a brief chat asked me to reserve the date, 18th July, as he wanted me to attend a special meeting on that day. After I had put the 'phone down, I checked my luach and discovered that the date, which was of course his 80th birthday, coincided with Shabbat.

So I immediately called back and told him that while I had to respect him as president of our country, I owed higher respects to the good Lord. He laughed and said he would try to make alternative arrangements for the previous day.

Two months later, in May, I was part of a delegation from the Inter-Religious Commission against Crime And Violence in the Cape which met the president in the cabinet room to urge him to request the authorities concerned to take more drastic measures to restore law and order. Our chairman, Archbishop Winston Ndungane, had asked me to "open the batting" by outlining our proposals. Madiba listened intently, and before replying in detail looked at me across the table.

"Cyril, after the meeting I need to speak to you."

After the press conference following the meeting, I duly went up to him. He took me aside from the others.

"You remember July 18th?" he asked.

"Of course," I replied.

"Well," he whispered, "I'm going to marry Graca Machel on that day."

I gave him a big hug, said I was delighted at the news and wished them both well. He emphasised that the event must be kept strictly secret. The moment was caught by a photographer from the Cape Times which published it the next day with a caption wondering what we were so happy about.

Speculation was widespread regarding the possible marriage, but

Parks Mankahlana, the presidential spokesman, vehemently denied the rumours and consistently brushed off all media enquiries.

On Thursday evening, 16th July, the President called me.

"Cyril, you remember what I told you about this weekend? Well, my wife-to-be and I would be delighted if you would come to my Houghton home tomorrow afternoon with your dear wife, and give us a blessing."

He explained that the wedding ceremony would take place on Saturday afternoon, but he wanted the involvement of all the religious denominations, so he was fitting me in beforehand. He repeated the need for secrecy.

So the next afternoon we duly dodged the press outside his home, and once safely in the lounge had the pleasure of meeting Graca, a really charming and intelligent lady. The only people present, apart from us, were the official reporter and photographer, the presidential spokesman and a senior bodyguard.

I gave them a rich blessing — that they should enjoy deep contentment for many years to come. Due to the tenderness of their personalities and the heartwarming care they always showed to others, I expressed the confident hope that they would achieve inner peace in their relationship together and abundant joy in their devoted companionship.

It was short and simple, and they laughed when I told them to kiss.

We had drinks and chatted and it was all rather delightful. On the way out I asked Mankahlana what he was going to say when the press found out about the wedding. He smiled and said he would cope with the situation.

One of Madiba's most endearing characteristics is his remarkable lack of pomposity and self-importance. The best-known and most beloved of the world's leaders, when he does anyone a favour he makes it appear the other way round. If the president of any other country had asked the Chief Rabbi to attend his wedding on a Saturday and been told it was not possible for religious reasons, that president would have been annoyed. Not so Madiba. He made special arrangements on that Friday afternoon to include the Jewish faith in the nuptials, and subsequently told a mutual acquaintance that I had done him the favour of fitting the blessing in before the Jewish Sabbath.

Having denounced the "false rumours" that the President was going to get married on his 80th birthday, and having called the police on the Saturday morning to remove the press corps on vigil outside the house, Mankahlana had a lot of explaining to do when at 4pm that Saturday afternoon Thabo Mbeki announced that the wedding had taken place.

The press went crazy, howled at the deceit, dubbed Mankahlana "Parks Pinocchio" and called for his dismissal. It was pointed out that although I had been there on Friday afternoon to bless the couple, on Saturday morning South African and foreign journalists were once again told there would be no wedding. Charged that his credibility as presidential spokesman had suffered irreparable damage, Mankahlana insisted that people — even a presidential couple — are entitled to their privacy.

On his short tour of Israel in October 1999, during which he introduced me to everyone as "my Rabbi," his statements on the Middle East situation were considered simplistic by many Israeli commentators. Russel Gaddin, the level-headed national chairman of the board of deputies, and I pointed out that the commentators failed to recognise how highly Mandela rates peace above all else and that his approach is to try and cut through the problems in order to reach a lasting solution. He not only asked for a purposeful Israeli approach to the whole "peace process," but impressed on the Palestinians the vital necessity of adjusting their mindset regarding Israel.

So which of Madiba's many qualities predominates? Is it the magnetic charisma, the innate charm, the easy air of authority of the natural leader, the amazing workload even in "retirement," his ready comprehension of complicated political affairs?

For me, it is his humanity, which is extended so naturally to all, especially the young. Great men have time for little children, and despite the rigorous demands of his office, I know often he has gone out of his way to help the blind, the maimed and the sick among them. As he was leaving a public function some years ago, a young white boy who was blind stopped him and asked that since he could not see him but wanted to touch him, could he run his hands over Madiba's face?

The patience shown by Madiba as he knelt down in fulfilment of the request, and the sheer joy on the blind boy's face, made it the moment of a lifetime.

At the opening of the Anne Frank Exhibition in Johannesburg, we were fascinated to learn from him that her Diary was one the most well-thumbed books on Robben Island: the inmates could so easily identify with her predicament, a young girl caught up in inhuman surroundings who yet dared to hope.

Nelson Mandela, after years of incarceration, has shown the world the way towards reconciliation, how to embrace one's fellows and reach out towards a better future. He has taught us all what it means to be a human being.

9. Much Truth, Little (So Far) Reconciliation

I couldn't believe my ears. While making a light lunch in our Cape Town flat, I was listening on the radio to the first hearings of the Truth and Reconciliation Commission.

The simultaneous translation from Xhosa was being given in a flat, unemotional voice but the details of the testimony were horrific enough. I could not believe that human beings could do such things to each other.

When the TRC was first mooted, there was consternation among many whites and a feeling of unease in the Jewish community. It was considered a mistake to probe the past; we had managed almost miraculously to achieve a non-racial democracy, why jeopardise further development by going backwards instead of forwards?

I disagreed with this view. I believed that we would be building the future on a false foundation if we failed to investigate and as far as possible uncover what had happened during the apartheid era. My problem was with the juxtaposition of finding out the truth on the one hand and the desired aim of promoting reconciliation on the other. These seemed to me antithetical companions.

At a conference of politicians, lawyers and clergymen to discuss the whole ethos of the TRC before the commission itself was set up, I expressed the view that "the more truth we discover, the less likely we will be able to reconcile. Exposure may well prove divisive."

I was promptly attacked as a "conservative" who failed to understand the pain of the victims, a pain that had somehow to be overcome prior to the building of our Rainbow Nation. Archbishop Hurley, just retired from Durban, agreed with me that if a proper job were done in uncovering the horrors of the apartheid era, it might well prejudice the chance of good relationships in the future.

Dr Alex Boraine, the TRC's deputy chairman, subsequently told me that he was convinced that as the aim was for restorative, not retributive, justice, we could indeed, once the bitter truth had been established, move onwards and upwards to a genuine process of reconciliation. Archbishop Tutu kept emphasizing that reconciliation based on falsehood, on avoiding the reality of all that happened, could never be a true form of reconciliation and would not last.

Reconciliation means that you achieve a point at which individuals, communities and groups are able to relate to each other without the baggage of the past interfering — this is because there has been either expiation or reparation or they have come to some kind of mutual understanding. However, in South Africa, now that the commission has finished its work, I feel that while justice has more or less been done regarding "the truth," reconciliation is still some way off.

Reconciliation between individual perpetrators and individual victims was partially achieved at some of the hearings, but the much wider area of relationships between the white beneficiaries of apartheid and the huge black population which suffered, and the other population groups in between, has hardly begun. So deep are the divisions along both racial and economic lines that South Africans cannot be considered to be much closer in any significant way as a result of the commission's work.

The task of true reconciliation, critical to the kind of future this country will have, still awaits us. Although a degree of understanding has been achieved and there was a marked absence of retaliation and vengeance, the long process to bring us all together in a workable way has hardly begun.

Amnesty is another problem. The defence forces and the police had apparently insisted to FW de Klerk that they would refuse to be part of the deal that gave birth to the new dispensation unless amnesty was a possibility. But the grounds on which amnesty have depended — full disclosure, and that the acts committed were in pursuit of political ends — were faulty. It was with horror that all lovers of justice learned that the perpetrators of the St James Church massacre and the murderers of Amy Biehl had been granted amnesty and released from prison. Serious repercussions for the rule of law are inherent in these decisions, in addition to which the commission's own adherence to the Norgaard principles was breached because victims in both cases were innocent civilians.

Nevertheless the revelation of the truth can be some kind of consolation and a first step on the long road to healing; people now know "what he did to me". That the deep pain has been assuaged is, of course, another matter, on top of which most of the victims and other relatives are dissatisfied with the meagre reparations, if any, distributed so far.

Regarding the involvement of religious communities with the commission, initially written statements were requested. The answers to the set questions were somewhat predictable and the exercise proved anodyne. Then we were told that each faith community would be summoned to special three-day religious hearings in East London to submit an oral explanation of its standpoint.

We suspected correctly that this would turn out to be a huge "confessional" exercise, from the Dutch Reformed Church which had colluded with the Nationalist government's racist policies to the minority religions, the "white" ones that had acquiesced in, or passively accepted, the apartheid regime. Moreover, black advancement in almost all religious structures had been painfully slow. In such an atmosphere, it would have been ludicrous and simply untrue to try to substantiate the view, often put to me by Jewish leaders, that "there was nothing to apologise for".

I met with the Board of Deputies and we decided that while we could justifiably make mention of the leading Jewish activists in the struggle to defeat apartheid, we would also admit the tacit acceptance of it by the general Jewish community.

In the hall where the hearings were taking place, Archbishop Tutu, the chairman, began the religious session with an apology for the Christian dominance of the South African scene, a dominance which had not always allowed respectful and fair treatment of other religions. On several occasions previously I had heard him on this theme and been most impressed with his breadth of view.

"What was the good Lord supposed to be doing before the Christian saviour came along — having a sleep?" he asked, a rhetorical question which allowed serious weight to be given to other denominations.

Nevertheless, Faried Esack, the maverick Muslim theologian, began his submission by berating Tutu for expressing such views while sitting before us "in his canonicals in a church hall".

Our team consisted of Marlene Bethlehem, the national chairperson of the Jewish Board of Deputies, my assistant Rabbi Ron Hendler and my colleague Rabbi Lewis Furman — both South African-born Rabbis, a fact I considered important for the purposes of the submission — and me. In our hotel the previous evening we had burned the midnight oil, polishing up our presentation and deciding exactly where to place the emphasis. At first light we continued our intense discussions.

Tutu welcomed us warmly and asked me to give the Jewish submission. Early on in my presentation I said,

"One of the greatest things that has happened in our country is that principles, concepts and values which are normally considered abstract have come gloriously alive in these historic times that we live through. The brotherhood and sisterhood of the human family has taken on increased meaning. Everyone knows the word 'Simunye,' — we must try to be one. The TRC has given new meaning to wrongdoing and forgiveness. These are not abstract, ethereal notions, but they are notions that get to the heart of the past of our country and to the soul of its future. The interfaith dialogue has moved beyond mere tolerance, discussion and debate to allow us collectively to try to create the building blocks for the future ..."

Proceeding to the crux of the matter I stated that "I would like to pinpoint the failings, as far as the Jewish community is concerned, of all that happened in the apartheid era. The Jewish community did not initiate apartheid. Many in the Jewish community did not agree with apartheid. Almost everyone in the Jewish community had a kind of awkward tension about apartheid. But most members of the Jewish community benefited in one way or another from apartheid."

I quoted Steven Friedman, the Director of the Centre for Policy Studies:

"No Jew who lived in South Africa during the apartheid period can possibly claim that his or her circumstances today are not in some measure a result of apartheid. Anyone who succeeded in business benefited from a right to economic activity which was denied others. Anyone who received a professional qualification, enjoyed a place at school, college or university which was denied to the majority on racial grounds alone. Anyone who enjoyed an authentic Jewish family life did so in a home which persons not classified as white, could neither own, nor occupy, save as a hired servant in which case they were not permitted to enjoy a family life of their own. Any member of our community who found a job in a corporation; or who was a skilled artisan probably occupied a post, from which those classified non-white were barred ... This context creates a profound personal and collective responsibility for every apartheid-reared Jew for it raises the possibility that their attainments today have been achieved only because of apartheid's role in denying to others what we now enjoy ourselves."

I was halfway through this quotation when Archbishop Tutu suddenly stopped me. Our team was taken aback because they thought he was going to protest at something I had said. But he leaned down and told me that I was speaking at such a rate that while my presentation was highly articulate the translators into Zulu and Xhosa and other South African languages had signalled to him that they could not possibly keep up with my speed.

It is a weakness of mine that I tend to speak too quickly and I had become so wrapped up in what I was saying that I had not realised that I had gone past the speed limit. So I slowed down.

Then I said: "In that the Jewish community benefited from apartheid, an apology must be given to this commission."

Having next quoted Professor Kadar Asmal who had several months before saluted the Jewish heroes of the anti-apartheid struggle, commenting that "the Jewish community of South Africa has produced proportionately more heroes in the struggle against apartheid than any other so-called white group," I mentioned that members of the Jewish community had also participated significantly in various protest groupings such as the Five Freedoms Forum, Jews for Justice in Cape Town, Jews for Social Justice in Johannesburg and the Black Sash.

As a prime failure of the general Jewish community had been one of passivity and silence, I went on to deal with the question of what silence connotes. It may be acquiescence, accommodation, cowardice or fear, but it may also be a question of discretion.

Here I quoted a Talmudic passage from Tractate Shabbat — this fascinated the many clergymen who were sitting as Commissioners — that debates the circumstances in which keeping silent in face of other people's misfortune may or may not be justified. I concluded this section with the normative view that "It is insufficient to stand apart from violations of human rights, and dissociation is inadequate where vocal protest is urgently called for and positive steps must be taken to rectify injustice".

Turning to the positive side I wished the commission to know about the extensive upliftment programmes which the Jewish community was undertaking, and gave different examples of the educational, welfare and agricultural endeavours of Tikkun. "We are applying Jewish skills, resources, expertise and know-how to be of maximum benefit to the upliftment programme ... We are trying to build bridges."

In conclusion I called for the opposite of apartheid.

"Finally, I want to say this: it's our job as religious people — if I may be bold to say so, the job of all of us — to try to apply the antidotes. What has emerged from the TRC hearings these past many months is horrendous, and the horror has affected us all. There is no one who has listened in on the radio or who very humbly has come to sit at the back and heard the testimony who hasn't been moved to tears. Because we have had here a record of inhumanity — the worst things that human beings can do to other human beings.

"What we need in our country now is to change because of that — to display the best that human beings can do to fellow human beings, not the hurt and the torture and the shame, but the love and the friendship and the mutual help to lift our country up. If apartheid was divisive, the antidote is building bridges, and coming together — a togetherness which will spell the great future of our country."

We thought the presentation to be quite adequate, and Professor Piet Meiring, a theologian of Pretoria University who was instrumental in organising the religious hearings, commented later that it was a clear, honest and valuable contribution to the proceedings.

We then had to answer the commissioners' questions which were insightful, such as wanting to know our Jewish community's viewpoint about the TRC. Rabbi Furman answered:

"I think that all that has emerged from the Truth Commission has deepened the sense of shame that we feel for being silent during that time. I think we have come to realise that apartheid was much more than an idiosyncratic political system and the brutality that has been exposed now is very similar to the brutality that our ancestors experienced in the past. I also think that the sense of shame has deepened my generation's commitment to inspire constructive action in the future."

The Reverend Bongani Finca then leaned over and looking straight at me asked my view on the issue of a wealth tax which had been suggested previously by Professor Eugene Terreblanche.

I answered as follows:

"That is a very pertinent question. Clearly equalisation is a very important issue. We in South Africa have topped the league for the last five years in the difference between the haves and the have nots. The biggest chasm in the world is here in South Africa. It is not in Asia or South America, but here. We have been top of the league according to United Nations figures. So clearly there is a responsibility. I am not an economist — only a preacher — but I have already heard favourable comment over the weekend from some Jewish businessmen. It was at a reception on Sunday and these businessmen said it would be only fair and proper if there was some kind of wealth tax in order to re-distribute wealth. There were one or two fears mentioned because we already are the most highly taxed country in the world in real terms. There was also a feeling that it may prove to be a disincentive for investment. I personally have always said, living in Johannesburg where so many white-owned houses have swimming pools and there is not even one public swimming pool in Alexandra, that the situation is obscene and immoral.

"I would put my weight behind the suggestions made last week. Whether my voice would be persuasive enough, I am not sure. But I feel that religious communities have to endorse practical programmes for re-distribution."

We were then thanked and dismissed, but I soon realised, when I was accosted by one of the many reporters, that my support for the wealth tax was going to hit the headlines. Even though Professor Terreblanche's suggested tax was minuscule, the very idea had ruffled the feathers of all those who would have to pay it if it was introduced. It is paradoxical to say the least that the black majority of our country usually demands much less than the white minority expects, while at the same time the white minority reacts with horror as if the end of the world has come every time they are asked to put their hand in their pocket.

Needless to say I was subjected to a barrage of criticism, and pressure was put on the Board of Deputies to disagree publicly with my views. To her credit, Marlene Bethlehem firmly resisted, and issued a statement saying how impressed all those present had been with my submission. As I have continually emphasized the necessity of the haves helping the have nots, it would have been quite hypocritical of me to have categorically rejected the wealth tax. With hindsight such an answer would also probably have caused a great deal of anti-semitism. In any event, I instinctively felt that the TRC in its conclusions would recommend some form of wealth tax. In the event, not only did they suggest that, but also five more similar taxes, including a once-off levy on corporate and private income and that each company listed on the Johannesburg Stock Exchange should make a once-off donation of one percent of its market capitalisation.

Subsequent to the religious hearings, Rabbi Hendler and I gave input to the Reparation and Rehabilitation Committee with specific regard to trying to bridge the cultural divide between initiators of upliftment projects and the recipients, and to ways and means of breaking down the reluctance of many advantaged towards being of practical assistance to the disadvantaged.

The TRC was moderately successful. I believe it formed an important part of the growing world-wide movement towards political and national accountability. Judge Richard Goldstone has done humanity a service by ensuring that the perpetrators of atrocities in Rwanda and the former Yugoslavia be brought to book, while the attempts to extradite Pinochet to Spain are a salutary reminder that dictators may have to account years later for their actions. That the world no longer stands idly by while human rights are being violated was demonstrated by Nato's intervention in Kosovo, though of course there has unfortunately been scant intervention in central Africa or, for that matter, in Burma and Tibet.

The TRC examined the past, exposed a multitude of horrors, and certainly helped to clear the air. Whether this knowledge of the past improves our ability to move forward together to build a better country remains to be demonstrated.

10. EGBOK!

Is Judaism optimistic or pessimistic?

Given the history of pogrom and persecution over so many centuries, it would not be surprising if an innate and engrained sense of hopelessness engulfed the Jewish frame of mind and found fixed expression within the faith itself.

Yet the tendency favours the optimistic approach. At the time of creation, G-d Himself pronounces a positive appraisal: "And G-d saw all that he had made and behold it was "tov me'od" — exceedingly good." And at the end of time, when all humankind will have progressed in harmony and peace to achieve its goal, the "golden age" of the Messiah will come to pass. The world will not end with a whimper nor in disarray, but with the glorious establishment of the Kingdom of Heaven on earth.

So in between times, why be gloomy?

True, the Talmud tells us about the over two-year long dispute between the schools of Hillel and Shammai as to whether it were better for man not to have been created than to have been created. The conclusion is defeatist — it were better for man not to have been created. But the verdict may have been occasioned by the acute difficulties of the times, and in any event is redeemed by a characteristic addendum — since man has been created, let him behave himself!

In more positive vein, the Talmud quotes a popular saying: "A person should pray for peace even to the last shovelful of earth," that is until the last clod of earth is thrown on one's grave, meaning that one should never despair — never, not even to the last moment — of Divine mercy.

Like a golden thread this optimistic outlook weaves its way through Jewish history. A remarkable instance is provided by Jeremiah the prophet, who in the year before the destruction of the First Temple by the Babylonians, redeems a field in his native village near to Jerusalem so that it will remain in the family. The enemy was already approaching and the land was worthless.

But he pays "seventeen shekels of silver," the full market price in normal times, to redeem it, for he looked beyond the darkness of inevitable defeat to the dawn of Israel's restoration, when houses and fields would once again be freely bought and sold by the people.

The selfsame defiant and inextinguishable hope shines through Anne Frank's famous Diary. Trapped like a bird in a cage in the narrow attic in Amsterdam's Prinsengracht, all too aware of the of the Nazi tyranny around her, her lively spirit refused to succumb to the horror. Never giving up her resolute trust in humanity, she felt able to write: "In spite of everything I still believe that people are really good at heart."

Whether a sufficient degree of optimism surrounds the future of South Africa, and therefore of its Jewish community, is highly debatable. Opinions seem to vacillate from one extreme to the other, from the disaster scenario which, ignoring areas of undoubted achievement, writes off any chance of it coming right — "What makes you think South Africa is any different from all the other African countries?" — to a utopian vision that blissfully disregards very real problems.

That the equilibrium — assuming there is one in this volatile situation — can easily be disturbed was brought home to me in no uncertain terms on Rosh Hashanah two years ago. Wishing to be positive on the first evening of the New Year, and to counteract the negativity which was so prevalent, I delivered a purposeful sermon in the popular Pine Street Synagogue on the theme "yi'heyeh tov" ("Everything will be all right").

I cited the lovely custom of dipping an apple in honey at the beginning of all our New Year meals as an augury of well-being, of goodness and sweetness, in the coming year. This was not I insisted anything to do with superstition — Jewish people are not allowed to be superstitious, keinenhora! — nor was it an exercise in wishful thinking. Rather it was a time-honoured affirmation that the future would be better than the past, that the tsoros of the past year would disappear, giving way to the multiple blessings of the year ahead.

Illustrating the necessity of looking on the bright side, I mentioned the bravery of the Marin family whose Claremont home had been destroyed by a fire bomb. They had all overcome the horrendous incident and had summoned the courage to face the future with confidence.

Waxing eloquent, I went on to insist that we must never give way to despair, that we did not have the right to give up, that we must not allow a huge question mark to hang over our future. "If we do not believe we have a future, then, G-d forbid, we will not have one," I opined.

The derashah was politely received and there were some nods of approval, even those firmly disagreeing with the tenor of my remarks appreciating the motivation which prompted them.

The morning after Yom Tov a woman telephoned. She was not angry but clearly very upset.

"I want you to know, Rabbi, that my son was murdered last month when his car was hijacked. So I could not agree with a word you said. In fact I cried all the way through your sermon."

She paused to collect herself. "I can see why you want to build up confidence in the future. It's part of your job as leader. You even sounded as if you really believe there's a chance." There was another pause. "But Rabbi, you will forgive me, won't you, if I cannot identify with it."

I could not think of anything sensible to respond to her, so apologised for having upset her, albeit unintentionally, and wished her long life.

Even for those of us fortunately not victims, putting a good slant on things may not be easy. But it is not impossible.

A balanced assessment of what has been achieved since 1994 would include the government's delivery of water to over three million people — as a patron of Professor Kadar Asmal's National Water Conservation Campaign, I am full of admiration at the manner in which he successfully tackled the host of problems involved in clean water provision — and the setting-up of some 567 clinics throughout the country for primary health care.

The government's fiscal discipline — a great tribute to Trevor Manuel's determined handling of the economy — has withstood the volatility of world markets. In the key area of job creation agreement has been reached so that government, business, trade unions and community organisations have together embarked on ambitious, labour-intensive programmes which promise more opportunities for the younger generation.

We now have diplomatic contact with 164 countries around the world and, despite the prevalence of crime, tourism is prospering so that we have progressed in the table of Countries To Be Visited from being 53rd in the world in 1990 to being 25th in 1998.

No one is suggesting everything is rosy and it will take several generations before the deprivation of the under-privileged is removed, but the process is under way and the huge concerted effort to eradicate poverty, motivated by an almost across-the-board consensus, has begun in earnest.

Nor should the negative factors adversely affecting the Jewish community be allowed to obviate the many positive ones.

On the one hand, the South African Jewish community is declining numerically, primarily due to emigration, although the figure for "remigration" is relatively high at 13%: thirteen people out of every 100 who leave this country, return here. (The vocabulary of migration is three-fold: emigration for those who leave, remigration for those who leave and come back again, and semigration for those who move from Johannesburg to Cape Town.)

On the other hand, the community is for the most part cohesive and closely knit. The extent of assimilation and the rate of intermarriage are statistically the lowest in the diaspora. A Jewish social welfare worker once told me she knew of a Jewish "drug group" in a fashionable district of Johannesburg which insisted on indulging with fellow Jews only: they would not smoke dagga with non-Jews! In a country as heterogeneous as South Africa, the external pressure is also a decided factor, each different ethnic and religious group huddling together for warmth.

The Jewish community is very centralised and well organised. It enjoys the full range of synagogal, Zionist, cultural and charitable organisations, most of which are vibrant. Despite the gradual reduction and eventual withdrawal of official subsidies to Jewish educational and welfare institutions, the community is still sufficiently wealthy, and sufficiently generous, to be able to cope.

Additionally, on the plus side the community is represented in the highest echelons of government and the judiciary, and Jews play a prominent role in the economy and in public life. While the government of the day is favourably disposed towards the Jewish community, on the negative side it is also favourably disposed to the establishment of a Palestinian State.

From time to time, as is only to be expected, there are anti-semitic statements and incidents — the Welsh-Jewish novelist Bernice Rubens accurately describes anti-semitism as "a light sleeper" — but by and large any expression of bigotry and racism is frowned upon and in fact illegal.

Concerning every aspect apart from crime, for every problematic and unsuccessful feature there are two to three reliable and effective ones. In the comparatively short time during which the new dispensation has been operative, our circumstances have been characterised by an inevitable mix of advance and setback, progress and failure. Only the immature expect everything to come right overnight. Only the blinkered fail to recognise where improvement is being attained.

A generation gap is noticeable between the older members of the community, many of whom, to use the telling phrase of Mervyn Smith, President of the African Jewish Congress, are living in "internal exile," and the younger generation, a sizeable section of which is eager and willing to embrace the new South Africa. When the highly competent Rabbi Yossy Goldman, Chairman of the Southern African Rabbinical Association, produced a pamphlet proclaiming "Fourteen Reasons for Staying in South Africa," it was largely frowned on by the older generation, many of whom are literally "yesterday's people," but praised by the younger generation.

In this situation our attitude is crucial.

Every transitional period is fraught with difficulty, but if we maximise the problems and downplay the achievements, if our approach is half-hearted and apathetic, if we permit gloom and pessimism to debilitate us, if we are struck with inertia, if we allow all our hopes to be frustrated by despairing of ever reaching a sustainable future, we shall never overcome.

Instead we should do everything possible to foster and encourage a spirit of optimism, which will activate us to participate willingly and fully in the exhilarating challenge of nation building. So very much has been achieved in our country in the past few years. We have been through the most remarkable, redemptive process of transition to democracy, a thrilling and bloodless revolution. Despite all the tensions, unity in diversity is gradually becoming the reality.

Of course it is likely that the South Africa of today and tomorrow will involve far greater risks than elsewhere, but it also offers far greater opportunities and the deeply satisfying reward of personally participating in the historic pursuit of building a better society. To capture for oneself the essence of the challenge, to take it on board and go for it, is the call of the hour.

In contradistinction to some whites who bemoan their loss of status, the reduction of their privileges and the fall in their standard of living, most black people — whose circumstances have not yet improved in any significant measure — are positive.

We should all join hands and toyi-toyi together on the road ahead.

Before the first elections in 1994, a radio station coined the acronym EGBOK. Notwithstanding the negative, racist and vulgar definitions people made up for it before its true definition was announced, it actually stands for, as we know, "Everything's Gonna Be OK".

If we can become believers in the future, maybe it will.

V

FESTIVE

1. New Year Wishes

There are two things wrong with the standard New Year greetings, printed on thousands of cards and so cheerfully expressed in most conversations: "A Happy New Year and Well Over the Fast".

As everyone who has been to cheder knows, the Hebrew phrase Shanah Tovah means not A Happy New Year but "A Good New Year".

Now if one's happiness derives from goodness — being good makes us feel happy — then of course the greeting is in order. But I know an awful lot of people who are very happy when they aren't being good!

Moreover, I have never understood the meaning of the phrase "Well over the Fast". Does it mean *well* over the fast — that is, that we should not, G-d forbid, suffer any ill effects from fasting? Or does it rather mean well *over* the fast — thank G-d it's come and gone for another year?

It really is an inappropriate phrase, because the Torah specifically instructs us that on Yom Kippur we must "afflict ourselves". We are supposed to have an uneasy fast. We are supposed to be reflecting on all the flaws in our character, about all the things we did in the past year which we shouldn't have done, about all the things we should have done which we didn't do. "A Happy New Year and Well Over the Fast" indeed!

As the old year vanishes and the new year beckons, of course all of us have hopes and wishes, desires and dreams. A major purpose of the Rosh Hashanah festival is to help us contemplate, define and pin-point what we really want from life, exactly what we request from G-d and precisely what we should seek from ourselves.

There is a host of obvious wishes. First and foremost for health and strength throughout the coming year for the members of our own family, and for all our friends and associates. With typical Jewish optimism, we even pray for the health of those who, unfortunately, are grievously ill: Abi Gezunt, as we say in Yiddish, "Just be healthy!"

And we pray for sustenance, material success, in the coming year.

Our shares should go up, and — please G-d — the rand should not keep going down.

One suspects there are those who have two prayers. Their own business should thrive in the year ahead, while that of their competitors should not enjoy quite such a good year. And the tour operator prays for sunshine and the umbrella manufacturer for rain, and the good Lord, with merciful providence, will answer — albeit not simultaneously — both requests.

And everyone hopes in the coming year for nachas, a lovely Hebrew word denoting "joyous satisfaction" and "elation of spirit," usually provided by children and grandchildren, and flowing especially from their achievements. In standard 10, coming up to matric, may they get As in all subjects (and as Bobba will tell you, they're good-looking with it).

Those fortunate enough to be celebrating a family celebration in the new year pray all will go well on the great day. The parents of the barmitzvah boy fervently hope their son's voice will not break before he has to sing for the first time in synagogue; the mother of the bride prays her daughter will look her best, resplendent under the chupah. And that Aunt Beckie will not upset too many members of the family.

And those who have no simchah to look forward to, earnestly add the extra prayer that in the year ahead their son or daughter should find their life's partner — Miss Exactly Right or Mr Almost Perfect — so that they, too, may have cause to celebrate.

There are of course more subtle wishes, yearnings of the heart, of the mind and of the soul. The lonely pray for company, the busy pray for solitude. The research worker, trying for years, prays for a breakthrough. The artist prays for the flow of inspiration. The mediocre pray for the touch of brilliance to their lives. And the unloved pray for love.

Everyone has dreams and hopes and wishes — it's a New Year!

A higher level of wishes is contained in the prayers we offer in the synagogue during the High Holy Days, the New Year and the Fast of Atonement. To be sure the pleas for health and strength, prosperity and success are valid, and they have their rightful place in our petitions to heaven for the coming year.

But — and the point is vital — long before we ask G-d for personal blessings, we petition Him in the Amidah to grant three special wishes: one for the world, one for the Jewish people, and one for the society in which we live. These petitions are supremely relevant.

The first wish, for all humanity, is that G-d should impose His fear throughout the world. It seems a strange request. The doctrine of the fear of G-d is one of the most unpopular and unfashionable in religious teaching. We ought no longer, it is maintained, hold before people's eyes the fear of heaven.

Ah, but suppose the fear of G-d does not mean the fear of invoking divine punishment but instead fear of desecrating G-d's name, the dread that heaven may form a bad opinion about our behaviour, the valid fear of what G-d thinks of us. The crucial contemporary weakness of our civilisation is the very absence of such fear, a lack of recognition that we are constantly answerable to the higher authority of the Sovereign of the Universe.

When the fear of G-d, the forerunner to the love of G-d, spells obedience to the dictates of conscience, when it means we tremble before Him, afraid of behaving in an unworthy or disreputable manner, such fear is a virtue and an ennobling factor for our civilisation.

Where there is no fear of G-d, there is fear of man. Without the consciousness that G-d looks down on all we do, there is no limit to the evil humans can (and do) perpetrate. Tyranny reigns, violence erupts and there is a trampling of the most basic rights. Each afraid of the other, instead of fearing G-d, man makes a jungle of the world that is supposed to be a garden.

The second wish, a Jewish one, is for honour for the people of Israel, and for the blessings of "joy to Thy Holy Land and gladness to Thy city". In synagogues throughout the world Jewish people pray every New Year for Israel, seeking divine help in the solution of seemingly insoluble problems, for an amelioration of the vexed situation which has gone on for so long, for an end to the heartache, that this year Israel should be blessed with real, authentic, palpable, lasting peace.

A country only the size of the Kruger National Park, Israel has achieved more in fifty years than any country in world history; Israel has the right to exist with honour among the community of nations. The dream of a peaceful, as well as a successful, Israel is passionately expressed at the outset of the year.

The third and last wish is for true happiness — "then shall the righteous see and be glad, and the upright shall exult and the pious triumphantly rejoice".

No generation has pursued happiness with such determination as ours, and how elusive a target it has proved to be. So many avenues of gratification have been sought — drugs of tempting variety, orgies of permissiveness, the frantic search for new sensation. Yet all the time we run away from reality, at every turn mistaking pleasure for happiness.

Happiness, to be genuine, must engage the whole personality, the spirit and the soul of the human being. It is to be found in involvement, not escape; in using time, not killing it. The sense of contentment we invariably experience when serving G-d and reaching out to be of service to others surpasses any fleeting joy in pandering to ourselves.

So we do not pray that everyone in the whole wide world become happy, rather that the righteous, who deserve it, should be happy. And with that prayer comes the hope that we, too, some day will join their illustrious company.

These are worthwhile New Year wishes: for a safer world, for honour for Israel and for deep personal contentment. May they come true for us one year soon.

2. "The New Me"

After forty-five years of loyal service to the same company, the time came for the worker to retire. The chairman of the firm, wishing to emphasise to all members of staff the importance of loyalty and longevity, arranged a lavish farewell party for him. He presented him with the customary gold watch and praised a devoted worker who had remained at the same job for so many years.

"It isn't really true," the old man said in his speech of thanks, "that I've had forty-five continuous years with the firm. I've been at the same job, at the same desk, in the same part of the factory, for all this time. So it's more correct to say that I have had the same year, exactly the same year, forty-five times over."

Judaism is not interested in the passage of time as such, but rather in how we can utilise time in order to make the future an improvement on the past. If each year is merely to be a repeat performance, with the same fixed interests and identical experiences, the same levels of commitment and the same limited horizons, then there is no real cause to celebrate the passing of time. Making a photocopy of one's own life is a terrible waste.

In this light, Rosh Hashanah presents the truly optimistic view that we can all indeed try to change for the better.

Am I making the most of my life? is the striking question it poses in the intense quest to urge us towards self-improvement. Do we really have to go around with our own "Use By" date, with the information stamped on the sole of our right foot — "Best by the end of this year"?

Nevertheless, with their understanding of human nature, the rabbis were very much aware of the many obstacles along the path of trying to become better. The first, and by far the most difficult, is our inability to admit to ourselves that we are not quite as good as we think we are. Just as the mirror at the fun fair distorts our physical image, so an inflated opinion of our personal worth is liable to produce contortions by exaggerating our qualities and underestimating our deficiencies.

The Midrash explains the fact that G-d created us with two eyes, not one or three, so that we would all have one eye to see the good points of everyone around us and the other eye to enable us to see our own faults. Oi, do we mix them up! We are all experts on everyone else's faults, using one eye to scrutinise their behaviour closely, while the other eye blissfully fails to see our own defects and continues to look steadfastly on our limited virtues.

"Oh wad some pow'r the giftie gie us, to see oursels as others see us!" — the poet Robert Burns's rhetorical prayer — is no easy task, the flaws in our own character rarely being acknowledged at source.

Similarly, Rabbi Samson Raphael Hirsch refers in his teaching on repentance to "the little defender" within each of us, which exists side-by-side with our conscience. Whenever we have done anything wrong, and in our heart of hearts we know it, this defender is always able to provide abundant excuses to justify our every action, or a multitude of reasons in mitigation of our conduct.

In hiding from our eyes a true picture of ourselves, we effectively block any chance of self-betterment and remain the prisoners of our own past. A truly honest appraisal of our inner self plus an unflinching scrutiny of our actions are the first vital steps in the struggle to improve, and despite the fact that it goes against the grain, the Jewish New Year demands this incredibly difficult exercise.

A further difficulty, again very much in line with human nature, is that we are all creatures of habit. The Talmud goes so far as to say that if someone commits a sin and then repeats it, that sin becomes permitted to that person. "What on earth are you taking about?" the Talmud remonstrates with itself.

In answer, the Talmud suggests that before the person commits that particular sin for the first time, he or she will have pangs of conscience, will say "Should I?" or "Shouldn't I?", will ask "Am I letting myself down?"

However, once they have dealt with all these questions and committed the sin, the second time round they do not go through the whole process again — so it is as if that sin is no longer forbidden and has become permitted to them. Breaking the force of habit is another stiff challenge in the long road towards repentance.

By far the most unpopular word in today's vocabulary is sin. The old, classical distinction between right and wrong — a clear-cut "Thou shalt" and "Thou shalt not" — an awareness of what is morally acceptable and what is beyond the pale, is no longer operative. Any sense of guilt has been replaced in our time by psychological jargon — neurosis, maladjustment, non-conformity and ambivalence. As a result, responsibility for wrong-doing is placed everywhere, except where it belongs. The higher demands of religion do not stand a chance in this atmosphere which insists that, while there may be wrong-doing, there are never any wrongdoers.

How reactionary our festival prayers seem in comparison with their harping on sin and the need for confession, their insistent emphasis on wrong-doing and the necessity of gaining atonement. Yet, if in any way we wish to become better, we have to recognise the sheer reality of sin, of our propensity to it and our responsibility for it.

Instead of something outside the person always being blamed — that we are the unwitting victims of heredity or the environment, or that our mother gave us the wrong breakfast cereal when we were children — instead of always seeing in front of our eyes a huge sign which reads "It wasn't me!" — we have to bow our head humbly, acknowledge our shortcomings and promise to endeavour to do better in the future.

That we do not have to remain in the rut, but can win a victory over ourselves to become better, is the dynamic annual challenge of the Ten Days of Penitence at the beginning of every year. Finding our true destiny by realising the potential within us can often prove to be an exhilarating, as well as a difficult, exercise.

The renowned mystic, Rabbi Nahman of Bratzlav, once deliberately woke up his congregation by pointing to a certain member of his flock — "Look at this man," he exclaimed, "he's been dead for five years but nobody has bothered to tell him."

In more serious vein, Rabbi Nahman sought to define the agony of the various types of exile. A person may be separated from his or her family, or banished from the country of their birth, or even estranged from G-d, but the worst galut of all, he suggested, was exile from oneself.

Improvement is a life-long pursuit not limited to age. A lovely Chassidic interpretation of the famous phrase in Psalms, "Cast us not off in our old age," re-makes the phrase as "Cast us not off to a time when we feel old". In other words, even when we are old, we should not feel old.

Vital to the success of the New Year is that somehow we ourselves become new.

3.   Following Through

How long does the impact of Yom Tov last?

This is not such a disrespectful question as it first appears and is of some legitimate concern to those who put so much into the preparation of the Holy Days and into officiating during them. Looking round the congregation a few minutes before the end of the fast on Yom Kippur, one often gets the feeling that the entire day of fasting and praying and seeking forgiveness will unfortunately dissipate very quickly.

Some people who do not travel on Yom Kippur park their cars in close vicinity to the shul when they arrive on Kol Nidrei night. As soon as the fast is over, waving cheerful greetings to all and sundry, they dash like mad to their cars — a kind of Jewish Le Mans Sprint — start up the engine as quickly as possible to see who can get away first and then race for home, or to wherever they are breaking the fast.

A half an hour later, whisky in hand and nibbling at their favourite nasherei, all thoughts of the fast are completely and blissfully forgotten.

There is a well-known technique in the world of sport called "following through". Imagine for a moment the striker in football aiming at goal, or a batsman poised to score a four, or golfers driving off from the tee — the movement of all these players must not cease at the moment of impact with the ball. To be effective, they all have to follow through with the action.

What difference does this technique make? one may well ask. Surely the ball has already been struck so that what the sportsman does afterwards is immaterial? Not so. Experience teaches that unless there is the intention of following through and unless that intention is fulfilled, the swing is adversely affected and the ball falls short of the target. What the player does after contact is absolutely crucial to success.

In a very real sense, what we do in the days and weeks after Yom Tov validates our observance of the festive season. If we go straight back to normal, exactly the same as we were before, the whole purpose is defeated. But with a follow through — that is, a fixed resolve to continue the momentum of the Holy Days and allow their impact to influence our lives so that we are carried forward on a higher plane — our keeping of them is worthwhile.

Some spiritual dividend must be apparent: prayer; attending synagogue more often; fitting in the time to attend a weekly shiur; giving at an improved level. Something — anything — as long as it stems from our Yom Tov resolve to reach up for, and achieve, a higher standard.

To help ensure that the festivals do not fade away, a number of quaint customs has arisen in Jewish communities over the centuries and they are diligently observed to this day by many families.

After Succot, the etrog is not thrown away, but its peel is placed in the spice-box to be sniffed at the weekly havdalah ceremony. The fronds of the lulav are preserved from one year to be used as binders in the next. Even the willow, beaten on Hoshanah Rabba is not discarded — the following Passover it is added to the furnace in which the matzah is baked.

Having done one mitzvah with these items, we go on to do another, and thus the flavour of Yom Tov lingers on for many months, the benefit remaining with us.

Similarly, in the field of Torah education, on Simchat Torah we also follow through, reading the beginning of Genesis from a second scroll, a few minutes after we have finished reading the end of Deuteronomy in the first scroll. Could we not have left the last Sidra on its own, and celebrated a glorious climax to the public reading of Scripture? But the Torah, too, is a continuum, precious in its inexhaustibility, and they only may finish who are pledged to restart.

The most important way we follow through is by continuing traditions handed down to us from the past, and that with loving care we in our turn hand them on intact to the next generation. The great enigma of Jewish survival against the odds, argued about by so many philosophers, historians, and theologians, can be solved very simply.

The Jewish people, and Judaism as a religion, have stood the test of time, the beliefs and practices, the values and ideals, spanning the generations. Because to Jewish people the proof that our faith is strong is not just that we keep it. It is that our children do.

4.   The Many Faces of Freedom

A constant source of inspiration, the story of the Children of Israel's exodus from Egypt established a precedent for all humanity.

The Festival of Passover is the most Jewish of festivals in that it celebrates the birth pangs of the people redeemed from the crucible of Egyptian bondage. Yet its message about the real meaning of freedom is valid for everyone today.

No idea is so abused in our modern vocabulary as freedom. In a huge variety of situations, the concept of freedom is invoked as a justification for a particular philosophy, political movement or style of behaviour.

Yet whenever freedom for some is at the expense of others, or wherever freedom connotes licence to do what we want to do and not what we ought to do, then real freedom is tarnished and the precious ideal is made to stand on its head.

Designated "the season of our freedom," Passover celebrates an altogether positive definition. Freedom denotes "liberty" and not "taking liberties" — a wise man once said that the difference between the two is as great as the difference between G-d and gods. Similarly, true freedom is utilised to cultivate the best that is within us. True freedom recognizes obligation and is a blessing to everyone.

When the Children of Israel came up out of Egypt, the Bible tells us that "a mixed multitude went up with them". In addition to the Israelites there were other downtrodden minorities who yearned to be free, but acknowledging that freedom is indivisible, the Israelites did not refuse them but invited them to join with them on the trek to redemption.

Freedom can never be restrictive. The famous German pastor, Martin Neimoller, who was a leader of the religious opposition to Hitler, blamed himself when he was arrested by the Nazis.

He wrote: "In Germany they first came for the communists and I didn't speak up because I wasn't a communist. Then they came for the Jews and I didn't speak up because I wasn't a Jew. Then they came for the trade unionists and I didn't speak up because I wasn't a trade unionist. Then they came for the Catholics and I didn't speak up because I was a Protestant. Then they came for me — and by that time no one was left to speak up."

Many centuries had to pass after the Exodus before the United Nations in 1948 proclaimed the Universal Declaration of Human Rights, re-affirming that "everyone has the right to freedom of opinion and expression; this right includes freedom to hold opinions without interference".

Between the statement of the ideal and its fulfilment there lies a world of anguish, and the cry of the politically and religiously oppressed is still disturbingly widespread in our enlightened times.

Likewise, the most persistent delusion at the beginning of the 21st century is that the individual must be totally free to do what he or she wants to do, to follow their own inclinations.

Life without any discipline can so easily lead, as we know only too well, to disaster. The essential paradox of freedom is that throwing off all restrictions and indulging ourselves does not make us free; rather, we become the slaves to our baser passions.

The rhetorical question "It's my life, isn't it?" may well contain some veracity, but if it means one is free without constraint to follow one's predilections, it usually ends up meaning "It's my life to ruin, isn't it?" As the famous 20th century song puts it - "I'll do it *my* way."

Moreover, the gift of freedom should be utilised to help others. A freedom which is insensitive to suffering, which does not care in any way for the condition of fellow human beings, is deficient. Freedom never means standing on the sidelines, pampering oneself while those around us are hungry.

From personal experience, the Israelite slaves of old understood the nature of suffering, and so their descendants are charged to identify with all who are bereft of comfort and who have less than their fair share of human dignity.

The horrendous details of the current poverty in our country — that more than half the population is below the poverty line, and that a quarter of the children suffer some form of malnutrition — should move all those who are able to take remedial action. Surrounded by urgent need, only the selfish consider themselves totally free to ignore the cry for help.

Thus Passover is a passionate affirmation of the right kind of freedom — a glorious and expansive freedom, a freedom which challenges us to use it wisely, a freedom dedicated to furthering human progress.

So on this festival, Jewish people everywhere deliberately go back 3 500 years to the momentous events surrounding the Exodus, to recapture the agony of slavery and the ecstasy of Divinely-gained freedom, and in order to emphasise the high purposes for which they were rescued.

It is a worthwhile exercise, for in the remembrance of yesterday lies the hope for tomorrow.

5.   The Dance of Pesach

Pesach seems to me to involve three important steps: one backwards, one sideways and one forwards.

The first requirement is a giant step backwards. We travel back 3 500 years to the momentous events accompanying the birth of our people. We return to our roots, go back to our origins, re-live the beginning of it all.

In many different ways Almighty G-d is known to us — we can appreciate Him during prayer in the depths of our soul, we recognise the reflection of His image when our fellow human beings show goodness, and we see Him at work continuously in nature, the super-power of the universe.

But the Jewish experience of G-d is above all in the arena of history when He intervenes on our behalf. Thus the Passover Festival commemorates a historic act of deliverance. We deliberately go back through time to remember the slavery and the redemption, the shame and the honour, the sorrow and the gladness, the freedom and the responsibility, all bound together in the pages of our early history.

Commenting on the Biblical line, quoted in the Haggadah, "It is because of that which G-d did for me when I came forth out of Egypt," the rabbis insist that "in every generation a person must consider himself as if he *personally* came out of Egypt".

Celebrated in Jewish homes throughout the world, the colourful Seder ceremonies are actually living history lessons. The abundant symbols, the unusual menu, the deliberate contrasts, the questions of the children and the answers of the parents, the stimulating toasts — such an impressive re-enactment of the Exodus has vivid impact on the Jewish commitment of young and old alike. Around the home table, the ties that bind us with the past are bonded anew.

A glorious flight of the religious imagination, we bridge the time gap, cross back over the years, so that we become personally involved. We, too, were there at the very beginning! A people which does not know about its past deserves no future, so we deliberately go back to the past to derive strength for the present and impetus for the future, that all our yesterdays may prove a blessing for tomorrow.

The second requirement is a step sideways, a conscious movement out of the small circle of our self-interest towards the wider area of the world around us. This is a direct challenge to us to help those in need. Pesach, the annual reminder of Egyptian slavery, should serve to imbue us with insight into the feelings of the unfortunate and an understanding of their plight. We, whose ancestors were slaves in Egypt, downtrodden, afflicted and robbed of all dignity, should know the heartache of the oppressed. It is quite fascinating that the Seder service begins by pointing to the matzah, the unleavened bread — "This is the bread of affliction our ancestors ate in the land of Egypt" — and then goes on with the invitation, "Let all who are hungry come and eat".

But three-and-a-half millennia separate the two phrases — "the bread of affliction they *used* to eat" and the invitation asking "all who are hungry *now* to come and eat". This apparent non sequitur challenges our social conscience to the core. For the remembrance of past hunger should prompt us to alleviate present hunger.

This step sideways — "to put ourselves in other people's shoes" — is a prerequisite to being of practical help. A doctor cannot treat a patient unless he or she also feels a little pain. A social worker cannot tackle problems if those in trouble are mere case numbers instead of fellow human beings in difficulty. Similarly, the haves cannot assist the have-nots unless they personally identify with their predicament.

Thus Jewish people are deliberately reminded of the afflictions and miseries of the slavery of Egypt, so that the quality of their sensitivity to suffering, annually honed by the observance of Pesach, will become of positive value to the needy around them.

The final requirement is a step forwards. This is a challenge to each of us individually not to stay at the same spiritual level, not to be self-satisfied, but to lift ourselves from the old routine and attempt with every fibre of our being to make some spiritual progress.

The song in praise of G-d's abundant kindness — "Dayyenu! We would have been satisfied" — must never be pronounced in terms of self-satisfaction.

The rabbis consider leavened foodstuffs, which are disallowed throughout the entire festival of Pesach, to be symbolic of sour characteristics. Leaven is regarded as a symbol of fermentation and corruption, and likewise man's tendency to sin is viewed as a process of moral fermentation. They therefore explain the commandment, "No leaven shall be seen with thee," to refer not only to the necessity of destroying all the leaven in the household, but to the necessity of eradicating it from deep within ourselves as well.

What is the point of ridding the whole household of the sour chametz influence and leaving it still within us?

Indeed, the saintly Rabbi Hayyim Yosef David Azulai of Jerusalem used to pray when searching for leaven on the evening before Pesach, "May this candle also light up the innermost recesses of my soul to remove from there all unworthiness and impurity".

So Pesach involves three steps: one backwards into history in order to strengthen our identity; one sideways into the reality of the world around us to inspire us to be of help; and one forwards towards a vision of ourselves, not as we are — but as we can be.

This Pesach dance — a sort of Pesach Tango — is a religious exercise of great importance. If we can perform it, it guarantees that we will truly live up to the idealism encapsulated by the festival. For we then become better as Jewish people, better as human beings and a little better in ourselves.

6.   The Gentle Nudge

If the Ten Commandments were to be given today, how would we react to them?

Three-and-a-half thousand years ago our ancestors assembled at the foot of Mount Sinai, and to their great credit, having previously unconditionally agreed to accept whatever G-d would instruct them, promptly pledged themselves to be committed and faithful to the commandments.

Our response would be somewhat different. For a start, the heavenly marketing techniques — with respect — leave much to be desired. Acceptance nowadays is never automatic. "Ten Commandments? Could we start with five, and see how we get along? Or how about a trial period, say a month, to see whether in fact we like them?"

More than this, if the Revelation were to take place today and the Decalogue to be enunciated for the first time, we would have serious objections to the format, content and indeed to the whole approach.

In this day and age, it grates terribly on the ear to have the law laid down for us in such an authoritative way. We much prefer the gentle nudge, to be coaxed and nursed into commitment. "Come on, try it. It's not so difficult. You can do it. You know you can!" Nowadays we do not need commandments. We want encouragement.

In this connection, the story is told of the small American businessman who bought a little shop and the rights to the one parking lot directly in front of it. The first thing he did was to have No Parking painted prominently on his parking space.

And every morning in the first week when he came to open the shop, another car was already occupying his parking spot, and at considerable inconvenience he had to find an alternative one. So he called in the painter and had the sign changed to Strictly No Parking!

This did not make the slightest difference. So he called in the painter again and this time tried Don't Even Think Of Parking Here! He continued to be pre-empted.

So he thought long and hard, and then asked the painter to paint You Don't Really Want To Park Here, Do You? Lo and behold, the next morning the parking space was empty. He had struck the right note for our age: Don't order people around, make them feel mean rather than guilty.

There is an awesome directness and clarity about the Ten Commandments that is also disconcerting to our modern-day ears. The words actually mean what they say. They are not abstract, avoidable principles, but demand that we actually carry them out.

Between the commandment and the fulfilment of it lies the shadow of our 21st century style of living. "Thou shalt have no other gods beside me" — what, can we not try genetic engineering and cloning ourselves? Play at being G-d? "Remember the Sabbath Day to keep it holy" — but Saturday is a day on which I want to do things that are not necessarily holy. "Thou shalt not commit adultery" — but suppose someone is caught in an unhappy marriage, what is he or she supposed to do? "Thou shalt not steal" — not even from the Receiver of Revenue? Not even a little bit?

There is a well-oiled and widespread evasion routine which goes as follows: "Of course the commandments are valid in theory, but they're not really meant to be put into practice." Pause. "All right, they do require to be put into practice, but they apply to other people, not me." Pause. "Okay, if you insist, they do apply to me as well, but please not now — later, much later, some time in the distant future."

Yet a further drawback is that nowadays we tend to be much more interested in our rights that in our duties. In every area of civil society, the justifiable clamour for rights — human rights, gender rights, constitutional rights, labour rights — must not be allowed to obviate the parallel necessity of fulfilling our obligations. While correcting obvious injustices, and while recognising the crucial and indispensable role of the Bill of Rights, it remains true that the well-being of society rests not only on the protection of the rights of the individual — the individual taking from society — but just as much on the individual's exercise of responsible conduct towards other people.

Because of this imbalance, the Ten Commandments, not a Bill of Rights but a list of obligations, do not have quite the appeal they should have.

So if the Decalogue were to be revealed for the first time today, coming from on high to an unsuspecting world, the reception would be somewhat cool to say the least. These injunctions are too clear-cut — we love the grey areas between the permissible and the indictable. They are too demanding — G-d is our father, He does not also have to be our lawgiver. They interfere with our lives; we can make up our own rules as we go along.

In contradistinction to the Biblical view that the Children of Israel readily accepted the covenant and all its conditions, the Talmud tells us in the name of Rav Avdimi Bar Hama that the Israelites were forced into compliance. Commenting on the phrase, "And they stood beneath the mountain," he states that the people were gathered not at the foot of the mountain, but literally beneath it. This means that the Almighty picked up the whole mountain, suspended it over the heads of all the people, and thundered at them, "If you accept these Commandments, it is well. But if you do not, I shall drop the whole mountain on top of you, and here shall be your graves."

Irrespective of acquiescence, the Ten Commandments had to come to the world. As was the case with the characters in Mario Puzo's The Godfather, they were an offer we could not refuse.

7. Wind Blown Leaves

I have lost at least half-a-dozen Succahs to inclement weather over the years.

More than any other festival in the Jewish calendar, Tabernacles, when we leave the house and try to live, or at least to eat, in the temporary booth in the garden, is subject to the elements.

In the London autumn the wind can often be too strong for the flimsy structure of a do-it-yourself Succah. Sometimes in October it is so cold that some kind of floor covering, old carpeting or cork tiling, is to be highly recommended.

The main enemy is rain. Soaking the branches on top, dripping through to spoil the decorations, making everything so wet and miserable, the festival — designated "the season of our joy" — can be anything but that.

One of the most well-thumbed sections of the Code of Jewish Law are the paragraphs telling what to do when it rains on the first evening of Succot.

How hard does it have to be raining before one is exempt from making Kiddush in the Succah and eating there? If it is bucketing down and you start the meal in the house and then, lo and behold, the rain stops, what do you do? If you are eating in the Succah and it begins to rain, how long do you have to persevere before returning to the comfort of indoors?

In England where pine leaves are used for the traditional s'chach covering — laurel is a far safer bet — the wind and rain combine to ensure that your chicken soup usually has more pine needles than noodles.

Trying in difficult circumstances to fulfil the commandment of living in a temporary booth throughout the duration of the festival has been a Jewish pre-occupation throughout history.

When a grandson was born just before Succot to the famous spiritual head, Shammai, in order that mother and son could fulfil the mitzvah, he took away most of the rafters and roof over her bed and covered it with leaves. On an urgent mission to the Imperial Court in Rome, Rabbi Akiva constructed a Succah on the poop of the ship crossing the Mediterranean. Rabban Gamliel, who was part of the delegation, did not approve.

When they woke up on the first morning of Succot they found that the frail construction had been carried away by the wind. Turning to his colleague, Rabban Gamliel joked, "Akiva, where is your Succah now?"

Their descendants have experienced many a similar fate.

In our first house in Kenton, I erected what I thought was a perfectly sound Succah just outside the French windows of our lounge. The first night Yom Tov went like a charm, but the next evening a storm began as we entered the Succah. We had just finished drinking the Kiddush wine when there was an ominous cracking sound. We just managed to get back into the lounge before the whole edifice collapsed.

As Edgware is an outlying district of London, it can often be very cold in the evenings, and one night I actually espied frost on the boughs of our Succah. On one occasion in St John's Wood, we had invited a large number of congregants to lunch with us in the Succah, but the weight of the rain, which had been falling all morning, caused the whole structure to cave in, and although the rain then stopped, we had no Succah to eat in. At Hillel House we enjoyed a beautiful modern Succah in an enclosed patio — at least fifty of us at a time could eat in it — but even there on occasion, the elements defeated us.

In South Africa, the non-Jewish public has the fixed belief that as soon as the Jewish festival of Tabernacles commences, so does the rain.

Coming from the northern hemisphere, I invariably take the precaution of spreading a tarpaulin over the whole temporary roofing of the Succah, just in case. Several years ago, just as Yom Tov came in, Johannesburg was hit by monsoon weather. Most of the Jewish community — and it is so wonderful to see the large number and variety of Succahs — trust to luck and do not cover their Succah, so I was one of the very few, after I had avoided the flood as I removed the tarpaulin, to fulfil the mitzvah of saying the blessing "to dwell in the Succah" on that first evening.

But when the weather smiles, there is no injunction of the Bible more deeply satisfying than that of living in the Succah. Jewish religious practice offers such marvellous and stimulating contrasts — if we can come close to G-d by praying, fasting and contrition on Yom Kippur, can we not also feel close to Him in the natural surroundings of the Succah?

In the evenings during Succot, looking up at the greenery of the boughs and the just visible stars through the foliage, there comes a wondrous sense of belonging to the world as it was made, not as man has made it. A feeling of deep contentment engulfs us. The covering of leaves symbolises the sheltering care of G-d, the best security there is, and promises for us all the blessing of peace.

It is not easy to think of G-d in the lounge. TV, a hi-fi system, sumptuous furniture and wall-to-wall carpeting are not altogether conducive to lofty thoughts. The indispensable paraphernalia of current living, micro-wave ovens, laptop computers and cell phones, are likewise not innate with spirituality.

But in the Succah, close to nature, it is easy to think of the Divine Creator of the universe.

8.   The Touch of Beauty

The only instance in the practices of our people where everyone performs the mitzvah in the most beautiful way possible is the manner in which we kindle the lights of Chanukkah. The basic fulfilment is that only one light be lit. Those who wish to fulfil the mitzvah in a more beautiful way — mehadrin — kindle a light, each one for himself, within the same household. Those who wish to fulfil the mitzvah in a most beautiful manner - mehadrin min hamehadrin - our universal custom, kindle one light on the first night, and keep adding a candle until the candelabrum is complete.

The concept of Hiddur Mitzvah — the notion that commandments should be fulfilled in a beautiful way as befits their status — has its source, according to our sages, in the phrase in the Song of Moses, "this is my G-d and I shall prepare a habitation for Him," which carries the alternative Hebrew meaning "this is my G-d and I shall beautify Him," that is to say act beautifully before Him when performing the commandments.

The Rishonim differ as to whether this source is direct, which would make the commandment to adorn the mitzvot with beauty a Torah one, or whether it is rather just an indication from scripture, which would make it a rabbinic one. If indeed this was a Torah obligation, then initially we would have to fulfil all injunctions in a beautiful manner, otherwise it would not count as having done the mitzvah. But the requirement is rabbinic, so that if one has failed to beautify the mitzvah, it nevertheless still stands.

However, in the same way that we say a berachah and mention the Name of Heaven every time we fulfil a commandment, it is recommended, although not mandatory, that we fulfil every mitzvah in the most beautiful way possible. Surely for Hashem only the best is good enough!

The rabbis categorise several different forms of beauty. Firstly and obviously there is the beauty of the mitzvah object itself. For example, a succah should be beautiful, a shofar, a Sefer Torah, a tallit and so on. The object indicates the enthusiasm of the performer and if the trouble is taken to obtain a beautiful object, clearly the person wishes to honour Hashem and to be inspired when performing the mitzvah.

Another successful way of fulfilling Hiddur Mitzvah is to surround the object itself with beauty.

The Mishnah in Bikkurim informs us that the annual first-fruits were brought up to Jerusalem with great pomp and ceremony, the ox carrying the fruits having its horns overlaid with gold with a crown of olive leaves on its head. Everything surrounding the first-fruits was made a fuss of and beautified, thus enhancing the mitzvah.

A fascinating additional way of adorning the mitzvah is to ensure that one is able to fulfil it in the most satisfactory way. For example, one is instructed not to eat on the afternoon before the seder of the first night of Pesach in order that one will have a good appetite to ful-fil the commandment to eat matzah. The reason for this, according to Rashi, is hiddur mitzvah, that to eat the matzah when we are really hungry, rather than on a full stomach, constitutes a far better way of impressing us with the significance of the commandment.

But although beautifying the commandments is important, the rabbis were very anxious that we should not overdo it. Tefillin are black — one of the reasons presumably being not to embarrass the poor — but it is surprising how much a pair can cost and how much one-upmanship exists regarding the quality of writing, parchment, stitching and leather. So to what extent should one take the obligation to beautify the commandments?

The Gemara informs us we should add "up to a third," the author-ities differing as to whether this means we should add a third of the size of the object itself, for example, with an etrog, or whether it means to add a third to the value, and involve ourselves up to that amount in additional expenditure in order to beautify the mitzvah.

Because the temptation exists to go overboard, especially with items such as buying an etrog, it is highly advisable to retain a sense of balance. A decade ago a renowned Jerusalem Rabbi summoned all his students before the Festival of Succot and instructed them to buy their respective wives a new dress for Yom Tov rather than spend the money on a more beautiful etrog.

A dissenting view on the whole issue is presented in the Talmud by Abba Shaul who reminds us that beauty of character is much more important than external beauty: "As Hashem is gracious and merciful" so should we all follow His example and try to show kindness to our fellows.

Interesting conflicts of Jewish religious law also arise with hiddur mitzvah. In the clash between eagerness and enthusiasm to fulfil the mitzvah, called zerizuth, and the obligation to beautify it, which takes precedence? For example, if one is buying a tallit, should one wait a few months until one can afford to buy a more beautiful one, or buy whatever one can afford at present? The rule is that the person should buy the tallit immediately and not wait. Enthusiasm is also a praiseworthy characteristic.

Also with the law of bal tashchit, that we are not allowed unnecessarily to destroy anything, the question is asked whether in the writing of a Sefer Torah, we are able to rewrite a column which was not written quite so well, for the sake of overall beauty. Although there were no mistakes in the column, we do in fact allow it to be removed and buried, in order that the scribe can do it again and thus safeguard the beauty of the written text.

Although we are keen on the concept of hiddur mitzvah, we do not allow it to have dominance over the essential fulfilment of a command. In the case where a person has sufficient oil to fulfil the Chanukkah commandment with hiddur mitzvah and keep adding to the light each night, but his neighbour unfortunately does not possess any oil at all, the person is required to give up some of his oil so that both he and his neighbour may fulfil the basic mitzvah.

The philosophical basis underlying the concept of hiddur mitzvah is crucial to an appreciation of halachah itself. Never designed to be automatic or a reluctant obligation, the mitzvah ought not to be dismissed as quickly and conveniently as possible.

Crucially, the mitzvah displays the outer expression of inner conviction. The coordination of the two is quite vital — the physical exertion of fulfilling a commandment and the beautiful way it is observed reflect back on our sincerity, on our motives, and even on our basic belief in the value of fulfilling the commandment in the first place. The person who approaches the obligation to fulfil the commandment with zeal and imagination and a desire to do it in the very best way possible, will indeed derive a maximum of spiritual satisfaction.

The touch of beauty is thus more than an aesthetic consideration. By consistently endeavouring to fulfil commandments in as beautiful a manner as possible, we bring spiritual beauty to our lives and truly validate the service of our Maker.

VI

HUMANITARIAN

1.   Tears Upon Tears

Following a series of barbaric incidents on the East Rand in the early nineties that continued even after the release of Nelson Mandela, all spiritual leaders roundly condemned the inhuman behaviour which was such a disgrace and which was prejudicing any chance of a peaceful new South Africa.

The Johannesburg Star carried a photograph at the time, showing a black 15-year-old girl from one of the townships, and she was crying. The previous tears she had copiously shed had dried up on her face and left their visible mark down the side of both cheeks.

She had begun to cry again, and you could see from the photograph that the rivulets of tears would flow down exactly the same path on her face. We were not told in the caption why the girl was crying. Perhaps her parents had been murdered or she was very hungry or she had no place to live. But she was clearly bereft of all hope. Our country had been reduced to tears upon tears, fresh tears on top of dried-up tears.

Sickening levels of violence are the worst blight on any country. The Bible is quite adamant about the corrupting nature of violence and its demoralising impact on all that is good in human nature. Whatever the underlying causes, political, economic, social or psychological, violence wreaks havoc on the fabric of society and must never be condoned.

The Rabbis of old stated that whereas the generation of the flood in Noah's time committed every possible transgression, their fate was only sealed when they put forth their hands to violence — "for the earth is filled with violence because of them," and concludes G-d, "I will therefore destroy them from the earth".

Listening to the evening news during that period, every single item was about murder or mayhem: children in the KwaZulu Natal midlands being hacked to death, taxi killings in Pretoria, a farmer and his wife butchered on an isolated farm in the Free State, and a brutal bank robbery that afternoon in a suburb of Johannesburg.

That each and every human being is altogether precious is a fundamental scriptural teaching. The Mishnah asks why, at the time of creation, G-d created many animals, birds, fish and insects, but when it came to the human race only one, Adam, was created.

The deliberate creation of only one human being is to emphasise, we are told, how very precious is each and every individual. Everyone in his or her own right is a microcosm of the universe, so that the twin obligation devolves on all of us to help preserve every single human being and never to destroy any human being. Each of us is a world in our own right.

Similarly, our concern must be extended towards everyone. Commenting on the Biblical verse "And ye shall love the stranger, for ye were strangers in the land of Egypt," the 19th century German-Jewish philosopher, Hermann Cohen, tells us that here, with its concern for the stranger, the Bible is teaching us humanity.

If one helps a member of one's own family, or one's own community, or a co-religionist, or someone from one's own ethnic group, it is to be expected. But when one helps someone who is not a member of the family, or from one's own religion, colour, or race, one asserts the triumph of a common humanity. This person, too, a fellow human being, created in G-d's image, is worthy of my concern.

The golden rule of the Holiness Code in Leviticus — "And you shall love your neighbour as yourself" (and oh, do we love ourselves!) — was never more apposite. For in our own day the "global village" has made us all neighbours, if only we had the moral fibre to realize it.

A lack of sensitivity is inadmissible in the religious view of humanity. In a significant gesture at the Seder service, as we solemnly mention the Ten Plagues, everyone around the table dips a finger into the full cup of wine in front of them, and dabs it on the side of the wine saucer or the plate. Others have the custom, as each of the plagues is mentioned, of actually pouring a few drops of wine from the cup onto the plate below.

One reason given for this custom is that we must display some sympathy for the Egyptians who suffered from the plagues. Although they deserved them, and Pharaoh by his stubbornness brought them on his own people, it would be churlish to gloat over our enemy's misfortune, so we deliberately spill the wine in mindful consideration of their discomfort. When fellow human beings suffer, our cup can never be full.

There are those who tell us that human rights are the most important desideratum for our new world order. Others insist on duties, responsibilities and obligations each to the other, if our society is ever to come right. Still others, and this is the crux of the matter, point to basic human feelings as the real answer. If only we could identify with the predicament of others, use our imagination a little to put ourselves in their place, feel their circumstances, acknowledge their problems, join in with their hopes. When our human feelings are properly in tune, our world will begin to change for the better.

In an illuminating illustration the Talmud teaches us that life, every life, is infinitely valuable. In a case where a person is thrown off a roof by a would-be murderer, but someone else kills the falling person by shooting him through the heart with an arrow before he hits the ground, the second criminal is also guilty of murder. But, you could well argue, the person was hurtling towards the ground and was going to die anyway. Ah, but the victim still had a few moments of life left, so the second person in expediting the death, albeit by a very short time, is guilty of a capital offence.

When we forget that life is infinitely valuable, we belittle the very foundations of our civilisation and we betray the purpose G-d sets for our existence. Hence it is absolutely imperative in our tempestuous times that we recreate a sense of the intrinsic value of life. Our most urgent task is to inculcate the healthiest respect for the life of all fellow human beings made in G-d's Divine image.

That our current society, racked by violence, can turn the corner and reinstate basic respect presents an awesome challenge. One single incident of hijacking does not traumatize the victim only, but often adversely affects the victim's family, the victim's neighbours, the victim's friends, the victim's colleagues and the victim's peer group. Everyone around, instead of being able to rely on decent standards of behaviour, becomes suspicious, wary and clouded with pessimism.

A rare exception to this rule is a young man called Clinton Fuchs. He was shot at, and badly wounded, in the hijacking of his car in the Jewish suburb of Glenhazel and subsequently lost one eye. Instead of feeling sorry for himself, he remained incredibly cheerful and determined to overcome his disability and was quite soon back at his favourite hobby of jogging. Courage, however difficult to assert in the present circumstances, is also an answer.

Two opposite trends are in force. The first and more obvious is violence with its callous disregard of others, its mounting tally of innocent victims, the damage it does to the ordinary scene with security checks and searches, its ever-threatening menace.

The second is altruism, a growing movement in which more and more thousands participate, helping for example to alleviate disease, famine and flood wherever they occur. By stretching out a hand to those they do not even know, and probably never will, they proclaim a victory for the human race. Thus do the extremes touch. The terrorist blows up someone he does not know; the altruist helps someone he does not know.

In answer to the objection that one's capacity to love should surely be exercised for the benefit of one's own family and one's own people, rather then reaching out to love the whole of humankind, the saintly Rabbi Abraham Isaac Kook, the first Chief Rabbi of the Holy Land in the modern era, taught that an intense love of all creation is essential.

We have to love humanity, the whole of humanity, before we can really love our own people. If we do not have love for the whole of creation which G-d has made, an all-encompassing love for the totality of mankind, then we cannot really love our own people. The direction is important. Instead of beginning with the centre of the circle as one's own people and widening one's commitment outwards to the periphery, we should rather embrace the whole circle and work inwards towards the centre which is our own people.

The chauvinistic stance which enshrines exclusivity for one's own group is, with this view, shown to be flawed. Not only is it intrinsically wrong to follow such narrow loyalties; in the end it is self-defeating because we cannot be good Jews if we are not good human beings, and only if we are able to love others can we reach up to the highest standard of loving ourselves.

I have a recurring nightmare. It concerns the way the 20th century will be viewed in years to come.

In the middle of this century, say the year 2050, looking back on the 20th century what will the historian say about us? The startling difference between the outstanding scientific, medical and technological advances, and the totally disproportionate lack of progress in moral well-being, in establishing world peace and displaying true humanity, will assuredly be noted.

"Clever people," the historian will say. "They could perform heart transplants, they landed on the moon, they could see sports events on television in any part of the world as they were taking place. Clever people! They harnessed nuclear power, they could surf the web, they could communicate with cell phones."

And then the historian will look at the world wars, at the Holocaust, at the inhumanity of Vietnam, Cambodia, Bosnia, Rwanda and a thousand other war-torn regions.

"Who were these 20th century people," he or she will ask, "who had such sophistication in technology and such immaturity of soul, who were able to reach up to the moon but incapable of reaching out their hands each to the other?"

Such a verdict will be deserved, but is it too much to hope that the new century can at least begin on a high note of moral awareness?

In the 1960s Bob Dylan used to sing the song, "Blowin' in the Wind". He posed the question — to our shame still unanswered — "How many ears does a man need to have before he can hear people cry?"

2.   The Moral Repudiation of Apartheid

The concept of human rights is among the first and foremost in Jewish classical sources. Tracing back the whole of the human race to one sole origin, the Bible teaches that all human beings have one creator and one ancestor, the human father.

Notwithstanding differences produced by external conditions, all human beings are thus related each to the other, a relationship which imposes on everyone the duty of safeguarding human dignity and of striving to be of mutual help. The Genesis narrative further proclaims all people to be equal. Since the whole of humanity is descended from the same source, no one can say that his or her lineage is superior.

The characteristic feature of the Jewish teaching is its total application, the generality of the concept demanding its acknowledgement concerning fellow citizens and strangers alike. Moreover, this applicability is independent of any merit or guilt; the mere fact that one is human warrants the full entitlement to human rights. As everyone is created *imago Dei*, the union of the human family subsumes an inherent responsibility at all times and in all places to behave in a proper and virtuous manner.

The interdependence of mankind is pivotal. Aware of the bonds which unite the human family, one can never justify abusive action. The Jerusalem Talmud in Tractate Nedarim explains the futility of one person hurting another by comparing it to a man cutting meat. The knife slips and inadvertently cuts his other hand. Would that man then strike the first hand in retaliation?

Hence, if human beings would only see themselves and their fellows as all part of one and the same organism, they would never think of maltreating anyone, because in reality such treatment is damaging to themselves.

In Jewish tradition, the bystander to inhuman conduct is considered guilty, almost to the same degree as the perpetrator. Integrity cannot be maintained in the midst of compromising situations nor in the face of evil is one allowed the luxury of "sitting on the fence".

The rabbis ask why all the Egyptians drowned in the Red Sea when it was the Egyptian royal power alone that was responsible for demanding the atrocities? The answer is clearly given in Seder Eliyahu Rabba — "because it is stated towards the beginning of the book of Exodus 'and Pharaoh commanded all his people' to drown the new-born Israelite males in the river Nile". Pharaoh's royal decree was proclaimed throughout the Land of Egypt, and yet no single person could be found to speak out against such cruelty. From this one learns that the Egyptian people at large were considered guilty and therefore deserved the fate that befell them in the Red Sea.

By contrast with the moral failure of most of the Egyptians, the midwives practised civil disobedience and refused to carry out Pharaoh's command to kill the males at birth. Although the Babylonian Talmud tells us that the midwives were Hebrews, a counter-tradition supported by Philo, Josephus and Abravanel insists that in fact they were Egyptian midwives assisting the Hebrew women in childbirth. After all, it was unlikely that Israelite women would kill their own, so in this view it is logical to suggest that Pharaoh instructed Egyptian midwives to kill the infant Jewish males.

Because the midwives did not shirk their moral responsibility under the pretext of adhering to superior orders, they were rewarded for their courage. The text states that they "feared G-d," a term invariably used in scripture to denote the universal element in religion which humanizes our conduct.

Understanding that divine law transcends man-made law, Judaism would strongly propound that those who have the courage to disobey an unjust civil law are in fact expressing the highest respect for law itself.

Fundamental to human rights is the indispensability of political liberty. That freedom is indivisible is a central axiom of the Jewish ethical standpoint. At the very outset of Israel's nationhood, over two hundred years were spent in abject slavery, in order to instil in Israel that throughout their future they were never to treat others as badly as the Egyptians had treated them. The heightened regard for human rights and the innate sense of social justice which this experience inculcated were meant to ensure that throughout its history the Jewish people would display sympathy for suffering humanity and endeavour to champion the cause of the underdog.

It is worth noting that Archbishop Desmond Tutu in giving evidence in 1981 before the Commission of Inquiry into the affairs of the South African Council of Churches stated that the story of the Exodus is a paradigm for all who are oppressed: "The G-d of the Exodus is a liberator G-d who leads His people out of every kind of bondage, spiritual, political, social and economic".

Nor is the excuse admissible that in order to be a good citizen one must always follow the law of the land. The Talmudic principle dina de-malchuta dina, "the law of the land in which one dwells is the law to be followed," first enunciated by the third century teacher Samuel to Babylonian Jewry, is limited in scope primarily to fiscal matters and in no way extends to the acceptance of discriminatory legislation against whole sections of the population.

In pointing out that the halachah gives sweeping powers to the constituted government, Jewish or otherwise, Rabbi Basil Herring in his study of Jewish ethics and the halachah reminds us that "it did not empower the citizen to surrender the use of his moral conscience ... civil disobedience has a long and honourable tradition in the halachah."

Against the argument that it is courting danger to challenge authority and that the exercise may well prove futile, traditional Jewish sources suggest that it is not for the protester to judge the outcome, but that the wrong must be opposed irrespective of the consequences.

An illustration is afforded by the following account from the Babylonian Talmud in Tractate Shabbat.

"R. Zeira once said to R. Simon: "You must censure the Exilarch's court." He replied: "They won't listen to me." R. Zeira retorted: "You must censure them all the same." This accords with R. Aha, who said that the only time G-d ever reversed Himself with regard to a benign decision was when He said to His scribe: "Go through the city, through

Jerusalem, and put a mark upon the foreheads of the men who sigh and groan over all the abominations that are committed in it." (Ezek. 9:4). The Holy One said to Gabriel: "Go mark the foreheads of the righteous with an X of ink so that the angels of death do not harm them, and the foreheads of the wicked with an X of blood so that the angels of death do harm them." Hearing that, Justice spoke up and said: "Lord of the Universe, what's the difference between them?" G-d answered: "Why, these are wholly righteous and those wholly wicked." Justice replied: "[But,] Lord of the Universe, they [the righteous] could have protested but did not." Said He: "But I know that even if they had protested no one would have listened to them." Said she: "Lord of the Universe, *You* knew it, but did *they*?"

In contradistinction to this view, Tosefot on this passage offers a cautionary note by indicating that in a situation in which it is quite clear that the ruling authority will dismiss the protest out of hand, one may be justified in keeping silent. There is no moral compulsion to speak out when one's words will be brushed aside. Indeed, the effect of the protest may be to harden the transgressors on their misdirected path and make the situation even worse. Sometimes discretion is the better part of valour.

It must be emphasized, however, that in Judaism the normative view prevails. It is insufficient to keep apart from violations of human rights, dissociation is inadequate where vocal protest is called for and positive steps are urgently needed to try to rectify the injustice.

Judaism dismisses with contempt the oft-repeated assertion that religion and politics do not mix. Thoroughly comprehensive in nature, the Torah seeks to govern every area of human activity, while prophet after prophet denounced the social evils of their times and thundered against corrupt leaders and unjust rulers. Religion is more than ritual and ceremonial. Only when its principles and values are directly applied to everyday life does it come into its own.

The entire purport of Jewish moral teaching, together with the essential lesson of Jewish historical experience as the most consistent victim among the peoples of the world, should have moved the community to oppose apartheid.

As the small but vociferous group, Jews for Social Justice, expressed it in a 1985 newsletter:

"Our history of persecution imposes a special duty on us to protest any form of discrimination against any people. Judaism is a religion of faith expressed in action; therefore its teachings about human dignity and social justice make it unacceptable for us to be guilty of the complicity of silence in an oppressive society."

A few Jewish individuals within the community, notably the late Chief Rabbi Louis Rabinowitz z'l, bravely challenged the evil system but that the community in general did not, is a matter of record.

Distancing oneself from the anguished cry of the majority in one's own midst and myopically pursuing one's own interests, whether personal or communal, can never be morally justified. As the American-Jewish philosopher, Abraham Joshua Heschel, once wrote,

"Indifference to evil is more insidious than evil itself; it is more universal, more contagious, more dangerous. A silent justification, it makes possible an evil erupting as an exception becoming the rule and being in turn accepted."

3. Giving And Taking

Two phenomena of modern living impact on our attitude to the needs of others.

Urbanisation, which attracts most of the world's peoples to live in huge, sprawling cities and which has virtually denuded rural areas in many countries, has not brought about increased levels of concern for the poor and destitute.

Quite the contrary. Urbanisation has bred a cruel paradox - the more people, the less concern; the larger the city, the greater the loneliness.

This degree of impersonality — how many of us know the names of the people living in the same apartment block or the same street as we do? — is at odds with the second phenomenon, the "information explosion". This, in tandem with the new technologies of the last decade of the 20th century, affords us rapid and detailed knowledge of floods, earthquakes, and hurricanes as soon as they occur and reminds us of the hungry and deprived.

A prize-winning photograph, which went round the world a few years ago, depicted a young Sudanese girl dying of starvation. As she was lying almost lifeless on the ground with no energy left to move, a vulture, a few metres away, watched and waited to pounce.

There was a great deal of media debate about this photograph: some commentators questioned whether the picture had been posed and others asked why the photographer had not been concerned with giving the little girl food rather than snapping the picture.

Awareness of need surely carries responsibility with it. Closing our ears and eyes to heart-rending accounts in newspapers and on radio and television is a betrayal of our sophisticated communications system, by means of which we know but seldom care.

In our day and against this background, the three distinguishing features of Jewish charity take on added significance.

The first imperative is that we are not allowed to refuse the call for help. The Midrash relates the story of two rabbis living in Tiberias who were stopped by a beggar while they were hurrying to join the queue for admission to the bath house. Not wishing to be delayed for any reason, they told the beggar they would answer his plea and give him some alms on their way back. Unfortunately, when they returned from the bath house, they discovered the beggar lying dead in the street.

Stricken with remorse, they resolved that as they had not dealt kindly with him when he was alive, they would personally attend to the traditional ritual of purification and make all the funeral arrangements. So they unclothed him to wash his body in accordance with the required procedure and to their amazement found a money belt full of gold coins round his middle.

The Rabbis felt exonerated for clearly the "beggar's" request had been illegitimate. Then they remembered the statement of Rabbi Eleazar that if it were not for the fact that there existed unscrupulous people promoting spurious and non-existent charities, all of us would be guilty every time we refused a legitimate appeal.

"Come, let us be grateful to rogues," Rabbi Eleazar said, "for if it were not for them, we would be sinning every time we failed to give."

Fortunately very few appeals are not genuine, so Jewish religious tradition asks us, if we are blessed with the means, never to refuse.

The second point, on which Jewish tradition is very insistent, concerns the manner of giving. In each and every way possible the dignity of the recipient must be respected. For example, the Bible tells us that the Jewish farmer of old had to leave the corner of each field called peah, a basic minimum of one-sixtieth, to the poor who came at harvest time to reap for themselves. Instead of being lined up in a row and given a handout, the morale of the needy was protected in that they themselves were required to cut the crop in the corner of the field and harvest it.

The genuine feeling that they themselves had contributed to collecting the corn reduced the notion of mere charity and protected their sensitivities.

We must always try to find the least humiliating way of giving. In this vein, the Torah instructs us that when we are face to face with the poor, giving should be accompanied by a kindly word. When we can achieve that, we are not only giving money but a little human warmth with it.

A famous example of protecting the feelings of the poor is given in the Mishnah, which describes a room of secret charity called The Whispering Chamber, close to the Temple. It was a large hall, dimly lit, with a big table at one end, on which there were three baskets. This arrangement was for the benefit of poor people who had formerly been wealthy; their experience of poverty was obviously more bitter than those who were used to being poor. People who wished to donate to those who had fallen on hard times would come in quietly and place their offering in one of the baskets.

Those who required help would come and take what they needed, not more, from one of the baskets. Thus no one knew whether the people going in and out were donors or recipients, safeguarding in a unique way the feelings of the poor. The Talmud records with pride that the baskets were never empty.

Whereas Maimonides made a great virtue of anonymity, the Berditchever Rebbe preferred that in times of great poverty those who could afford to help should come face to face with the poor. This way they would be more aware of the realities of need and more prepared to offer practical help. A lesson here for today's South Africa?

A further amazing example of sparing feelings is that the Torah prohibits a creditor from invading the debtor's house to obtain a pledge against the loan he has given him. We are told in Deuteronomy that the creditor must stand outside and the debtor will bring out the pledge. This proscription displays the highest level of respect for a fellow human being, because it recognises that however poor a person may be, he still has the right to be ba'al ha-bayit, the lord of his home.

The third Jewish teaching is that no-one is ever exempt from the obligation of giving charity. The Shulchan Aruch, in an otherwise surprising law, legislates that anyone who is being supported from the communal charity chest is nevertheless not free form the responsibility of giving charity. In order that he himself might donate a little, he is deliberately given a little more than he requires.

The vital point here is that no one, even the poorest of the poor, is ever allowed to stop giving charity. In the course of time his circumstances might well improve, and should he, heaven forbid, become accustomed not to give any charity, he will continue in that way. Judaism does not allow any exceptions: the taker must also be a giver. No one can be permitted to give up giving.

Why people donate has been researched and has revealed a variety of motivations. Some people give only when there is a crisis; recent events in Kosovo are an example of when this happens. Some give for ideological reasons, the current upliftment projects in South Africa being an example of this. Some give due to the pressure of society; they are not really interested in the cause but would feel mean if they did not. Some do it for personal fulfilment; by identifying with the plight of others, they discover new dimensions to themselves.

In our time, when so much affluence and such widespread poverty exist side by side, the way in which charity is apportioned is critical. Transcending one's own needs to reach out to others is a noble act, which Judaism enhances by asking us to remember emotional, as well as practical, needs.

Utilizing their possessions for double benefit, those who respond to the needs of others by regularly sharing what they have, are truly blessed.

4.   Caring And Sharing

From early in the days of communism, the story is told of the party secretary who was sent to a rural area to instruct the populace about egalitarian principles. After an hour's address, he tested his listeners.

"Ivan, if you had fifty cows, what would you do?"

Ivan immediately replied, "I would keep half of them and give the other half for the benefit of the people."

"Good," said the speaker. "And you, Igor. Supposing you had a dozen horses?"

Igor dutifully answered that he would keep half of them and give the others to the people.

"Tell me, Vladimir, if you had two chickens, what would you do?"

There was an embarrassed silence. Vladimir scratched his head and stroked his chin.

"What's the problem, Comrade Vladimir? Tell me, if you had two chickens, what would you do?"

"The problem, Comrade," said Vladimir, consternation in his voice, "the problem is — I have two chickens!"

Redistribution of any kind is a difficult exercise for those asked or pressed to assist the poor. A major controversy since the dawn of the new South Africa has been caused by the debate over the ways and means of eradicating poverty.

On the one hand there are those, mainly from the white elite, who argue that you cannot bring about greater prosperity by imposing punitive measures by taking resources away from the rich and giving them to the poor.

Well over a century ago Abraham Lincoln put it this way, "You cannot strengthen the weak by weakening the strong. You cannot help small men by tearing big men down. You cannot help the poor by destroying the rich."

Quite so. But the appalling reality of poverty cries out for alleviation; it asks all those who are able to help to make honest attempts to effect some degree of amelioration.

The widespread reluctance of big business to grapple with the gigantic problem was lamentably demonstrated by the reaction to Professor Sampie Terreblanche's proposal for a "wealth tax". At the business hearings of the Truth and Reconciliation Commission, he suggested that 0,05 percent of assets over R2 million — he subsequently raised the level to R10 million — should be paid as a special apartheid reparations tax.

Despite the fact that most big companies spend far greater sums on their social responsibility programmes, and the pronouncement of government leaders that if big business had any moral sensitivity, it would volunteer to provide the funds, the howl of protest from the business sector indicated that Terreblanche had touched a raw nerve.

It is relevant to note that a totally different attitude is emerging among some of those responsible for global financial strategy. Noting that around 1,3 billion people across the world live on less than $1 a day, World Bank president James Wolfensohn in his 1998 report stressed the necessity of focusing on social issues: "Without equity we will not have global stability; without a better sense of social justice, our cities will not be safe and our societies will not be stable."

A radical re-think also comes from his senior vice-president, Joseph Stiglitz, who has emphasized that the new economics must have a human context, guiding the genuine development of the world's backward countries and their transformation. It is also salutary to hear ultra-successful speculator George Soros complain that "the free market capitalist system [is] intrinsically riddled with conflict," that abrupt capital flow reversals are damaging to the global economy and calling urgently for massive international regulation of speculative capital.

What is desperately needed in South Africa as a first step towards changing the situation is an honest recognition of the problem, a shift by whites from their myopia and sheltered surroundings to an awareness of, and empathy for, the deprived millions so close to them.

The gap between the haves and have-nots is becoming even wider. The statistics in South Africa at the end of the 20th century are staggering: ninety percent of the nation's wealth is in the hands of some ten percent of the people; ninety-three percent of the unemployed are black Africans. Whereas in Japan the gap between top and bottom earners is 7:1, the ratio in South Africa is 100:1; and the poorest forty percent of households, about 18 million people, have to live on a monthly sum of R352,53. Too many of Africa's children are ill-housed, ill fed, illiterate and ill, and the awesome task is how to give them a better future.

South Africa is often described as a first world country in a third world setting. But when the first world meets the third it can easily become second rate, a situation which the privileged think should be avoided at all costs. Yet millions of underprivileged people would certainly rejoice at the chance to shift their standards upwards.

Not just the statistics but the realisation that the ideological base of most economic systems is faulty should impel us to discover new ways of tackling poverty. In a recent encyclical, Sollicitudo Rei Socialis, the Pope roundly condemned both collectivism and capitalism "which in different ways subordinate human beings to larger ends".

In truth both systems have failed to encourage the required progress. The death of communism was greeted by the free world with elation. Based on the admirable objective of human equality, it faltered in its lamentable failure to understand human nature. The reverse criticism is now being levelled at free market economies that pursue wealth creation almost impervious to anything other than market factors, stubbornly refusing to transcend the chase for personal gain by joining to it the responsible promotion of social good.

To solve the dilemma, the writer Paul Johnson has coined the phrase "compassionate capitalism" — a free market economy with moral purpose. The idea is that excess wealth should be siphoned off and utilised for housing, hospitals and schools. He does not underestimate the fact that heavy taxation frustrates the creation of wealth — "killing the goose that lays the golden egg" — but his noteworthy idea that "it is possible to run capitalism in tandem with public policies which make use of its energy while steering it in a moral direction" has not yet received the attention it deserves.

That it is possible to do this has been shown by countries such as Sweden, Holland and Japan, all of which have managed to achieve high levels of fiscal growth while at the same time giving their citizens admirable social welfare services.

All those who have the financial and intellectual capacity to point the way towards significant change — government leaders, world economic leaders and corporations — should cooperate to create the right climate for reducing poverty.

At both the Poverty Summit and the Jobs Summit held in 1998, all sectors of society were urged to band together in the "war" against poverty. There was no shortage of recommendations — a once-off "redistribution" tax, setting aside the apartheid debt, greater support for entrepreneurs, community-based infrastructure projects and legislation requiring companies to make social investments — but the will to implement them still needs to be summoned.

A measure of government intervention, although the business sector loathes any official imposition, aimed at the reduction of poverty is also needed. The task of government is not to give preference to policies that protect the well-being and comfort of the few but rather to engage in activating policies that create opportunities for the many. As Thabo Mbeki has pointed out, "the richest and middle income groups have been largely the beneficiaries of public spending in the past ... to address inequality, policies must target the poor ..."

A further vexed problem is that socio-political reconciliation depends crucially on reparation. The recognition that the past iniquities of the apartheid era can only begin to be rectified by an acute sense of responsibility towards repairing some of the damage has yet to emerge. As Judge Richard Goldstone of the Constitutional Court has observed: "What hope is there of racial harmony if those so seriously disadvantaged by past discrimination are not assisted to overcome that disadvantage? And can those of us in the white community who were the beneficiaries, willing or unwilling, of that abhorrent system claim with any fairness a hold on those benefits at the cost of perpetuating the imbalances?"

Until that realisation dawns, a number of steps can still be taken. A low-rate capital gains tax — effective in Canada and Australia where it is their main form of tax on the wealthy — should be introduced. On the other hand, because current incentives are all too sparse — certain limited and specific educational contributions are tax-exempt — government would do well to encourage higher levels of donation in the spheres of health, welfare and education by seriously expanding the range of exemption. (This paragraph was written prior to the presentation of government's budget for 2000, which begins to tackle both these areas.)

Wealth is comparative and Dr Franz Auerbach of the World Conference on Religion and Peace has proposed that those earning a fairly decent salary should pledge the equivalent of one month's income, to be paid in three monthly instalments, to the President's Fund.

Globalisation carries enormous risks. Thus far the developing countries have not been the ones to profit from it and just as debt relief does not automatically translate into poverty relief, so the forces of globalisation may bring instability and more suffering.

Nonetheless, awareness of the interdependence of human beings and of the issues they face is a healthy feature of today's international financial world. We need this awareness now in full measure in South Africa.

That the haves must help the have-nots in our country at this time is not merely an economic or political or social necessity. It is a moral imperative.

5.   The Incomplete Family

A great heartache of South African Jewish life is the sad fact that so many families are incomplete.

Happy indeed are those who have all three generations, grandparents, parents and children, with them in South Africa. For most, some are missing. Many schoolchildren have big brothers and sisters living abroad, and grandparents sometimes have most, if not all, of their children and grandchildren spread across the world. One of my colleagues, Rabbi Lewis Furman, calls the photographs periodically sent to relatives in South Africa "the paper children".

My wife and I had been here only a few weeks when we visited the large Waverley Synagogue one Shabbat morning. At the berochoh, three elderly women approached me and said they would like a word when the proceedings had finished. I dutifully sought them out when almost everyone had gone home.

They explained that they were grannies and that all their grandchildren lived abroad. Although they were in their mid-seventies, they informed me that they worked part-time every week solely to afford the airfare to visit their far and dear ones.

"We can't live on photos alone," one of them indignantly told me.

"Nor on videos either," said another.

"We have to keep the family connected somehow," insisted the third.

I asked them how far they had to travel, and the one with the longest journey told me: from here to Australia, then to Israel, then on to Britain, and from there to Canada.

"So what do you want from me?" I asked. There was a brief silence.

"We just wanted you to know the situation we're in. It's very depressing, but we're trying to make the best of it. What we really want from you is to try to persuade as many people as possible to stay. We know it's not so easy but the more who stay, the fewer will be in our position."

So my wife and I learned about the "Granny Run," a fixed part of our communal scene. These grannies are to be greatly admired because they still work, long after they should have retired, so as to be able to spend a precious few weeks, sometimes only days, of togetherness with their own flesh and blood.

True the emptiness and the aching void can be partially allayed by telephone, fax and e-mail, but not even the most sophisticated electronic contacts can compare with actually being together. These grannies do not begrudge whatever it costs in time, effort and money to keep the family together.

Less fortunate are the forgotten parents who reside in our Jewish old-age homes. While the homes themselves are indeed comfortable, more like homes than institutions — though an institution can never be a home — many of the old folk simply do not hear regularly from their children and grandchildren. Some of them do not even get a telephone call before Yom Tov.

An acute sense of missing out on the warmth of Jewish family life is present on occasions such as Rosh Hashanah, and, of course, the Seder nights.

The few family members who are able, financially as well as in terms of time, really do a mitzvah by coming back home to South Africa to spend Yom Tov, and how deeply their visits and presence are appreciated.

A beautiful, spiritual dimension of togetherness was afforded us on one of our first visits to Cape Town. Our dear friend, Rabbi Eric Kaye, now living in the United States, was at that time the rabbi of the Gardens Synagogue, the mother congregation of South African Jewry. We were staying over during Shabbat at his home and he and his wife Bess had kindly invited two dozen guests — leaders of the congregation and of the Board of Deputies — for Friday night dinner.

When we had finished singing Shalom Aleichem and Eishet Chayil, Rabbi Kaye, who incidentally is a Cohen, blessed his youngest son Monty with the traditional priestly blessing with which fathers bless their children on Friday evenings.

He then paused, and while we were all still standing, he closed his eyes and lifted his arms, and said out loud — "this is for Larry" — Larry at the time was studying at yeshivah in the States. He pronounced the blessing as if his son was there with us.

He then said — "this is for Sorrel" — Sorrel was then studying in Jerusalem. Again he closed his eyes, lifted his arms, and blessed Sorrel as if he was present.

The experience was extremely moving, because of course his children knew, despite the difference in time and place, that wherever they were in the world their father was blessing them at the Friday night table. How profoundly meaningful for the bonds of unity between parents and children and children and parents that the blessing was pronounced over their absent heads. Thus does family love overcome geographical distance.

The incomplete family threatens a "larger" area than the family itself. Demographic statistics incorporate a crucial component called "the dependency ratio". This is compiled by calculating the number in the younger generation, children and students, to which is added the number in the older generation, mainly retired people, thus giving a total of all those who are dependent.

This is then compared with the number of those earning a living, and in a position to maintain other members of the family as well as themselves.

Obviously every viable community requires a solid middle group of economically active persons who can support and care for the young and old not earning a living. Because South African Jewry is haemorrhaging at the immediate post-graduate level, a brain-drain in the 25-30 year age group, a problem of great magnitude looms in the near future. We are already becoming a community with a "missing middle".

Recent statistics show that while an overall average of one in four Jews intends ("fairly likely" plus "very likely") to migrate within the next five years, in the 20-30 year age group no less than half intend to leave. While it also true that there are often problems to be overcome in settling elsewhere, these statistics constitute a troubling dilemma.

An additional worry is that up till recently most elderly Jewish people were financially independent and managed quite comfortably on their own, but nowadays an increasing number of old people are being dumped by children and grandchildren who emigrate abroad, leaving the community to carry the main burden of looking after the old and impecunious members of their family.

I caused something of a furore several years ago by calling for a tax on all South African Jews living abroad of $250 per family a year. Given that the people who would be asked to donate had been born and educated here, and because one would have imagined that some degree of interest in "us" would remain after they had left these shores, the request was not, in my view, so outrageous. But, although it was followed up by some well-wishers abroad, the response to date has been poor.

If South African Jewry is not rapidly to become a tale of the old and the poor, it is vital to prop up the crucial middle section by somehow or other discouraging that age group from leaving these shores.

This is not easy. The question — "Why don't you stay and give South Africa a chance?" — is considered by many to be a chutzpadik question because choosing where one wants to live is a basic personal right. Yet the fact remains that if a proportion of our newly-qualified accountants, lawyers, doctors, scientists, businessmen and engineers cannot be persuaded to stay, we will rapidly face acute problems of survival.

Furthermore, the moral aspect needs to be emphasised as it is one of the factors that should be taken into account. Where is a qualified doctor of more value? In Australia or Canada, or in the South Africa of today?

While emigration figures tend to be exaggerated, probably because many people who talk about leaving actually do not, the problem of the incomplete family is with us with a vengeance. It is evident that a significant minority of our Jewish university students has already decided to leave the country right after graduation, and on the other hand that a significant minority, proud of South Africa, is resolutely determined to live here and make a meaningful contribution. In between these groups, a large number of young people are undecided. A large question mark hovers over their future.

Instead of leaving such crucial decisions to family conferences and peer group pressures, a healthy and vigorous debate throughout our community ought to be held on this whole issue, with all the pros and cons being sensibly weighed up and, if possible, dispassionately considered. On the plus side, some of us find this country an invigorating and challenging place; on the other, the threat of criminal violence is debilitating. On the one hand, South African Jewish life is of a high quality; on the other, the country is struggling through its transformation, which puts economic and other stresses on society.

Emigration may be seen as a trade-off between competing factors, but at least the issue ought to be thoroughly canvassed before decisions — quite often wrong ones — are made. On the outcome, after all, the well-being of our community may depend.

6. Helping To Put Things Right

The extent of poverty in this country is appalling. We all know the facts, but we shrug our shoulders when confronted with them because it is difficult to translate them into the real terms of misery and deprivation or to put ourselves into the position of the millions of unfortunate people.

What is always required is a defining moment, something which happens to make the full reality of the predicament hit home.

It happened to me on a visit, some years ago now, to a school outside Nigel in a district called Jameson Park. This school had the worst facilities in the world. It was a primary school for about 200 black pupils and they were housed in the tumble-down shacks of the old Witwatersrand Gold Mining Company which had closed down many years ago.

Situated in the middle of open fields, apart from the shacks, the school had no amenities whatsoever. In place of toilets, the pupils had to utilise the overgrown grass. Most of the children, some of them only six years old, had to walk eight kilometres in the early morning to get to school from Duduza township on the other side of Nigel, and then had to walk back again every afternoon.

The three classrooms, if you can dignify these facilities with such a term, were dark. They were far too hot, the sun shining on the tin roof. Holes in the roof meant that when it rained the pupils invariably got wet. There was no door, just a sheet of hardboard which doubled as the blackboard.

There were three teachers for the three crowded class rooms. Sitting three to a desk, meant only for two, the pupils were being taught basic arithmetic with the use of beer-bottle tops. One teacher, newly qualified, was trying to teach English to pupils who spoke Sotho only — they were on one side of the classroom — and on the other side to those who spoke Zulu only.

Quite the most moving thing about our visit, we were a group of 18 representatives of Jewish organisations from Johannesburg, was the spirit of the children. Despite the appalling conditions, they seemed happy. They had a school to go to, they were learning, and they sang a selection of songs for us with great gusto.

On the way home we discussed how we could try to be of help in this situation. The resolve was born then to commence with Tikkun — a graphic Hebrew word meaning repair, improvement, helping to put things right — the Jewish community's organisation to help the disadvantaged in our country. The idea was that we would highlight traditional Jewish roles in helping the needy, something which has been done by Jewish people for their own and for the general community throughout history, that we would aim to harness Jewish community resources, that we would attempt a series of welfare projects and that we would encourage individuals to volunteer their skills and expertise. Clearly something had to be done.

The Talmud enunciates a principle of crucial importance which is the basis for such work. That principle is called "mipnei darchei shalom," for the ways of peace.

This means that the manner in which we relate to non-Jewish people should be governed at all times by the dictates of harmony and by the desire for peaceful co-operation. We do not live in a world full of Jewish people only and therefore our relationships with all others must be governed by care and consideration of their needs, thus contributing to a peaceful society.

The Talmud tells us — "we do not prevent the non-Jewish poor from gleaning [in Jewish-owned fields], from collecting the forgotten sheaf, nor from gathering corn in the corner of the field because of the ways of peace. Our Rabbis have taught: we provide charity to poor people who are not Jewish just as we provide to the Jewish poor."

According to the Babylonian Talmud, the duty to include non-Jews when giving charity devolves on both the Jewish community as a whole and on individual Jews. It must be noted that the needs of fellow-Jews are accorded priority. But what the Talmud is telling us is that we must never treat our own as if they are the only people with needs. Thus we are fully entitled to give priority to Jewish charitable causes and Jewish needy persons, but not exclusivity. To give only to the Jewish poor is thus un-Jewish. It has been well said that charity begins at home but does not end at home.

To be sure, the Talmud also enunciates the obverse principle — "mishum eivah," to avoid enmity — meaning that the failure in given circumstances to help a non-Jewish person, or any imagined insult to him, might well lead to persecution of the local Jewish community. For example when idolatry was widespread, it was forbidden for a Jewish midwife to attend a non-Jewess in delivery — it would be helping an additional idol-worshipper to enter the world — but wherever this could cause bad feeling, it was nevertheless permitted.

In similar vein, in the case of a Gentile sending a gift on one of his festive days, say a Christmas present, to a Jewish acquaintance, the latter was instructed to accept it if refusal might be regarded as insulting.

To promote the ways of peace is not a principle with pejorative connotations but is altogether positive. Indeed Rabbi David Hoffmann, the distinguished head of German Orthodox Jewry at the time of the First World War, points out that the concept is deliberately called for the *ways* of peace, and not just "for the sake of peace". In other words, what is being attempted is the purposeful building up of harmonious relations between Jewish and non-Jewish communities by means of a range of practical efforts which can engender good will. The ways of peace have to be created and pursued.

Tikkun covers a wide range of programmes. Programmes to alleviate hunger include the Mitzvah Bin: when the Jewish housewife goes shopping she is asked to buy an extra tin or packet of non-perishable food and place them in the attractive Mitzvah Bin at her synagogue. The food goes to needy organisations such as the Street Children's Alliance.

In the field of education the range of projects includes literacy programmes such as those at Ossac, a black adult education school at the Oxford Synagogue in Johannesburg. Pupils attempt the IEB test in English and Maths and there is a high success rate. There is nothing more joyous than seeing someone over 50 who has been denied an education, but who has come every evening to study, passing the examination. The glow on that person's face when he or she receives a certificate is wonderful to behold.

Skills are also taught — such as pattern cutting, dressmaking and machine knitting — and the fashion shows when the pupils display the clothes they themselves have made are hugely popular.

Tikkun, under the able leadership of my co-chairman Bertie Lubner, who has an infectious commitment to the new South Africa, our chief executive officer, the energetic Herby Rosenberg, our ubiquitous development officer Mrs Nono Ntlhane, and thanks to the organising ability of my wife as coordinator of projects, is going from strength to strength.

On a recent visit to our agricultural project at Rietfontein, Madiba was thrilled at the success of the bakery we have established there, at our farmers' cooperative which grows organic vegetables and at the facilities of the nearby school we have adopted. Significantly he referred to "the white hand of help" which when willingly extended could make all the difference to the transformation process and change despair into realistic hope.

Israel is currently helping seventeen African countries with crucial items such as solar heating and water preservation and we are hoping that Ben Gurion University's agricultural expertise will help us to make Rietfontein a model to be replicated in other deprived rural districts of the country.

When the Jukskei River overflowed after torrential rains at the beginning of this year, the Tikkun Young Adults group initiated a mammoth relief effort, transporting blankets, food and clothing to Alexandra township. Tikkun is also heavily committed to ameliorating the problem of inner city decay; the Hillbrow project at Temple Israel aims to provide an exciting range of formal and informal activities for the deprived street children of the area, to teach them basic skills to enable them to earn a living and to occupy their leisure time — a brass band and soccer team are already in action — so as to keep them out of mischief. Reeva Forman's enthusiasm for this project is an inspiration to everyone involved.

Recently we were given a large batch of end-of-range winter coats by an anonymous donor from Sydenham Synagogue. Having sorted out the sizes, we distributed them to "residents" — mostly living on the street — of Hillbrow. None of them had ever owned a new garment in their lives and they heaped blessings upon us. We gave them outer warmth but they gave us a feeling of inner warmth.

Many other Jewish organisations participate in outreach programmes. The King David Schools in Johannesburg are of ongoing benefit to East Bank School in Alexandra with computer studies and science and similarly the Herzlia Schools in Cape Town regularly assist schools in Khayelitsha. The He'Atid programme, founded by the Krok twins, Abe and Solly, with Mizrachi, takes groups of young professionals to Israel for specialized courses in entrepreneurial and banking skills, courses which are so successful that almost everyone gains promotion on their return.

The Selwyn Segal Centre, a home for the mentally and physically handicapped in Johannesburg, is twinned with the Nokatula Centre in Alexandra township. The Union of Jewish Women engaged for many years in encouraging mothers in Soweto to be interested in their toddlers' education and is now very active in the field of rape victims' support. ORT runs high quality courses teaching scientific and technical skills.

Among the notable individuals who have inspired and implemented upliftment programmes, Helen Lieberman of the Cape runs a project called Ikamva Labantu which provides employment for very many black people, including the blind. They make toys and bead decorations that are sold all over the world.

Not only educational and welfare but also sporting and cultural activities are organised. Maccabi arranges sports days for Soweto youngsters, and from time to time there are joint concerts, black choirs and Jewish choirs singing together.

In the current anguished situation of colossal need we are

challenged to relinquish self-interest, apathy and indifference, and instead progress with moral sensibility towards an identification with the underprivileged. A consciousness of the historical role we are called on to play at this time should be with us, as well as the understanding that unless we strive to make this a better world for the needy millions to live in, it cannot be the kind of world in which we ourselves can ever really be contented.

Hence Jewish commitment to upliftment programmes must become stronger and wider, a deliberate effort to commit ourselves to courses of action which will contribute meaningfully to the future of South African society.

This work should also be seen in a greater context. Professor I Mayor of Unesco succinctly sums up this challenge:"for human beings to be worthy of the name, they must belong to the human species and experience that sense of belonging. If they know and feel themselves to be members of the human family they will have no difficulty in assisting their fellow beings ... We must think globally while acting locally so that human solidarity may flourish."

The critics may say that since South African Jewry is numerically small we must look after ourselves, that we have neither the resources nor the energy for outreach tasks. Yet non-involvement is not a Jewish option. In the South Africa of today we are under a definite moral obligation to contribute our Jewish talents and expertise for the benefit of the population at large. It is important to appreciate that this does not entail giving up any of our Jewish beliefs, practices or communal activities; it does entail giving to the best of our ability.

Espousing the honourable viewpoint which aspires to replace despair with hope, we can play our part in making the caring society a reality.

7.   On Being Human

That life is precious is one of the maxims we all take for granted, unless of course we have the misfortune to be in a war zone, caught up with fleeing refugees, or happen to live in a country where the crime rate is so high as to make life cheap.

An inspiring example of the value of life came my way quite by chance while visiting the Middlesex Hospital in West Central London in 1965. During my customary rounds to see the patients, I found that an elderly Jewish man was not in his bed, so I went to look for him and found him in the Day Room.

We were the only ones there and were chatting amiably when another patient, he must have been in his eighties, approached the Day Room and was about to enter when he suddenly collapsed. The nearest nurse rang the emergency bell, shielded the patient with a screen, and within a minute the team of specialist doctors and nurses set to work trying to revive him.

As he had collapsed just outside the door, the other patient and I were not able to get out. I deliberately turned him round so that he could not see what was going on, but I was spellbound by the frantic efforts at resuscitation. I recall distinctly that there was a large pane of glass in the door of the Day Room, the bottom half of which was frosted over, but the top half clear.

So I could not see exactly what they were doing, only their faces, as they strove to revive him. It was deeply moving. I know these were professionals and it was their job to try to save life but they were so devoted to their task: grimly earnest and utterly determined. I have never witnessed such intense concentration.

Unfortunately, despite their strenuous efforts, they failed, and after twenty minutes gave up. When they had taken the poor dead man away, I managed to leave. The faces of those doctors and nurses frantically trying to bring life back to an old man have remained with me ever since.

There are people around who will do everything possible to

preserve life. One of my Kenton congregants, Cyril Benson, who unfortunately passed away a few years ago, once took me aside after I had given a shiur on the Talmudic principle of Pikuach Nefesh — that everything must be done to save life and that all other laws, such as those of Shabbat, are laid aside whenever life is in danger.

He told me quietly that in a skirmish in North Africa during the Second World War, in the middle of a very hot day, he had been seriously wounded and left for dead. In considerable pain, he eventually lapsed into unconsciousness.

When he woke up many hours later he was in a medical tent eleven miles away. On inquiring how he had got there, he was informed that some nameless private had picked him up and carried him on his shoulders all the way through the desert to the medical tent. The soldier, who had to carry his rifle and heavy regulation pack, as well as him, in the heat of the day, had not left his name but simply brought him in, laid him gently down, mentioned where he had found him, asked for a drink of water and promptly returned to his unit. Cyril owed his life to that soldier who had not even wanted any thanks.

Making the most of life in difficult conditions and adverse circumstances is another good test of our humanity. Johannesburg has a most caring organisation which looks after the mentally and physically handicapped of all ages. It is called Selwyn Segal and it is a tribute to all that can be achieved against the odds.

Under the energetic directorship of Jack Shapiro, who refuses to accept limitations of mind or body, every member of the Selwyn Segal family is urged to develop his or her talents. Jack has pioneered whole new areas of stimulating interest by utilising drama, music and art. Occasionally Selwyn Segal presents musicals to the general Jewish public and the standard is invariably high.

No one is ever allowed to sink into the rut of self-despair; everyone is challenged and horizons are always expanded. Nowhere in the world are the handicapped accepted in such an inspirational way nor treated, despite their incapacities, as normal human beings. It speaks volumes for South African Jewry that all the members of the Selwyn Segal family are made very welcome at any shul they visit on a Shabbat morning and given honours such as opening the Ark.

In other countries of the Jewish world the mentally restricted and physically handicapped, especially those suffering from Down's syndrome, are institutionalized a long way from centres of Jewish residence, but to its great credit South African Jewry welcomes them everywhere and makes a big fuss of them.

My wife and I entertain them annually at home for Shabbat day. We have sumptuous meals, loud communal singing and party games and a great time is had by all. Just before Shabbat goes out, we are thanked by them with numerous individual speeches, and because they come from the heart, they are the best thanks we ever receive.

Similarly, visiting Camp David in the Magaliesburg for their annual summer programme is always a thrill. Fun is not the prerogative of a privileged few but the right of all, and the magnificent recreational facilities, the sheer beauty of the setting, and the exhilarating programme guarantee all the campers a thoroughly enjoyable holiday.

The ability to relate so well to fellow human beings and to encourage them to reach up to try and achieve the best within them is the ethos of Selwyn Segal and Jack Shapiro's constant ambition. Because G-d does not make mistakes — there are "no children of a lesser god" — the compensations for disability are substantial. For instance, they are capable of showing uncomplicated and natural affection. Totally without contrivance or selfish motives, the feelings of these very special people are expressed in a truly genuine way. Their capacity to love is an example to so-called normal people.

Sensitivity to other people's feelings whatever the situation and the fixed desire to prevent any form of humiliation are always reliable hallmarks of one's level of humanity.

When my wife and I first came to South Africa and were settling into our new home, our domestic workers treated us with too much deference. My wife is the last person on earth to put up with this so she summoned all the staff for a meeting with us to explain what she wanted.

She told them she knew they would all work hard for us and that on our part we would try to look after them properly, but she would be grateful if they would not use expressions which indicated any inferior status.

"Do not call my husband 'master'," she instructed them.

They turned to me.

"What shall we call you?" they wanted to know.

"Call me 'rabbi'," I answered.

"And what does 'rabbi' mean?" they asked me.

"It means 'master'!" I replied honestly. And then of course had to go into a long explanation about Rabbi meaning master in the sense of teacher and not denoting any untoward superiority.

In our world today there is not enough of what Stephen Smith of the Beth Shalom Holocaust Centre at Nottingham in England calls "the humanity of humanity". I suppose many of us are so busy looking after number one that we have little time to be truly human, but fortunately there are a sufficient number of examples around of those who do care about their fellow human beings and who go out of their way to help them.

Among the ones I have known are Rabbi Eddie Jackson — Eddie and I were in lodgings together in Cricklewood as students — whose care as a pastor was a source of great strength and comfort to his congregants, my friend Peter Morgan of London — one of the Kindertransporte children — who since his retirement fills every moment of the day with helping others, as if the hatred of the Nazi Europe of his childhood has to be personally redeemed by his extraordinary kindness, and my cricket companion Colin Bliss, a bachelor who spends all his spare time in supporting good causes.

They challenge the rest of us to discover deeper levels of response towards others. When we do respond, in addition to the intrinsic reward of improving our relationships by increasing our humanity, we come to know ourselves the better. For the great paradox of self-realization is that in reaching out to others we find our true selves.

In the early 1950s some American scientists, interested in what materials human beings are made of, actually worked out our chemical contents. An average man, 1,8 metres tall and weighing 75 kilos contains, they discovered, enough sugar to fill a small bowl, enough iron to make a nail of medium size, lime sufficient to whitewash a chicken coop, phosphorous for 2 200 match tips, enough magnesium for one dose, enough potassium to explode a toy cannon, and a little sulphur. The same scientists worked out that at the time the market value of these contents was $2.98.

From the spiritual standpoint human beings are composed of mind, heart and soul; created in G-d's own image, they can aspire upwards, belying the animal nature of their composition. Material man, viewed from the value of the chemical elements of his own body, is only worth a few dollars. Indomitable in spirit and just "a little lower than the angels," the real human being is priceless.

VII

SPIRITUAL

1.   The Efficacy of Prayer

Fascinating questions may be asked about every prayer in our prayer book, the Siddur.

Among these are the authorship; the religious theme of the prayer and its significance; its place in the order of the service; variations in the Ashkenazi, Sephardi and Chassidic ritual; the history of the prayer including any reaction towards it; and its relative importance, as shown by whether we stand or sit during its recitation.

However, one crucial question rises above all the others. How does the prayer produce the desired effect?

Jewish prayer is termed "the service of the heart" so it is apposite to ask about the mood a given prayer is able to produce, about the depth of spiritual feeling it engenders and the level of inspiration it arouses.

Appreciating that such sensitivities are doubtless highly subjective — different people are moved at different times in different ways — and while it could be argued that the whole subject is too personal and esoteric to allow for any meaningful treatment, and because of all mitzvot the personal input to tefillah is crucial to obtaining spiritual dividends, it may nevertheless prove helpful for our prayers to be subjected to such analysis.

The exercise is not done with any motive other than to enable us to gain deeper insights into the holy aim of the composers of our tefillot and in the hope of intensifying our consciousness of their purpose.

Because a variety of adjacent factors may be the source of inspiration, let us dispose of them at the outset.

The music on its own, irrespective of the words of the prayer, may be deeply moving. Kol Nidre, for example, is a very dry legal formula, in which the Sephardim cancel retrospectively a range of religious vows which may have been undertaken, and Ashkenazim cancel them from this Yom Kippur till the next one. It is highly technical and would normally be recited in plain speech, but because it is the opening prayer of the holiest day of the Jewish year and because of the hauntingly plaintive music to which the words are sung, all Jewish people find it very inspiring.

But the words and the music are at odds. Rabbi Nahum Rabinovitch, the illustrious head of the Yeshiva at Ma'aleh Adumim, points out that if anyone actually sang out loud the legal formula for the cancellation of the ownership of chametz on the morning before Pesach, they would probably be locked up in a lunatic asylum!

Similarly, one can be deeply moved by the setting. Many of our shuls are ideally constructed and beautifully embellished, and some of our shtieblach are powerhouses of tefillah sustaining everyone by their atmosphere of concentrated devotion. No matter what prayers we are saying we feel uplifted. No one could daven Minchah in the synagogue of the Ari in Safed, just as twilight is descending over the hills, and fail to experience a profound sense of the closeness of the Shechinah.

What has to be probed is the degree to which the words, style and approach utilised by the composer manage to convey in truly uplifting manner the particular religious message he wishes to impart.

The first key component is appropriateness. Does the prayer exactly match the mood, catch precisely the feelings of the participants?

The glorious climax to the Sheva Berachot, sung at wedding ceremonies and feasts, for example, contains every single word for joy. All the synonyms in the Hebrew language for simcha — to which the bride and groom on their great day are equated — gilah, rinah, dizah, v'hedvah — mirth, song, jubilation and merriment — are mentioned, so that the words themselves help to enhance the atmosphere of joy surrounding the festivities.

The hymn Yedid Nefesh, sung in many synagogues as Shabbat approaches and in many homes as part of Zemirot, contains the epitome of the praise of G-d — "hadur na'eh ziv ha-olam" — exquisitely beautiful is the Splendour of the world — thus allowing everyone around the family table to give voice to the adoration of the Almighty who has given us the holy Sabbath day.

The specific style selected for a prayer also plays a part in its power to move us.

Sometimes this is achieved by sheer simplicity: for example, in the Evening Service — "Blessed be the Lord *by day*; blessed be the Lord *by night*. Blessed be the Lord *when we lie down*; blessed be the Lord *when we rise up*."

Or sometimes this is achieved by deliberate contrast. Adon Olam begins by praising the Eternal Master and Creator of the whole universe, yet it ends with "the Lord is with me": He is a personal G-d, interested in little me!

Similarly, the first paragraph of Alenu is particularistic, emphasising that Israel alone has been chosen from among the peoples. But the second paragraph is universalist, the choice imposing on the chosen people the responsibility of testifying to G-d's name at all times and in every circumstance before the whole world.

A further component is the imagery employed. When on Shabbat we put the Torah scroll back in the Ark, we chant Psalm 29 about "the voice of the Lord".

Just as the revelation on Mount Sinai was preceded by thunder and lightning, so does this Psalm give us, in the words of Israel Abrahams in the Companion to Singer's Prayer Book, "a thrilling description of a storm, a verbal symphony in which the shattering peals of thunder reverberate round the hills, ending in peace and the calm after the storm".

This is a very vivid and effective way of reminding us that Hashem's voice, which speaks to us in the Torah, is the same Divine voice that rules over nature.

Descriptive power also comes to the fore in the Hymn of Glory, Anim Zemirot. Despite strong philosophical objections to its anthropomorphism — that is ascribing human physical and psychological attributes to the deity — the depiction of the Divine, varying from that of an old, grey Judge on the Day of Judgement to that of youthfulness, "with sparkling dew His head is covered/His locks with the dewdrops of the night", is deeply emotive.

Another factor is the treatment of the theme in hand. The personal prayer of the Chazan — "Hinneni" ("Here am I") — recited before the Musaf Amidah on Rosh Hashanah and Yom Kippur, is an example.

Due to his own human inadequacies and the daunting task of appealing to Hashem for forgiveness of the congregation's sins, the genuine Cantor is filled with trepidation. "Who am I?", he asks, to fulfil this responsibility. The plea, that although he personally is unworthy to entreat on behalf of the congregation, yet his supplications should nevertheless prove acceptable, is one of the most poignant, as well as one of the most honest, in the liturgy of any religion.

Another component is the religious motivation. Having said the blessings over the Torah in our early morning prayers every day, we are immediately required to learn a little, in case our daily activities prevent us from fulfilling the obligation, and the blessings would thus be in vain.

The deliberate choice of Mishnah — Eilu Devarim — reminding us that there is no limit to human kindness, followed by the extract from the Gemara Shabbat listing ten specific good deeds, constitute a gentle reminder at the beginning of the morning service that we should devote ourselves during the day ahead to fulfilling as many of these injunctions as possible.

The second major section of the Rosh Hashanah Musaf, the Zichronot, is another instance. The specific motive of this section is to make mention of the good deeds of our ancestors so that their descendants may claim a good New Year.

In asking Hashem to be good enough, as it were, to remember the piety of our forebears, we are accounting their zechut, their merit, as righteousness which we, as their children, deem to be to our credit. With such good ancestors, we are pointing out with chutzpah, we cannot be so bad after all! Hence Hashem should bless us throughout the future.

The most powerful feature in activating mere words so that they become elevated prayers, helping turn our thoughts, our hearts and our very souls toward our Father in Heaven, is the spiritual impact.

While Jewish prayer may be categorised into three major sections, Praise, Thanksgiving and Request, often it is the passionate appeals contained in the last category which give rise to the most heartfelt prayer. These requests are born out of tension. The person praying is in crisis because of the clash between his faith and his circumstances. He is in dire peril, in the depths of despair, yet his instinctive reaction is to cry out for salvation. Because he is in trouble on all sides, the only place to look is upwards.

The Book of Psalms, the greatest collection of poems describing side-by-side the anguish of suffering and the heights of exaltation, is used extensively throughout the Siddur. In the middle of the full Hallel, for instance, the Psalmist pours out his soul in the midst of his torment:"When I found nothing but distress and sorrow, I invoked the name of the Lord; I beseech you, O Lord, save me!"

When the person davening is able to identify with such sentiments, vindicating his trust in Hashem and asking Him for help amid the many anxieties of today, the prayer truly comes alive.

The Siddur is the outpouring of the Jewish spirit, over many centuries and in every country of Europe and the Near East in which our people have lived. We should think for a moment every time we pick up a Siddur that we are holding in our hand three-and-a-half thousand years of prayer, from Biblical extracts, to the Mishnah, to the personal prayers of Talmudic Rabbis which the people in general came to love, to the traumatic ups-and-downs of the Middle Ages, right up to the most recent addition, the prayer for the well-being of the State of Israel.

Our prayers are not one-dimensional, but a glorious blend of Jewish history and Jewish geography. Because Hashem's gift to Israel is the Torah, His people have consistently felt the obligation to reciprocate and give a precious gift — the Siddur — back to Him.

2.   Shabbat Bliss

It was late Wednesday afternoon, I was already twenty minutes late for an important meeting, and I was caught in a colossal traffic jam. I was six urgent phone calls behind. There were two engagements that evening at both of which I had to speak. I had a deadline for an article which had to be in by nine the following morning.

Suddenly amid the hooting of the cars and the cacophony of the rush hour, I thought of Shabbat and immediately the panic left me. Its innate peace, "Shabbat Menuchah," was only forty-eight hours away.

Of all the reasons given for the value of Shabbat, by far the most telling in our own day is its contrast with our frenzied week-day life. The more we are under pressure, the more we chase around, the more we are caught up in the rat race, the more Shabbat constitutes a lifesaver, a tranquil, blissful day.

The fourth of the Ten Commandments instructs us, "Six days shalt thou labour and do all thy work ...". The obvious question is: how can we complete all our work before Shabbat?

The answer is given that the minute Shabbat comes in we should consider it to be the case that all the work we wanted to do has in fact been done. Otherwise, instead of relaxing, we will be spending the whole of Shabbat worrying about the many things we wanted to do and just did not manage to fit in.

The trick is to switch off, to persuade ourselves that all the things we have to do have been done, or at least can wait till next week.

This once-a-week truce with our struggles, anxieties and everyday problems is a boon, and indeed gives us back our humanity. In an incisive American-Jewish video, everyone chases frantically around trying to fulfil their work routine. But everyone is so lost in the job, so caught up with the task in hand, that they have become literally faceless. The accountant's face is a calculator, the shopkeeper's a cash register, the office worker's a computer.

As soon as Shabbat comes in, their faces return to them. For one precious day they are human beings once more.

The great paradox of Shabbat is that all the negatives create a glorious positive. All those who regularly keep it and love it can testify that they do not go around all day bemoaning the fact that they cannot do this, they cannot do that, that this is forbidden and that is frowned upon. To the contrary, the escape from the frenetic weekday rush allows a genuine atmosphere of calm. All the tsoros of the previous week can recede into the background, and the worries, distractions and tumult of everyday life are cast off. We can truly relax.

Another of Shabbat's greatest joys is not to have to bother with the seemingly indispensable devices and gadgets which dominate our lives.

The telephone, especially the cellular phone, can often be a irritating nuisance, interrupting whatever we are trying to do. We can actually live for a whole day without radio and television, without videos and hi-fi sounds. There are six other days in the week to surf the web. Likewise, Hashem did not give us two legs, one in order to change gear and the other for the accelerator or brake pedal, but so that we can walk!

A very strong argument can be made out that by giving up all the trappings of our modern civilisation for 25 hours, we in fact become more civilised, masters of the technology surrounding us, not its abject slaves.

In attempting to achieve this oasis of Shabbat peace, the Code of Jewish Law, in addition to proscribing actual work and forbidding us to talk about it, also recommends that we try to avoid situations in which we would be tempted to think about our work.

Naturally, the law cannot prohibit our thoughts and anything can so easily trigger off reminders of work. Nevertheless it is a sensible safeguard to the tranquillity of Shabbat, to suggest that we do not deliberately put ourselves in places which will automatically bring our work to mind.

For example, the shopkeeper should not take a Shabbat afternoon walk down the main shopping mall because he will assuredly look at the prices his competitors are charging. Similarly, the farmer should not take a Shabbat walk round his property. He will make too many mental notes related to the farm.

This mood of genuine contentment which comes to all who banish weekday cares is altogether precious. Indeed, a leading Jewish psychiatrist once confided to me that in more than forty years of practice, he had rarely come across a Shomer Shabbat who had suffered a nervous breakdown.

The change of mood has a purpose. Not just to have a day off or a short holiday at the week-end, Shabbat offers the opportunity for the sanctification of life itself. Its free time can be devoted to reading, study, meditation and prayer with the community, and of course to devote time to enjoy our own home and to be with our family, with whom our connection during the week is attenuated.

One gets the impression that if it were not for Friday night, some parents might forget what their children look like. For the teenagers, too, enjoying themselves need not always mean getting out of the house but staying in to participate.

The breathing space allows us to reflect on the direction of our lives — to ask ourselves where we are going — and by reminding us that there are higher values than being a money-making machine re-invests us with dignity.

From the physical, psychological, artistic and spiritual points of view, Shabbat is a blessing, and at the start of the 21st century is more fundamental to our Jewish well-being than ever before. Just as when visiting an art gallery, we cannot see a painting properly if we stand right up against it, but have to retreat a few yards to appreciate it properly, so with our own lives. Standing back and reviewing from the vantage point of Shabbat what we have done in the previous week and what we intend to do in the coming week gives added purpose and direction to our lives.

The blessing touches the whole day. The food acquires the Sabbath taste. The forty winks become fifty winks - there is nothing to beat the Shabbos shloff. Nobody gives or takes orders about work, so that every man is his own master.

An interesting feature of South African Jewry is the mass attendance at Friday evening services. Due to the convenient time that
Shabbat comes in across South Africa — unlike other countries, such
as England — the admirable custom has developed over the years of
whole families attending the Friday evening services. The only trouble is that for many South African Jews Shabbat is reduced to Friday
night only, with Saturday becoming a day for shopping or golf — a religious version of Schubert's Unfinished Symphony. Fortunately many
of the younger generation are learning the pleasure of extending
Shabbat to Saturday as well.

"Cometh the Shabbat, cometh rest," the Rabbis tell us. Turning
from our weekday labours, Shabbat has the power to calm our minds,
soothe our hearts, and to remind us, once a week, that we have a soul.

3   The Essential Jewish Identikit

What makes us Jewish? The agonising, quarrelsome and in many ways destructive debate on "Who is a Jew?" — which has divided the Jewish world, the Orthodox from the non-Orthodox, traditional Israelis from most of American Jewry, due to irreconcilable views on Jewish personal status — is, surprisingly, not the most important consideration.

"What is a Jew?" is the key question for the Jewish present and the Jewish future. Accepting that we are Jewish, what does it mean to us? How do we evince our Jewishness? What responsibilities, if any, does it impose? What makes us tick Jewishly?

Reaching an agreed definition is no easy task. There are almost as many definitions as there are Jewish people. And to compound the difficulty, some of the attachments are so peripheral as to be embarrassing.

The former Bishop of Birmingham, Hugh Montefiore, who celebrated his Barmitzvah in the old Bayswater Synagogue in London, adamantly refused, on being ordained into the Church of England, to assent to the article of faith which declares that the Jewish people are forever damned because their ancestors who lived at the time of the Christian saviour failed to recognise him as such. It was, he insisted, an insult to the people of his birth.

In similar vein, Jean-Paul Lustiger who was born to Polish-Jewish parents, and who is currently Cardinal Archbishop of Paris (he may even become Pope, and if that ever happened, imagine the nachas of Jews everywhere — a Jewish Pope!) a few years ago roundly condemned certain revisionist historians who dared to doubt the authenticity of the Holocaust.

It seems quite difficult, having been born Jewish, to give up the connection altogether. Something, albeit tenuous, sticks. An acquaintance of mine who made the conscious decision to opt out of the Jewish community many years ago, told me when I happened to meet him by chance how avidly he reads a Jewish newspaper whenever it comes to hand.

Closer to the centre, but defective nevertheless, are those whose Judaism is almost exclusively gastronomic, a "chopped liver and gefilte fish" Judaism, which does not allow them to pass by a kosher restaurant without popping in for a traditional delicacy.

To others Judaism is an emotional concept, a mixture of feelings about the tragedy of the Holocaust and the emergence of the State of Israel. Sensitivity to anti-semitism, necessitating around-the-clock vigilance to defend the good name of Jewry, is also a widespread feature of post-emancipation Jewishness.

To yet others it is simply a matter of mixing with fellow Jews, of belonging to a Jewish country club or Jewish bowling club.

Many resent being asked about it. "What do you mean 'Am I a good Jew?' Of course I'm a good Jew. I go to shul on Friday night whenever I can. I love chicken soup with pirogen. I know the difference between a kugel and a bagel. I play a good hand at bridge. I take the family on holiday to Muizenberg every summer. What a chutzpah even to ask me! Of course I'm a good Jew."

Similarly, a survey commissioned by the Guttman Institute some five years ago to investigate the religious observance of Israeli Jews discovered most of the respondents considered themselves "traditional" — "Do I have a mezuzzah on my front door? Sure I do. Do you think I'm an Arab?" — although their overall standards would not really justify their self-assessment.

Often the common characteristics of a Jewish identity are so trivial that a positive and compelling definition, based on sound principle and solid practice, is difficult to find. Since you *are*, come hell or high water, Jewish, the prevailing philosophy seems to suggest that you don't have to *be* Jewish.

The point is confirmed by sociological research carried out during the past twenty years into the Jewishness of given districts of London Jewry. In one survey, those who filled out the questionnaire containing the standard probes into beliefs, opinions and conduct, actually complained that "the questions made us feel less Jewish than we really are".

Because subjective evaluations are so suspect — Woody Allen, on being asked his religion in the course of an interview many years ago, promptly replied, "I'm Jewish, but I have an explanation" — and because of the massive range of possible definitions, a look at a neutral study might throw some beneficial light on the topic.

An index of the dimensions of religious identity, and how to measure them, was compiled in the 1960s at the University of Chicago by the sociologists Glock and Stark and subsequently applied to Jewish identity by Professor Bernard Lazerwitz.

Eight key components were specified in this fascinating exercise — a jig-saw puzzle of the core pieces which fit together to constitute the "real" Jewish person or, if you prefer, the essential elements of the Jewish Identikit.

The first was "religious behaviour". Standard items such as synagogue attendance on the Sabbaths and Festivals forms this index. A sliding scale operates — consistent, inconsistent, infrequent, and none. Naturally, the sociologist is not interested in the personal answer, but only needs the information to help establish the trend.

Research has revealed a remarkable dissimilarity to be at work among the younger generation in the Jewish world of today. One arrow points out, towards assimilation and estrangement from the community, while the another points inwards, indicating a passionate commitment to Judaism.

In this "religious behaviour" index, for instance, a noteworthy difference was detected in the attitude of successive generations to the same religious ceremony. To most elderly Jewish housewives, lighting the candles on Friday evening is an integral part of Shabbat, a cherished commandment which creates the unique Sabbath atmosphere.

To many young Jewish housewives, on the other hand, lighting the candles on Friday night is a "quaint custom," "the neighbours do it, so we also do it," or "our parents are coming for Friday night dinner — they'll kill us if they don't see the candles on the table."

But the return to vibrant faith and meticulous practice is also very noticeable. When I first started in the Rabbinate some forty years ago, a middle-aged to elderly congregant would come up to me and say: "Rabbi, I don't keep this and I don't keep that, I don't know this and I don't know that, but I want you to know my late father, olov hashalom, knew the Rashi on the week's parashah off by heart, and my Zeida, zecher tsadik livrochoh, was actually a Rov in der heim."

Nowadays, a middle-aged to elderly congregant approaches me and begins the same way: "Rabbi, I don't keep this and I don't keep that, I don't know this and I don't know that, but" — here there is a different hechsher — "my son and daughter-in-law are so frum, they have a strictly kosher house and I have to be careful what I bring them. And my grandson, bless him, has just told me he is going to study at a famous yeshivah in Jerusalem, starting next year. He may even end up becoming a rabbi."

Across the Jewish world, the items most observed are circumcision, Barmitzvah and holding a Seder on the first night of Passover. Most Jewish people keep some of the laws regarding mourning. An average of just above six out of ten people fast on Yom Kippur. Kashrut, judged primarily by the purchase of kosher meat and the separation of meat and dairy utensils, in some countries is observed by 35 percent of Jewish homes, but the number eating kosher all the time (do people have a different stomach outside the home than in it?) is significantly lower.

The second dimension probed by Lazerwitz was piety. Concerned with the more intense religious practices, this is measured by items such as religious fasts. "Do you fast all day on Tishah b'Av?" the researchers asked the respondent. "What's Tishah b'Av?" some respondents have been known to reply.

Next comes the intellectual index, which covers formal religious education and less structured learning situations such as summer camps and adult study courses. The rise in the numbers attending Jewish day schools is clearly beneficial to, although not a guarantee of, a deeper Jewish identity. The popularity of adult Jewish education, especially classes in conversational Hebrew, the history of anti-semitism and mysticism, is testimony to the widespread thirst for Jewish knowledge.

The ideological dimension examines the extent to which the respondent subscribes to traditional beliefs. Key concepts such as reward and punishment, the after-life, and the doctrine of the Messiah may be probed, and not surprisingly in the whole area a massive degree of uncertainty was displayed in the respondents' answers.

The picture of Jewish identity that is being built up now moves on to consider the parental role. Given the importance of the Jewish home, this dimension, incorporated in the research into all the different denominations, has a special connotation and a deeper emphasis.

What a respondent's parents did for him or her religiously — childhood memories of home ceremonies and parental religiosity and how it was displayed — are explored, and what respondents, in their turn, do as parents for their children is investigated.

Pre-eminent in its influence, the Jewish home has inspired the individual to perpetuate Jewish tradition. In an ingenious visual display, that marvellous museum, Beth HaTefutsot, in Tel Aviv highlights the power and continuity of the Jewish home in a series of twelve line drawings depicting a Jewish living-room in different countries in different centuries.

One can see the interior of Jewish homes drawn in black pencil — from a 5th century home in the Caucasus to a 7th century Algerian home, from an 11th century Spanish home to one in Franco-Germany of the 13th century, and from 16th century Polish Jewry to an up-to-date apartment in New York.

At a glance one takes in the changes in fashion and style, the differences between one country and another, the disparity between one century and another. But the Jewish ritual objects have been coloured in — the mezuzzah on the door, the Shabbos candlesticks, the wine goblet, the Mizrach plate, the besamim box, the candelabrum for Chanukkah, the old Siddur and Chumash — and, despite the different times, the home is immediately recognisable as a Jewish one. Down through the ages, and despite being driven from one country to another, the hold of the Jewish home has persevered. Amid all the changes, the Jewish features have not changed.

The next index concerns the ethnic element, the extent to which concentration of friends and courtship lies within one's religious and ethnic grouping. Restricting social contact to one's own is manifestly an indicator of real identification, whereas openness to all groups, however laudable as a liberal maxim, often proves the passport to exiting the community.

So prevalent is the assimilatory trend, that it has been seriously suggested that if diaspora Jewish communities wish to survive, they should deliberately construct semi-ghettos so that while participating in commerce and pursuing their professions in the outside world, they can retreat to their Jewish enclave, their very own laager, for all other activities. Whether such a strategy would work is a matter of conjecture.

In his study of Jewish students at Oxford, which boasts an Oxford University Jewish Society, an Oxford University Israel Society and an Oxford University Cholent Society (which used to meet every Tuesday evening for the consumption of cholent, the Oxford intellectuals insisting that since cholent was so delicious it should not be restricted to Shabbat), Professor Bernard Wasserstein tested the ethnic dimension by asking: "Of your three best friends, how many are Jewish?" The answers clearly reflected the possibility of subsequent intermarriage.

The penultimate index concerns religious organisational activity and seeks to measure voluntary participation in the work of communal organisations. Much scope exists for such endeavours with a multiplicity of activities readily on offer.

Membership on its own does not necessarily indicate active interest, and serving on a committee — a hallowed Jewish pastime — does not necessarily include actually doing something to help the cause. So much time is spent at meetings, endlessly examining every possible angle of a quite elementary issue, that one often speculates on the ratio of words to deeds. Is it 10 to 1, that is ten hours of deliberation in committee to one hour of actual work? Or is the verbiage even more predominant?

This dimension is nevertheless valid. It often denotes genuine care for the welfare of key aspects of the community and the colossal amount of voluntary work undertaken is a tribute to the selfless band of activists who happily fulfil all sorts of tasks, ward off criticism and who, in so many instances, keep the community going.

Concern about co-religionists in the rest of the world is the last identity dimension. Whether we care about fellow Jews in precarious situations — in the countries of Eastern Europe, for example — forms part of this study.

The Israel component is pivotal. Since the establishment of the state, a key element of Jewish identity has been a sense of commitment, however vicarious, towards it, and with many of the younger generation "Israelism" is a more potent factor than Judaism.

Involvement with Israel, from casual holidays to the learning of Hebrew, to endeavouring to appreciate its complex politics, is a prominent feature of the programme of diaspora communities world-wide, and the notion of interdependence has taken firm root. Second best to living in Israel, attachment to it in some form or another is an indispensable plank of Jewish identity.

So these are the pieces that make up the Jewish Identikit. No one is obliged to score heavily on all eight, but if hardly any of them is present to some degree the claim to identify Jewishly wears a little thin. Certainly the acid test of these dimensions is a more reliable gauge than the psychological perspectives often advanced nowadays to substantiate identification.

In a study in the 1970s of Redbridge Jewry in London, Professor Barry Kosmin concluded that "religion is mainly a family-centred or crisis activity, as symbolised by Barmitzvah and the recitation of Kaddish." Being Jewish in this suburb of London had much more to do, he argued, with such issues as modes of dress, the type of house one lived in, the size of car one owned, and Jewish "mannerisms".

What of South African Jewry? That more intense Jewish commitment is a pronounced feature of Jewish life in South Africa, particularly among young adults in Johannesburg, is demonstrated by the results of the 1998 survey of 1 000 Jewish households conducted by the Kaplan Centre of the University of Cape Town and the Jewish Policy Research Institute of London.

The survey shows a remarkable resurgence of Jewish religious observance. South African Jewry has by far the highest percentage in the Jewish world in respect of items such as fasting on Yom Kippur, observing a Seder, separating meat and milk in the kitchen and attending synagogue weekly.

Regarding the latter, Professor Allie Dubb, in his 1991 Sociodemographic Survey, found that 21,7 percent attended synagogue at least once a week. The latest survey gives a figure of 39 percent, an amazing advance in the space of some eight years.

Jewish identity is remarkably strong with 49 percent feeling "extremely conscious of being Jewish" and 41 percent "quite strongly Jewish." Only one respondent answered "although I was born Jewish, I do not think of myself as being Jewish in any way."

Indeed, in comparing the statistics with those of Anglo-Jewry and American Jewry, Professor Kosmin of the Policy Research Institute described the South African community as "the Super Jews of the Jewish world".

Undoubtedly there is a growing Ba'al Teshuvah movement, evidenced by the proliferation of shtieblach and by the many hundreds of young Jews from non-observant backgrounds who have enthusiastically espoused Torah Judaism.

Among the reasons for this satisfactory state of affairs are the quality of Jewish day schools, which most Jewish teenagers attend; the spiritual intensity engendered by the Kolel and by inspirational rabbis; and the combined efforts of the charismatic Orthodox movements — Lubavitch, Ohr Sameyach and Aish HaTorah. Bnei Akiva is the most popular Zionist youth movement. Uniquely for the Jewish world, instead of fighting and competing with each other, all the Torah forces seem to have joined together to make such positive impact.

External reasons for this noteworthy resurgence include the paradoxical fact that apartheid reinforced ethnic cohesion, keeping the

Jewish community very much to itself and that the turbulent nature of the current crime-ridden transformation causes many teenagers to turn inwards to examine their roots. The insecurity of the "outside" scene pressurises them to look "inside" to find safety in traditional values.

South African Jewry may well be diminishing in size but the quality of Jewish religious life has never been better.

A final key component which I have always thought vital to true Jewish identity is a sense of Jewish history. A consciousness of our heritage and of the sacrifices to sustain it constitutes a powerful incentive to continue to preserve tradition. Throughout history, the Jewish people has cherished classic values and often been the conscience of the world. Mindful of our proud past, we can determine to live up to this ideal.

Most important, whatever else being Jewish means, it must bring joy as well as responsibility, and amid the welter of powerful ideals and abundance of precepts infuse everyday life with enhanced purpose and nobility.

4.   "Even Stevens"

The Talmud offers a unique and fascinating suggestion about our moral stance. It is that we should consider ourselves exactly balanced between righteousness and wickedness — in a 50/50 situation, half good and half bad — "even stevens".

To consider ourselves 100 percent good would not only be big headed and altogether conceited, it would also be untrue. As the book of Koheleth tells us, "There is no one on earth who doeth only good and sinneth not".

But we should not, on the other hand, see ourselves as thoroughly bad. However many unworthy actions we may have committed, it is wrong for anyone to brand themselves too far gone for redemption. Self-contempt and the notion that we are worse than we really are, are disincentives to improvement. The one person able to improve you is none other than yourself and the one door which is never closed is the door to repentance.

So, instead, the Talmud with deep wisdom suggests the correct stance is one of equipoise, a neat balance between goodness and badness, the needle measuring our self-appraisal pointing precisely to the middle. The aim of this suggestion, of course, is to exert maximum pressure on our behaviour. Since we are 50/50, the very next thing we do is of vital importance as it is going to tip the scales one way or the other.

And so the Talmud elaborates — "if one then proceeds to do a good deed, happy is he, for he has tilted the balance in the favour of merit. If he commits a transgression, oh dear, woe is he, for he has weighed down the scale of guilt".

Such an outlook is no mere fantasy, but can prove most beneficial. The next word we say can be kind or cruel; I must therefore try to speak kindly. My next action may be helpful or damaging; I must endeavour to make it good. My very next thought can be sweet or poisonous; my personal moral balance necessitates that the thought shall be a nice one.

This 50/50 approach is very much out of keeping with current educational psychology. Nowadays everyone is taught "to feel good" about themselves; nothing should be allowed to threaten their comfort zones. This view not only prevents progress in education — if the kids are already wonderful, what do they need to aim for? — but also runs contrary to the basic challenges of religion. Unless we feel uneasy about ourselves, we will never start to get better. If we forget that no triumph is ever gained without exertion, we remain stuck in a self-satisfied rut. So the "even stevens" approach is much needed if we are to attempt to do justice to our potential for improvement.

Having thus put us very much on our toes, the Talmud then takes a great leap forward and postulates exactly the same situation with the world. The whole wide world is also half good and half bad, half lovely and half horrible, exactly balanced. The arrow on its moral gauge, too, points to dead centre.

What an awesome responsibility this places on every human being, significantly adding to the pressure. For it is not our personal account only which is affected by our actions. More, much more, it is the continual well-being of the world as a whole. Every one of us holds in his or her hands the ability to move the world in the right direction.

There is something very constructive as well as daunting in this view. For with it, no person is insignificant nor any action inconsequential. Thus each of us helps or hinders, makes or breaks, builds or destroys.

Too often we resort to an alibi — "What I do doesn't really make any difference, the world is governed by such impersonal forces, there cannot be any lasting significance to my personal actions".

How wrong this familiar excuse is. There is no such thing as a small good act. Every day we can take the initiative. We can be welcoming and encouraging. We can extend our range of friendship. Wherever we go, we can touch the lives of others with benevolence, and in so doing play our individual part in helping to increase the overall aggregate of goodness in the world.

At the present juncture, with so many difficulties in our country and its abundance of problems, a question mark hovers over the future. Will there be peace and progress or will we slide back into dissension and malevolence?

So it is crucially important that the "even Stevens" approach galvanises us from our apathetic rut into positive action and that we try to tilt our personal balance in favour of good. For at the same time, the very same time, we will be helping everything to come right and contributing towards a better future.

5.   Approaching the Kotel

Come with me on my favourite walk. The sun is shining brightly and we are standing at the side of the King David Hotel in Paul Emil Botta Street. There are not many people around in the early afternoon as we walk downhill past the Pontifical Biblical Institute and the French Consulate, both very dignified buildings.

The road bends and we can see the beautiful — and expensive — residential development of King David's Village, Mamilla, which blends exquisitely with the landscape. Soon we are walking through Chutsot HaYotzer, the arts and crafts lane, an ideal setting for modern Judaica.

Excitement is mounting as the Old City approaches. Crossing over the busy main road, we look up at King David's Tower, and enter through the Jaffa Gate. There are different ways to the Wall, but we traverse Omar Ibn El-Khattab Square and turn into the Armenian Orthodox Patriarchate Road.

We continue past the seminary in the Armenian Quarter and skirt the Jewish Quarter, so beautifully restored, and cross through the milling taxis to the top of Batei Machase Street. Here we stop momentarily — the new, up-to-date Jerusalem is behind us and the panoramic view of the venerable, old city is in front of us.

There is no view quite like it in the world, and it has not changed much during the centuries. Behind us is end of the twentieth century, before our eyes could easily be tenth century or earlier. Both have their grandeur, but there is a stillness and an old-world charm about the Old City which seem to defy time.

We continue down the hill past Yeshivat HaKotel, from which the noise of Torah learning emanates, and come quickly down to the promenade and the security check at the entrance to the Kotel. The Wall is to our right.

Strange that a heap of stones can be so evocative, tugging at the heart strings, taking us back along the dusty road of history to the gloriously thronged Temple.

We are at the Wall. You must stand right up against it, stretch your arms high above your head and with open hands grasp the stones. Close your eyes and pray.

According to tradition, Jerusalem, G-d's home town, is the centre-point of the whole earth. As the dual form Yerushalayim indicates, there are two Jerusalems - the "Jerusalem below" is situated directly beneath the "Jerusalem above". It is the place where earth and heaven meet, where heaven kisses earth. It is the gateway to heaven.

Whenever we pray, wherever we are in the world, we have to turn towards the Holy Land. Inside Israel, we must face towards Jerusalem. In Jerusalem itself, we face the direction of the Wall. Our prayers, be it noted, do not immediately ascend on high; they have to scud along the earth till they get to the Wall, and only then do they go up via the site of the Temple to heaven.

So praying at the Wall is very special because here — and here alone — the prayers ascend immediately.

There are twenty-six rows of stones. The huge lower ones, some of them weighing over a hundred tons, date from Herod's Temple, directly above them are plainer Roman stones, above them are stones of the Saracen era, and right at the top are small bricks from medieval times.

Due to the exciting excavations of recent years, we now know that there are at least nineteen rows underground, and huge areas of the outer wall which existed at the time of the Hasmoneans have been uncovered.

How did the stones get there? The Midrash tells us that the poor people of Jerusalem were dismayed because they did not have any silver or gold, precious wood or fabrics to donate to the Temple while it was being built. So they resolved to donate the only thing they had — the work of their hands. They dragged the heavy stones from the Cave of Zedekiah and they built, as a labour of love, the outer walls of the Temple.

In the destruction of the Temple everything was obliterated, except this Wall, because what we build with our hearts lasts forever.

The cement holding the Wall together is also very special. Engineers will tell you that the only reason the Wall has withstood earthquakes, and survived the soil pressure behind it, is that the rows are terraced, each stone set back a few inches relative to the one beneath.

But traditionalists ascribe the unusual degree of stability to a totally different cause. Thousands and thousands of prayers, written on folded bits of paper, fill every crack and crevice of the Kotel. They are the best mortar. The wall is held together by the myriad pleas of the people of Israel.

Nowadays you can fax a prayer to the Wall and some kind Lubavitcher will place it between the stones for you. You can even dial a prayer on your telephone and the recipient at the Wall will place his cell-phone up against the stones. This modern age: you can pray at the Wall without being there!

The Wall has many different moods. When a lot of people are present it is joyous — the Barmitzvah ceremonies on Monday and Thursday mornings are a delight, particularly when an oriental boy in traditional costume is celebrating and his relatives are all ululating. But on a cloudy, windy day with hardly anyone there, the Wall can be frightening, awesome in its towering majesty.

On Tisha B'Av, the Wall cries for the glory of the Temple of old which has been lost. On Yom Yerushalayim, however, the yeshivah students dance in great joy for hours on end, and loudly chant every sentence from the Book of Psalms which makes mention of Jerusalem.

To be blessed at the Wall by the Cohanim — in Jerusalem the ceremony takes place daily — is always a privilege. On Fridays, when thousands of Moslems attend the Mosques on the Temple Mount, the prayers to Hashem of the Jewish worshippers below mingle with the prayers to Allah of the multitude of Moslems above. The same G-d understands and receives both sets of prayers.

The walk to the Kotel is always worthwhile, because the experience, deeply spiritual, always serves to strengthen identity with Am Yisrael. The Wall makes us think of our spiritual heritage and our personal effort towards preserving the Jewish future. The Wall is all we have left, a symbol of past destruction, and yet, because it is preserved, simultaneously the symbol of future salvation.

Capturing the unique attraction of the Kotel, Rabbi Abraham Isaac Kook, the Chief Rabbi of the Holy Land in the 1920s, used to say: "There are stones which are mere stones and there are hearts which are only hearts — but some hearts are made of stone and some stones cry out like hearts".

The Divine Presence, we are told, never departs from the Kotel. With its almost tangible holiness, there we can pray in the words of the Shabbat Shacharit Kedushah, "may You be magnified and sanctified in the midst of Jerusalem your city from generation to generation and unto all eternity. And may our eyes see Your Kingdom".

6.   Holiness Sublime

Towards the beginning of the Bible there is a great difficulty concerning the creation of man in that G-d says "Let us make man in our image".

The use of "us" is problematic. With whom was Almighty G-d deliberating? Some suggest He was speaking to the angels. Others suggest it is the plural of majesty, royal commands being given in the first person plural.

The Baal Shem Tov, the founder of Chassidism, has a lovely explanation. He explains that G-d was speaking to man himself, "Come, you and I together, let us make man. If you do not wish it, I can never make you into a real man. But if you do, together we shall succeed."

Living up to the spiritual potential which G-d has placed within us is the main challenge Judaism poses its adherents. It is the first religion in human history to demand the love of G-d, not just belief in G-d. "And you shall love the Lord your G-d" is proclaimed immediately after the declaration of faith: "Hear, O Israel, the Lord our G-d, the Lord alone".

The Italian Jewish commentator, Moses Hayyim Luzzatto, tells us that this love combines a yearning for the closeness of G-d and a continual striving to reach up for holiness. There should be delight in mentioning G-d's name, in occupying oneself with Torah and in uttering His praises. Such love demands total self and imbues all life with the pursuit of righteousness.

It is related of the saintly Rabbi Levi Yitzhak of Berditchev that his fulfilment of the commandments could never be mundane or pedestrian because G-d Himself had given them to us and asked us to perform them. Hence, on the Feast of Succot when he was about to reach for his lulav which was in a glass-covered chest, he thrust his hand through the lid and did not notice that he had cut himself. On Chanukkah, when he saw the holy candles burning, he was impelled to touch the flames. On Purim before the Megillah was recited he danced ecstatically round the bimah.

At the Seder when he said the word "matzah" he was so moved with fervour that he threw himself against the table and tipped over the seder plate and the wine, so that everything had to be prepared anew. He put on a fresh kittel, and like one about to taste the most exquisite cake, and not the dry flat unleavened bread, shouted out: "Ah! This matzah!"

Prayer is considered a most important holy activity. Not the sort of prayer which continually makes requests of G-d, but the sort of prayer which thanks Him for all life's blessings and desires to express the adoration of Him. Intensely emotional, this type of prayer is a vital means of attachment to the Almighty and a rapturous way of segregating oneself temporarily from earthly bonds in order to join in spiritual ecstasy to the source of all things.

When necessary, holiness can offer a powerful retreat. The question is often asked as to how believers managed to cope with the horrors of the Nazi holocaust. However many lost their faith, the answer for those who retained it lies in the ever-present sensation of mystical union with the divine, which allows indifference to material and physical adversity and views severe troubles with equanimity. Such a strong and pervasive feeling that one is never alone was powerful enough to sublimate the worst of experiences, so that they came through the chaos with their self-respect intact and — a phenomenon belying their hopeless condition — with an untarnished and ennobling belief in G-d and the world He created.

For most of us, at least a glimpse of the desired level is provided by Yom Kippur. However far we may have strayed from G-d, from our community, from our people, or from our true selves, the spirituality of Yom Kippur brings us back once again to the essence of our own souls and impels us to identify once more with our people and our Creator.

It is as if on Yom Kippur there are no barriers — of time or space, of history or geography, of this world or the next. On this remarkable day, we feel close to Jewish people the world over, we are together again for a few precious hours with the members of our family who are no longer alive but whose memory surrounds us with blessing, and turning away from the ordinary and grasping the holy, we can come nearer to G-d Himself.

The Midrash states that the high priest was especially privileged on Yom Kippur in that he experienced all the high holinesses coming together: on Yom Kippur, the holiest day, he, the holiest man, went into the inner sanctuary of the Temple, the holiest place, and pronounced the name of G-d, the holiest word.

This concurrence of acute holiness transported him to a higher level and allowed him to ask forgiveness for the sins of Israel. We, too, on a lower plane can try to immerse ourselves in the atmosphere of Yom Kippur, and raise ourselves to a higher spiritual plateau.

Rabbi Abraham Isaac Kook consistently refused to differentiate between the sacred and the profane, holding that there was no such category as secularity. He taught us that there is only "the holy" and the "not-yet-holy", a marvellously optimistic view of Israel's individual and collective aim and purpose.

According to him, nationality is not a goal in itself but only a step towards the Divine wish of human perfection for the entire world. He describes this universal concept beautifully in terms of an all-embracing song.

There are four types of singer, he tells us. There is one who sings the song of his own life and in that he finds adequate spiritual satisfaction. There is another who needs to sing the song of his people. He leaves the circle of his own self and attaches himself with a gentle love to the whole community of Israel. Together with her, he sings her song.

There is yet another who goes beyond the boundary of his people Israel to sing the song of humanity. His spirit extends outwards to the noble essence of human beings and he sings together with all of them. And then there is one who reaches out towards even wider horizons, so that he links himself with all existence and he can sing the song of all G-d's creatures.

This, he tells us, is the song of pure holiness — the song of the self, the song of the people, the song of humanity and the song of the whole wide world.

The most solemn affirmation the Jewish person ever recites is "The Lord, He is G-d," which is called out seven times by the congregation in unison as the fast of Yom Kippur draws to its close. An awesome climax to the day of prayer, contemplation, fasting and confession, the crucial factor is whether we really mean it.

For where, precisely, is the Lord the G-d of our lives? Is he G-d at home in the moral values which govern our domestic relationships and in our behaviour to each other? Is He G-d in business or our profession in that our ethics are in consonance with, and not a flagrant denial of, the principles He asks us to live by? Is He G-d in the community, everyone submerging personal vanity in the collective effort to glorify His name? Is He G-d in our innermost being, as real as our own selves?

It is by no means easy to remember in the daily round of existence that the Lord He is G-d, or to try to fulfil the injunction of the Shema to love Him at all times. Holiness, nevertheless, remains a necessary and persistent challenge, pursuing us in everything we attempt, impelling us to sanctify our humdrum lives, subliminally underpinning all we hope to achieve.

Until that blessed time comes when the darkness ceases and the shadows flee away, and the dawn rises to greet the day which is all day and not night, and the gates of heaven open to allow us to enter eternity and, going forward to our ultimate fulfilment, our soul ascends on high to rejoice in the light without end which is the glory of Almighty G-d.